# The
# Complete Book
## of SMALL
# BUSINESS
# FORMS &
# AGREEMENTS

## Gustav Berle, Ph.D.

**PRENTICE HALL**
Englewood Cliffs, New Jersey 07632

Prentice-Hall International (UK) Limited, *London*
Prentice-Hall of Australia Pty. Limited, *Sydney*
Prentice-Hall Canada, Inc., *Toronto*
Prentice-Hall Hispanoamericana, S.A., *Mexico*
Prentice-Hall of India Private Limited, *New Delhi*
Prentice-Hall of Japan, Inc., *Tokyo*
Simon & Schuster Asia Pte. Ltd., *Singapore*
Editora Prentice-Hall do Brasil, Ltda., *Rio de Janeiro*

10  9  8  7  6  5  4  3  2  1


**Library of Congress Cataloging-in-Publication Data**

Berle, Gustav
    The complete book of small business forms and agreements /
Gustav Berle.
        p.      cm.
    Includes bibliographical references and index.
    ISBN 0-13-174632-4
    1. Small business—United States—Forms.   2. Small
business—Law and legislation—United States—Forms.
I. Title.
HF5371.B47   1992
651'.29—dc20                                                    92-13096
                                                                     CIP

ISBN 0-13-174632-4

**PRENTICE HALL**
Professional Publishing
Englewood Cliffs, NJ 07632
Simon & Schuster. A Paramount Communications Company

**Printed in the United States of America**

# About the Author

Gustav Berle, Ph.D., has been a small businessman and university instructor for the past 40 years, culminating his career as marketing and communications director of SCORE, the Service Corps of Retired Executives, in Washington. SCORE is the largest volunteer business counseling organization in the world and is affiliated with the SBA. With SCORE, Berle has had 40 years of hands-on entrepreneurship, including 18 years as a university instructor. As a foundation, he has written and published nine small business books. *The Complete Small Business Book of Forms and Legal Agreements* is his tenth book. He is also author of *Green Entrepreneurs: Opportunities in the Environment* (1991) and the *Small Business Information Handbook* (1990).

# Introduction

The complexity of modern business life—even *small* business—and the on-slaught of demands from tens of thousands of federal, state, county and municipal agencies, makes it mandatory to utilize all the help you can get.

This collection of forms, agreements, and contributory comments is the result of dealing with thousands of small businesses across the United States. Considering that thousands of forms and legal agreements exist, one single book cannot claim to cover every possible problem that might arise. There are many good attorneys and accountants to share the problems, as well as federal, state, and volunteer business assistance offices.

However, many business management problems can be solved by the entrepreneur. The forms and agreements in this book are commonly used and popular. Many are forms that you might not have thought of, but whose use will streamline your business and certainly save you considerable time and money.

Some forms, such as W-2s and passport applications, have been deliberately omitted because they can only be submitted in original, not photocopied formats. All others, however, can be photocopied easily and should then be kept in a safe, accessible file. Some forms can be altered to suit your individual needs or serve as inspiration and a tickler-file for your personal imagination. Use them for your profit and enjoy the time you save to good advantage.

*Gustav Berle*

# How This Book Will Help You

Starting and operating a small business is a very difficult and hectic job. Forms and legal agreements are just part of the task. Forms are necessary for the orderly operation of the business and agreements serve the purpose of protecting you from unforeseen future conflicts.

This book will help to streamline your recordkeeping and provide instant access to scores of forms used in forming a business or successfully running one. Whether you are responsible for a large corporation or a one-person operation, you'll find this book an indispensable part of your daily business activities, with ready-to-use forms and agreements that deal with:

- Forming a business and setting it up.
- Preparing a lease for the premises or for needed equipment.
- Employing one or more associates and workers, either full- or part-time, inside or outside of the business premises.
- Purchasing supplies, inventory, transportation means, utilities, subscriptions, and services.
- Arranging for insurance coverage for persons and products.
- Planning sales, inventory, and warehousing controls.
- Vacation schedules, absences, hiring, and firing.
- Plans for the future that might include savings, investments, and pensions.
- Keeping track of all the necessary records, lists, cash flow, banking needs, and, of course, taxes.

## The 10 Commandments of Form Layout

These are some basic concepts preferred by forms experts. There are many variations—especially the ones *you* prefer or find more convenient. However, these guidelines come closest to standardization and efficient function.

1. Use 3-by-5 spacing: 1/3rd of an inch between lines for horizontal lines, and 5 spaces (-----) between vertical lines.

2. ULC design of form page: caption or information is placed in the upper left corner.

3. Caption each page so that even the apprentice clerk will have no doubt about the form's purpose.

4. Check boxes should be placed in front of the question.

5. Visual aids, such as screens, should be used to guide the reader, not just for decorative purposes.

6. Leave enough margins around the edges.

7. Self-instructions should be part of the form.

8. If the form is to be routed or passed on, indicate this on the form.

9. A clearly identifying code, number, and/or title should be placed somewhere on the form (such as a date, quantity, or identification).

10. Whatever you put on the form—lines, titles, instructions—should only serve to get the information desired.

Satisfying the requirements of your own needs and that of your employees, suppliers, and customers is just part of the job. To these basics you must add multiple layers of the federal, state, county, and municipal bureaucracy. Everything and everybody requires forms; many require legal agreements. You will find hundreds of examples, role models, and inspirations in this book. These forms, in conjunction with your accountant, lawyer, banker, and insurance representative, make a great management team. With these forms and agreements you will not need to call on the professionals as often, and you will be better prepared when you do. The unrestricted use of any business form or agreement in this book is yours. The saving in time and money of just a single utilization will more than pay for this companion's acquisition. And as a master file and continuing inspiration of needed forms and agreements, this volume will pay for itself over and over again.

# Contents

**Contents**

# SECTION ONE

# Business Forms and Letters

# 1.

# ACCOUNTING AND BOOKKEEPING FORMS

Control over the operation of a business is necessary for several reasons. The entrepreneur's own curiosity is satisfied by good accounting and bookkeeping records, as these will tell continuously whether the business is making money or not, how much it is making, and the origin of the profits. Good records will tell whether the business is charging adequately for its products and services, which resources are the best, which customers are paying promptly or, if delinquent, the nature and age of the delinquency. Records will point to the business's cash flow and assure that it can continue to operate or, if problems arise, where these problems are and perhaps even point to corrective measures. Last year's records will help prepare next year's forecasts. In the final analysis, bookkeeping records are mandated by local, state, and federal tax demands. These forms will provide guidance to most bookkeeping and accounting needs and may be duplicated as often as needed. For other related forms see sections 3 (*Financial*) and 7 (*Office and Company Operation*).

## ACCOUNTS RECEIVABLE/PAYABLE FORMS

Accounts Receivable are money owed on current accounts by a customer or client (debtor) to the business (creditor). Such entries represent uncollected or unsettled transactions and claims. Entries from this Accounts Receivable form should agree with the balance in the General Ledger.

Accounts Payable are the reverse of the above figures—representing the money owed by the business to creditors. Each entry indicates the purchase of goods or services from a supplier. A/P entries normally do not include money owed for salaries, rent, or interest on loans. If you do a great deal of business with one supplier, you may want to devote an entire Accounts Payable page just to that one resource. The balance in this form should also agree with the corresponding sum in the General Ledger.

# ACCOUNTS RECEIVABLE AGE ANALYSIS

*As Of:* _____     *Prepared By:* _____

| Customer Name | Present Balance | Current < 30 Days | Amounts Past Due | | | Remarks |
|---|---|---|---|---|---|---|
| | | | 31 to 60 Days | 61 to 90 Days | Over 90 Days | |
| | | | | | | |
| | | | | | | |
| | | | | | | |
| | | | | | | |
| | | | | | | |
| | | | | | | |
| | | | | | | |
| | | | | | | |
| | | | | | | |
| | | | | | | |
| | | | | | | |
| | | | | | | |
| | | | | | | |
| | | | | | | |
| | | | | | | |
| | | | | | | |
| | | | | | | |
| | | | | | | |
| | | | | | | |
| | | | | | | |
| | | | | | | |
| | | | | | | |
| | | | | | | |
| | | | | | | |

# SUMMARY OF ACCOUNTS PAYABLE

| Vendor's Name | Balance Payable | | | |
|---|---|---|---|---|
| | Balance at Beginning of Year | | Balance at End of Year | |
| | | | | |
| | | | | |
| | | | | |
| | | | | |
| | | | | |
| | | | | |
| | | | | |
| | | | | |
| | | | | |
| | | | | |
| | | | | |
| | | | | |
| | | | | |
| | | | | |
| | | | | |
| | | | | |
| | | | | |
| | | | | |
| | | | | |
| | | | | |
| | | | | |
| | | | | |
| | | | | |
| | | | | |
| | | | | |
| | | | | |
| | | | | |
| | | | | |
| | | | | |
| | | | | |
| | | | | |
| | | | | |
| Balance Forward | | | | |
| TOTAL | | | | |

## SUMMARY OF ACCOUNTS RECEIVABLE

| Customer's Name | Balance Receivable | | | |
|---|---|---|---|---|
| | Balance at Beginning of Year | | Balance at End of Year | |
| | | | | |
| | | | | |
| | | | | |
| | | | | |
| | | | | |
| | | | | |
| | | | | |
| | | | | |
| | | | | |
| | | | | |
| | | | | |
| | | | | |
| | | | | |
| | | | | |
| | | | | |
| | | | | |
| | | | | |
| | | | | |
| | | | | |
| | | | | |
| | | | | |
| | | | | |
| | | | | |
| | | | | |
| | | | | |
| | | | | |
| | | | | |
| | | | | |
| | | | | |
| | | | | |
| | | | | |
| | | | | |
| | | | | |
| | | | | |
| | | | | |
| Balance Forward | | | | |
| TOTAL | | | | |

# ANNUAL EXPENSE SUMMARY

FOR YEAR _____

| Month | Phone | Meals | Travel | Hotel | Enter-tainment | Misc. | Monthly Total |
|-------|-------|-------|--------|-------|----------------|-------|---------------|
| JANUARY | | | | | | | |
| FEBRUARY | | | | | | | |
| MARCH | | | | | | | |
| 1st QUARTER TOTAL | | | | | | | |
| APRIL | | | | | | | |
| MAY | | | | | | | |
| JUNE | | | | | | | |
| 2nd QUARTER TOTAL | | | | | | | |
| JULY | | | | | | | |
| AUGUST | | | | | | | |
| SEPTEMBER | | | | | | | |
| 3rd QUARTER TOTAL | | | | | | | |
| OCTOBER | | | | | | | |
| NOVEMBER | | | | | | | |
| DECEMBER | | | | | | | |
| 4th QUARTER TOTAL | | | | | | | |
| YEARLY TOTAL | | | | | | | |

NOTES _____

COMPANY CREDIT CARD SUMMARY

[ ] _____ # _____

[ ] _____ # _____

[ ] _____ # _____

[ ] _____ # _____

# ANNUAL SUMMARY WORKSHEET

## INCOME

Gross receipts from sales, fees, commissions, etc. _____

Returns, allowances, credits, etc. _____

Other income _____

## COSTS OF GOODS OR BUSINESS OPERATIONS

Inventory at year's beginning _____

Inventory at year's end _____

Purchases _____

Cost of personal use items _____

Materials and supplies _____

Other costs _____
_____

## DEDUCTIONS

Advertising _____
Bank Charges _____
Car and truck costs _____
Commissions paid _____
Dues & publications _____
Employee benefits _____
Freight & shipping _____
Insurance _____
Interest (business) _____
Legal & accounting _____
Meals & entertainment _____
Office expenses _____
Rent (business) _____
Repairs _____
Supplies _____
Taxes _____
Travel _____
Utilities & Telephone _____
Wages _____
Other expenses (specify) _____
_____
_____

# ASSETS/LIABILITIES WORKSHEET

NAME: _____    *TAXABLE YEAR ENDED* _____

I.D. # _____

| ASSETS | BEGINNING OF TAXABLE YEAR | END OF TAXABLE YEAR |
|---|---|---|
| **OTHER CURRENT ASSETS** | | |
| | | |
| | | |
| | | |
| | | |
| | | |
| | | |
| TOTAL | | |
| **OTHER INVESTMENTS** | | |
| | | |
| | | |
| | | |
| | | |
| | | |
| | | |
| TOTAL | | |
| **OTHER ASSETS** | | |
| | | |
| | | |
| | | |
| | | |
| | | |
| | | |
| TOTAL | | |
| *LIABILITIES* | | |
| **OTHER CURRENT LIABILITES** | | |
| | | |
| | | |
| | | |
| | | |
| TOTAL | | |
| **OTHER LIABILITES** | | |
| | | |
| | | |
| | | |
| | | |
| TOTAL | | |

# MONTHLY EXPENSES

*Individual*

Month _____

| Date | Meals | Hotel/Motel | Mileage | Other Transport | Enter-tainment | Misc. | Detail |
|------|-------|-------------|---------|-----------------|----------------|-------|--------|
| 1 | | | | | | | |
| 2 | | | | | | | |
| 3 | | | | | | | |
| 4 | | | | | | | |
| 5 | | | | | | | |
| 6 | | | | | | | |
| 7 | | | | | | | |
| 8 | | | | | | | |
| 9 | | | | | | | |
| 10 | | | | | | | |
| 11 | | | | | | | |
| 12 | | | | | | | |
| 13 | | | | | | | |
| 14 | | | | | | | |
| 15 | | | | | | | |
| 16 | | | | | | | |
| 17 | | | | | | | |
| 18 | | | | | | | |
| 19 | | | | | | | |
| 20 | | | | | | | |
| 21 | | | | | | | |
| 22 | | | | | | | |
| 23 | | | | | | | |
| 24 | | | | | | | |
| 25 | | | | | | | |
| 26 | | | | | | | |
| 27 | | | | | | | |
| 28 | | | | | | | |
| 29 | | | | | | | |
| 30 | | | | | | | |
| 31 | | | | | | | |

*Because of IRS Regulations, please indicate details of each expense.

# MONTHLY EXPENSE RECORD

| | |
|---|---|
| MONTH OF | _____ |
| SALESPERSON | _____ |
| ADDRESS | _____ |
| CITY | _____ |
| STATE | _____ ZIP _____ |

| TERRITORY | PRODUCT | COMPANY CHARGE CARD NO. |
|---|---|---|
| | | [ ] TELEPHONE |
| | | [ ] OTHER |

| Date | Trans | Parking/ Tolls | Hotel | Meals | Enter- tainment | Misc | Company Charge | Employee Charge | Cash | Daily Totals |
|---|---|---|---|---|---|---|---|---|---|---|
| | | | | | | | | | | |
| | | | | | | | | | | |
| | | | | | | | | | | |
| | | | | | | | | | | |
| | | | | | | | | | | |
| | | | | | | | | | | |
| | | | | | | | | | | |
| | | | | | | | | | | |
| | | | | | | | | | | |
| | | | | | | | | | | |
| | | | | | | | | | | |
| | | | | | | | | | | |
| | | | | | | | | | | |
| | | | | | | | | | | |
| | | | | | | | | | | |
| | | | | | | | | | | |
| | | | | | | | | | | |
| | | | | | | | | | | |
| | | | | | | | | | | |
| | | | | | | | | | | |
| | | | | | | | | | | |
| | | | | | | | | | | |
| | | | | | | | | | | |
| | | | | | | | | | | |
| | | | | | | | | | | |
| | | | | | | | | | | |
| | | | | | | | | | | |
| | | | | | | | | | | |
| | | | | | | | | | | |
| | | | | | | | | | | |
| | | | | | | | | | | |
| | | | | | | | | | | |
| | | | | | | | | | | |
| TOTALS | | | | | | | | | | |

*Payment Method* spans the Company Charge, Employee Charge, and Cash columns.

| IF SUBMITTED AS AN EXPENSE REPORT – SIGN BELOW | |
|---|---|
| Preparer Signature/Title | Date |
| Approval Signature/Title | Date |

| MONTHLY AUTO EXPENSE RECORD | |
|---|---|
| Less Cash Advance | |
| Less Charges to Company | |
| Balance Due   [ ] Company  [ ] Employee | |

# MONTHLY EXPENSE WORKSHEET

Month of _____

| | Expense | Amount | How Paid (check #, voucher) |
|---|---|---|---|
| 1. | Salaries and Wages | | |
| 2. | Telephone | | |
| 3. | Utilities | | |
| 4. | Insurance | | |
| 5. | Repairs/Maintenance | | |
| 6. | General Supplies | | |
| 7. | Office Supplies | | |
| 8. | Advertising | | |
| 9. | Promotions/Display | | |
| 10. | Automotive | | |
| 11. | Travel (other) | | |
| 12. | Rent/Mortgage | | |
| 13. | Interest | | |
| 14. | Loan Repayments | | |
| 15. | Postage & Shipping | | |
| 16. | Delivery | | |
| 17. | Entertainment/Gifts | | |
| 18. | Books/Subscriptions | | |
| 19. | Taxes | | |
| |   Social Security | | |
| |   Federal Excise | | |
| |   State Unemployment | | |
| |   State | | |
| |   Local | | |
| 20. | Personal Draw | | |
| | TOTAL | | |

*(Small Business Flexible Monthly Expense Schedule)*

# PERSONAL EXPENSE RECORD – WEEKLY

NAME:_____ FOR WEEK ENDING:_____ DEPT.____

| | SUNDAY | MONDAY | TUESDAY | WEDNESDAY | THURSDAY | FRIDAY | SATURDAY | TOTAL FOR WEEK |
|---|---|---|---|---|---|---|---|---|
| **FROM** | | | | | | | | |
| **TO** | | | | | | | | |
| **TO** | | | | | | | | |
| **TOTAL AUTO MILES** | | | | | | | | |
| Mileage | | | | | | | | |
| Gas – Oil – Lube | | | | | | | | |
| Parking & Tolls | | | | | | | | |
| Auto Rental | | | | | | | | |
| Local – Cab/Limo | | | | | | | | |
| Air – Rail – Bus | | | | | | | | |
| Lodging | | | | | | | | |
| Breakfast | | | | | | | | |
| Lunch | | | | | | | | |
| Dinner | | | | | | | | |
| Laundry – Cleaning | | | | | | | | |
| Phone & Telegram | | | | | | | | |
| Tips | | | | | | | | |
| Other | | | | | | | | |
| | | | | | | | | |
| Entertainment (please detail below) | | | | | | | | |
| **TOTAL PER DAY** | | | | | | | | |

## DETAILED ENTERTAINMENT RECORD

| Date | Item | Persons Entertained / Business Relationship | Place Name & Location | Business Purpose | Amount |
|---|---|---|---|---|---|
| | | | | | |
| | | | | | |
| | | | | | |
| | | | | | |
| | | | | | |
| | | | | | |
| | | | | | |

| | | |
|---|---|---|
| | **SUMMARY** | |
| Purpose of Trip:_____ | Total Expenses | |
| | Less Cash Advanced | |
| Remarks:_____ | Less Charges to Company | |
| | [ ] Me | |
| Date:_____ Signature:_____ | Amount Due [ ] Company | |

# GENERAL LEDGER

Account Number _____

Account Name _____

Address _____

Sheet _____ of _____

| DATE | DESCRIPTION | CHARGES | CREDITS | BALANCE | |
|---|---|---|---|---|---|
| | | | | CHARGES | CREDITS |
| | Amount Brought Forward | | | | |
| | | | | | |
| | | | | | |
| | | | | | |
| | | | | | |
| | | | | | |
| | | | | | |
| | | | | | |
| | | | | | |
| | | | | | |
| | | | | | |
| | | | | | |
| | | | | | |
| | | | | | |
| | | | | | |
| | | | | | |
| | | | | | |

# INCOME STATEMENT

For _____ (month) and year to date ended _____ , 19____
($000)

| | Current Month | | Year to Date | |
|---|---|---|---|---|
| | Amount | % of Sales | Amount | % of Sales |
| **REVENUE** | | | | |
| Gross Sales | _____ | | _____ | |
| Less sales returns and allowances | _____ | | _____ | |
| Net Sales | _____ | 100 | _____ | 100 |
| | | | | |
| Cost of Sales | | | | |
| Beginning inventory | | | | |
| Plus purchases (retailer) or | | | | |
| Plus cost of goods manufactured (manufacturer) | | | | |
| Total Goods Available | | | | |
| Less ending inventory | | | | |
| Total Cost of Goods Sold | | | | |
| | | | | |
| Gross Profit (Gross Margin) | | | | |
| | | | | |
| **OPERATING EXPENSES** | | | | |
| Selling | | | | |
| Salaries and wages | | | | |
| Commissions | | | | |
| Advertising | | | | |
| Depreciation (e.g., on delivery vans) | | | | |
| Others (detail) | | | | |
| Total Selling Expenses | | | | |
| | | | | |
| General/Administrative | | | | |
| Salaries and wages | | | | |
| Employee benefits | | | | |
| Insurance | | | | |
| Depreciation (e.g., on equipment) | | | | |
| Total General/Administrative Expenses | | | | |
| Total Operating Expenses | | | | |
| | | | | |
| Other Operating Income | | | | |
| | | | | |
| Other Revenue and Expenses | | | | |
| | | | | |
| Net Income before Taxes | | | | |
| Taxes on Income | | | | |
| Net Income after Taxes | | | | |
| | | | | |
| Extraordinary Gain or Loss | | | | |
| Income tax on extraordinary gain | | | | |
| | | | | |
| **NET INCOME (NET PROFIT)** | | | | |

# INVOICE

SOLD TO:               SHIP TO:

Name: _____     Name: _____

Address: _____     Address: _____

City, State, Zip: _____     City, State, Zip: _____

| Date | Order No. | Terms | Dept. | Ship Via | |
|------|-----------|-------|-------|----------|---|
| Quantity | Style No. | Description | Price | | Total | |
| | | | | | | |
| | | | | | | |
| | | | | | | |
| | | | | | | |
| | | | | | | |
| | | | | | | |
| | | | | | | |
| | | | | | | |
| | | | | | | |
| | | | | | | |
| | | | | | | |
| | | | | | | |
| | | | | | | |
| | | | | | | |
| | | | | | | |
| | | | | | | |
| | | | | | | |
| | | | | | | |
| | | | | | | |
| | | | | | | |
| | | | | | | |
| | | | | | | |
| | | | | | | |
| | | | | | | |
| | | | | | | |
| | | | | | | |
| | | | | | | |
| | | | | | | |
| | | | | | | |
| | | | | | | |
| | | | | | | |
| | | | | | | |
| | | | | | | |
| | | | | | | |
| | | | | | TOTAL | |

Salesman _____

17

# CONTRACTOR'S INVOICE

TO:

| | |
|---|---|
| | DATE |
| | CUSTOMER ORDER NO. |
| | ORDER TAKEN BY |

| | |
|---|---|
| JOB ADDRESS | STARTING DATE |
| JOB PHONE | |
| BILL TO | |
| ADDRESS | |
| PHONE | |

**DESCRIPTION OF WORK**

SIGNATURE

[ ] I HEREBY AUTHORIZE THE ABOVE DESCRIBED WORK TO BE PERFORMED.

[ ] AT OUR REGULAR RATES        [ ]    C.O.D.

[ ] FOR THE AMOUNT OF        [ ]    INVOICE

| WORK ORDERED BY | | TIME STARTED | |
|---|---|---|---|
| [ ] COMPLETE | | TIME FINISHED | |
| [ ] JOB INCOMPLETE | | TRAVEL TIME | |

| DATE | HOURS | TOTAL MATERIAL | |
|---|---|---|---|
| MECHANIC | | TOTAL LABOR | |
| | | PERMIT | |
| HELPER | | MISC. | |
| | | TOTAL AMOUNT | |

DEPOSIT PAID

BALANCE DUE

UPON COMPLETION

# INVOICE

**(YOUR NAME/ADDRESS)**

**Invoice No.:** _____
**Date:** _____

**SOLD TO:**

**Discount:** _____
**Shipping via** _____

_____

**Sales Tax** _____

| Item (# and description) | Quantity | Unit Price | Discount Price | Total Price | Sales Tax |
|---|---|---|---|---|---|
| | | | | | |

**Total Weight** _____
**Subtotal** _____
**Sales Tax** _____
**Shipping** _____

**Total** _____

# SERVICE INVOICE

**SOLD TO:**                                    **SERVICE AT:**

_____          _____
_____          _____
_____          _____

| Make of Equipment | Model No. | Serial No. | Date Repaired |
|---|---|---|---|
|  |  |  |  |

## ⋅-PARTS USED-⋅

| Quantity | Description | Price | | Amount | |
|---|---|---|---|---|---|
|  |  |  |  |  |  |
|  |  |  |  |  |  |
|  |  |  |  |  |  |
|  |  |  |  |  |  |
|  |  |  |  |  |  |
|  |  |  |  |  |  |
|  |  |  |  |  |  |
|  |  |  |  |  |  |
|  |  |  |  |  |  |
|  |  |  |  |  |  |
|  |  |  |  |  |  |
|  |  |  |  |  |  |

| Date | No. Hours | Rate/Hour | Amount | | | Total | |
|---|---|---|---|---|---|---|---|
|  |  |  |  |  |  | Tax |  |
|  |  |  |  |  |  | Total Labor |  |
|  |  |  |  |  |  | Total Bill |  |
|  |  |  |  |  | GUARANTEED FOR 30 DAYS | | |
|  |  |  |  |  | AGAINST FAULTY LABOR | | |
|  |  |  |  |  | AND MATERIALS ONLY | | |

**Comments:**

_____
_____
_____
_____
_____

**Service Man:** _____     **Signed:** _____

# INVOICE STATEMENT

DATE: _____

ACCOUNT NO. _____

AMOUNT REMITTED:

$ _____

*PLEASE DETACH AND RETURN WITH YOUR REMITTANCE*

| DATE | INVOICE NO. / DESCRIPTION | CHARGE | CREDIT | BALANCE |
|---|---|---|---|---|
| | PREVIOUS BALANCE BROUGHT FORWARD | | | |
| | | | | |
| | | | | |
| | | | | |
| | | | | |
| | | | | |
| | | | | |
| | | | | |
| | | | | |
| | | | | |
| | | | | |
| | | | | |
| | | PLEASE PAY THIS AMOUNT | | |

*THANK YOU FOR YOUR BUSINESS*

JOURNAL

Number: _____

Month of: _____

| Date | Description | Charges | | | | | Credits | | | |
|------|-------------|---------|---------|---------|---------|---------|---------|---------|---------|---------|
| | | Accounts Receivable | Accounts Payable | General Ledger Acct. No. | General Ledger Amount | | General Ledger Acct. No. | General Ledger Amount | Accounts Payable | Accounts Receivable |
| | Amount Brought Forward | | | | | | | | | |
| | | | | | | | | | | |
| | | | | | | | | | | |
| | | | | | | | | | | |
| | | | | | | | | | | |
| | | | | | | | | | | |
| | | | | | | | | | | |
| | | | | | | | | | | |
| | | | | | | | | | | |
| | | | | | | | | | | |
| | | | | | | | | | | |
| | | | | | | | | | | |
| | | | | | | | | | | |
| | | | | | | | | | | |
| | | | | | | | | | | |
| | | | | | | | | | | |
| | | | | | | | | | | |
| | | | | | | | | | | |
| | | | | | | | | | | |
| | | | | | | | | | | |
| | | | | | | | | | | |

# EXPENSE JOURNAL

| Meals & Enter-tainment | Office Expenses | Rent | Repairs | Supplies | Taxes | Travel | Utilities & Telephone | Wages | Auto Expense | | Miscellaneous | |
|---|---|---|---|---|---|---|---|---|---|---|---|---|
| | | | | | | | | | Mileage | Expense | Description | Amount |
| | | | | | | | | | | | | |
| | | | | | | | | | | | | |
| | | | | | | | | | | | | |
| | | | | | | | | | | | | |
| | | | | | | | | | | | | |
| | | | | | | | | | | | | |
| | | | | | | | | | | | | |
| | | | | | | | | | | | | |
| | | | | | | | | | | | | |
| | | | | | | | | | | | | |
| | | | | | | | | | | | | |
| | | | | | | | | | | | | |
| | | | | | | | | | | | | |
| | | | | | | | | | | | | |
| | | | | | | | | | | | | |
| | | | | | | | | | | | | |
| | | | | | | | | | | | | |
| | | | | | | | | | | | | |

# EXPENSE JOURNAL (Cont'd.)

| Date | Check Number | Payee | Advertising | Bank Charges | Commissions | Dues & Publications | Employee Benefit Programs | Freight | Insurance | Interest | Legal & Professional Legal |
|------|--------------|-------|-------------|--------------|-------------|---------------------|---------------------------|---------|-----------|----------|----------------------------|
| | | | | | | | | | | | |
| | | | | | | | | | | | |
| | | | | | | | | | | | |
| | | | | | | | | | | | |
| | | | | | | | | | | | |
| | | | | | | | | | | | |
| | | | | | | | | | | | |
| | | | | | | | | | | | |
| | | | | | | | | | | | |
| | | | | | | | | | | | |
| | | | | | | | | | | | |
| | | | | | | | | | | | |
| | | | | | | | | | | | |
| | | | | | | | | | | | |
| | | | | | | | | | | | |
| | | | | | | | | | | | |
| | | | | | | | | | | | |
| | | | | | | | | | | | |
| | | | | | | | | | | | |
| | | | | | | | | | | | |
| SUBTOTAL | | | | | | | | | | | |
| BALANCE FORWARD | | | | | | | | | | | |
| TOTAL | | | | | | | | | | | |

24

# INCOME JOURNAL

Month of _____, 19____

| DATE | GROSS SALES | | | | | | | | OTHER INCOME | |
|---|---|---|---|---|---|---|---|---|---|---|
| | CASH SALES | | CREDIT SALES | | RECEIVED ON ACCOUNT | | RETURNS/ ALLOWANCES | | | |
| 1 | | | | | | | | | | |
| 2 | | | | | | | | | | |
| 3 | | | | | | | | | | |
| 4 | | | | | | | | | | |
| 5 | | | | | | | | | | |
| 6 | | | | | | | | | | |
| 7 | | | | | | | | | | |
| 8 | | | | | | | | | | |
| 9 | | | | | | | | | | |
| 10 | | | | | | | | | | |
| 11 | | | | | | | | | | |
| 12 | | | | | | | | | | |
| 13 | | | | | | | | | | |
| 14 | | | | | | | | | | |
| 15 | | | | | | | | | | |
| 16 | | | | | | | | | | |
| 17 | | | | | | | | | | |
| 18 | | | | | | | | | | |
| 19 | | | | | | | | | | |
| 20 | | | | | | | | | | |
| 21 | | | | | | | | | | |
| 22 | | | | | | | | | | |
| 23 | | | | | | | | | | |
| 24 | | | | | | | | | | |
| 25 | | | | | | | | | | |
| 26 | | | | | | | | | | |
| 27 | | | | | | | | | | |
| 28 | | | | | | | | | | |
| 29 | | | | | | | | | | |
| 30 | | | | | | | | | | |
| 31 | | | | | | | | | | |
| TOTAL FOR MONTH | | | | | | | | | | |
| BALANCE FORWARD | | | | | | | | | | |
| TOTAL | | | | | | | | | | |

## PROFESSIONAL ACCOUNTING RECORDS

The following two forms are essentially alike. One is an open one that allows the user to keep track of time in any preferred increment—1/4 hour, 1/2 hour, one hour. The second form is already calibrated for quarter hours. Most professionals, like lawyers, like to account for their professional consulting time in 15-minute segments. In this manner they can more accurately charge for small services, like a phone call, dictating a short letter, or looking up a reference. It has been the experience of many professionals who keep account of their services more elastically, that only half of their time is charged for. For this reason a professional must either keep track of his working time in almost minute increments, or take a general time period and arbitrarily double it, in order to account for all of his or her time spent on a client's behalf.

| HOUR | DIARY | TIME HRS. | MIN. |
|------|-------|-----------|------|
|      |       |           |      |
|      |       |           |      |
|      |       |           |      |
|      |       |           |      |
|      |       |           |      |
|      |       |           |      |
|      |       |           |      |
|      |       |           |      |
|      |       |           |      |
|      |       |           |      |
|      |       |           |      |
|      |       |           |      |
|      |       |           |      |
|      |       |           |      |
|      |       |           |      |
|      |       |           |      |
|      |       |           |      |
|      |       |           |      |
|      |       |           |      |
|      |       |           |      |
|      |       |           |      |
|      |       |           |      |
|      |       |           |      |
|      |       |           |      |
|      |       |           |      |
|      |       |           |      |
|      |       |           |      |
|      |       |           |      |
|      |       |           |      |
|      |       |           |      |
|      |       |           |      |
|      |       |           |      |
|      |       |           |      |
|      |       |           |      |
|      |       |           |      |

## PROFESSIONAL CHARGE SHEET

# PROFESSIONAL TIME RECORD

| | PERSON | CHARGES | | PAID | | BALANCE | |
|---|---|---|---|---|---|---|---|
| 7:00 | | | | | | | |
| 7:15 | | | | | | | |
| 7:30 | | | | | | | |
| 7:45 | | | | | | | |
| 8:00 | | | | | | | |
| 8:15 | | | | | | | |
| 8:30 | | | | | | | |
| 8:45 | | | | | | | |
| 9:00 | | | | | | | |
| 9:15 | | | | | | | |
| 9:30 | | | | | | | |
| 9:45 | | | | | | | |
| 10:00 | | | | | | | |
| 10:15 | | | | | | | |
| 10:30 | | | | | | | |
| 10:45 | | | | | | | |
| 11:00 | | | | | | | |
| 11:15 | | | | | | | |
| 11:30 | | | | | | | |
| 11:45 | | | | | | | |
| 12:00 | | | | | | | |
| 12:15 | | | | | | | |
| 12:30 | | | | | | | |
| 12:45 | | | | | | | |
| 1:00 | | | | | | | |
| 1:15 | | | | | | | |
| 1:30 | | | | | | | |
| 1:45 | | | | | | | |
| 2:00 | | | | | | | |
| 2:15 | | | | | | | |
| 2:30 | | | | | | | |
| 2:45 | | | | | | | |
| 3:00 | | | | | | | |
| 3:15 | | | | | | | |
| 3:30 | | | | | | | |
| 3:45 | | | | | | | |
| 4:00 | | | | | | | |
| 4:15 | | | | | | | |
| 4:30 | | | | | | | |
| 4:45 | | | | | | | |
| 5:00 | | | | | | | |
| 5:15 | | | | | | | |
| 5:30 | | | | | | | |
| 5:45 | | | | | | | |
| 6:00 | | | | | | | |
| 6:15 | | | | | | | |
| 6:30 | | | | | | | |
| 6:45 | | | | | | | |

## STATEMENT (GENERAL)

DATE: _____ 19____

_____

_____

_____

| | | | | | | |
|---|---|---|---|---|---|---|
| | | | | | | |
| | | | | | | |
| | | | | | | |
| | | | | | | |
| | | | | | | |
| | | | | | | |
| | | | | | | |
| | | | | | | |
| | | | | | | |
| | | | | | | |
| | | | | | | |
| | | | | | | |
| | | | | | | |
| | | | | | | |
| | | | | | | |
| | | | | | | |
| | | | | | | |
| | | | | | | |
| | | | | | | |
| | | | | | | |
| | | | | | | |
| | | | | | | |
| | | | | | | |
| | | | | | | |
| | | | | | | |
| | | | | | | |
| | | | | | | |
| | | | | | | |
| | | | | | | |
| | | | | | | |

# BUSINESS DEDUCTIONS RECORD

Business Name _____

Business Address _____

_____

Social Security or
Identification No. _____

Year Ended _____ 19____

Form _____

| COST OF GOODS SOLD: | | | | | |
|---|---|---|---|---|---|
| Inventory at Beginning of Year | | | | | |
| Merchandise Bought for Sale: | | | | | |
| | | | | | |
| | | | | | |
| | | | | | |
| | | | | | |
| Salaries & Wages: | | | | | |
| | | | | | |
| | | | | | |
| Other Costs: | 〈 | | | | |
| | | | | | |
| | | | | | |
| | | | | | |
| TOTAL | | | | | |
| Less: Inventory at end of year | | | | | |
| COST OF GOODS SOLD | | | | | |

| CONTRIBUTIONS: | | |
|---|---|---|
| | | |
| | | |
| | | |
| | | |
| | | |
| | | |

| Contributions Carryover: | | | |
|---|---|---|---|
| Year of Origin | Unused Prior Years | Used This Year | |
| 19 | | | |
| 19 | | | |
| 19 | | | |
| 19 | | | |
| 19 | | | |
| TOTAL | | | |
| Total Subject to 5% Limitation | | | |

| TAXES: | | | |
|---|---|---|---|
| F.I.C.A. | | | |
| Federal Unemployment | | | |
| Federal | | | |
| | | | |
| State Sales Tax | | | |
| State Franchise Tax | | | |
| State Auto Licenses | | | |
| State Unemployment | | | |
| State Income Tax | | | |
| State | Tax | | |
| State | Tax | | |
| State | Tax | | |
| Real Estate Tax | | | |
| Personal Property Tax | | | |
| City | Tax | | |
| | | | |
| TOTAL TAXES | | | |

| SCHEDULE | LINE | | |
|---|---|---|---|
| | | | |
| | | | |
| | | | |
| | | | |
| | | | |
| | | | |
| TOTAL | | | |

| OTHER DEDUCTIONS | | |
|---|---|---|
| Advertising | | |
| Auto – Truck | | |
| Accounting – Legal | | |
| Collection | | |
| Commissions | | |
| Dues and Subscriptions | | |
| Freight & Express | | |
| General – Miscellaneous | | |
| Heat, Light, Power and Water | | |
| Insurance | | |
| Janitor and Cleaning | | |
| Laundry | | |
| Office Expenses | | |
| Postage | | |
| Printing | | |
| Refunds – Allowances | | |
| Repairs | | |
| | | |
| Supplies | | |
| | | |
| Telephone & Telegraph | | |
| Travel | | |
| | | |
| | | |
| | | |
| | | |
| | | |
| TOTAL OTHER DEDUCTIONS | | |

# 2.

# EMPLOYMENT/PERSONNEL FORMS

From the day a business opens its doors, a policy for hiring employees is needed. This need exists whether the employee or employees work on the business's premises, outside of the premises as external representatives, or as homeworkers. Hiring employees imposes obligations. Since crystal balls are not part of the hiring process, the employer must anticipate even the most unexpected and farfetched problems at some unknown time in the future. For all these reasons it is important to have the proper forms that establish a businesslike relationship between employer and employee—even if the latter is a family member or relative. An important ingredient of an employer-employee relationship is the references—which should be verified in all cases. Another factor to consider is the company's—even the individual entrepreneur's own concept—way of running the business. If the house rules are not spelled out before employment commences, then small transgressions can grow into major obstacles and even law suits. In addition to numerous commonplace forms, this section also contains a suggested company policy handbook. You may add or subtract from this, or change the ingredients and wording to suit your situation—but produce one for each employee, full- or part-time, stranger or relative, and make sure it is read and understood. It is the key to a happy and productive employer-employee relationship.

There are numerous employment application forms, employment record forms, earning record forms, separation forms, and so on. Some typical and useful ones are included here which you may wish to use as is, or change to suit your individual business needs. All employment or personnel forms are incisive to a degree—they probe into the employee's past and present life. For this reason such forms have to be kept in utmost confidence and the employee must be assured that such is the case. There are occasions when the confidential information in employment records may be divulged to outsiders—such as a credit institution to whom the employee has applied for a loan or major purchase, an insurance company about to write a policy on the employee, or another company to whom the employee has applied. It is possible, too, that law enforcement agencies can make inquiries about the employee.

## EMPLOYMENT APPLICATION AND AGREEMENT

(Please Print)                        Today's Date _____

Name_____        _____
            Last Name                          First Name & Middle Initial
Address_____ Telephone_____
            Street
                                            Soc.Sec.No._____
_____   U.S. Citizen: Yes /__/   No /__/
       City          State      Zip Code   Minimum Salary $_____
Position Desired _____
How did you find out about this employment opportunity? _____
Are you willing to work overtime on short notice? _____
Can you arrive at work on a timely basis? _____ Date you can start:_____

### EDUCATION

| Name and Location of School | From(Year)to(Year) | Grad? | Major Subject | Degree |
|---|---|---|---|---|
| High | | | | |
| College | | | | |
| Other | | | | |
| | | | | |

### RECORD OF EMPLOYMENT

PRESENT (OR LAST) POSITION:
    Name of Firm_____Supervisor/Mgr._____
    Business Address_____Telephone_____
    Type of Business_____ Salary $_____Per_____
    Dates Employed: From_____To_____ Reason for Leaving_____

    Your Duties and Specialty_____

NEXT PREVIOUS POSITION:
    Name of Firm_____Supervisor/Mgr._____
    Business Address_____Telephone_____
    Type of Business_____ Salary $_____Per_____
    Dates Employed: From_____To_____ Reason for Leaving_____

NEXT PREVIOUS POSITION:
    Name of Firm_____Supervisor/Mgr._____
    Business Address_____Telephone_____
    Type of Business_____ Salary $_____Per_____
    Dates Employed: From_____To_____ Reason for Leaving_____

### CHARACTER REFERENCES

| Name and Address | Place of Employment | Title | Telephone |
|---|---|---|---|
| 1. | | | |
| 2. | | | |

Name and address of relative or friend through whom we can locate you or who we could
contact in case of emergency:_____

Typing speed: _____ wpm
Shorthand speed: Standard _____ wpm; Speedwriting _____ wpm; Stenotype _____ wpm
Adding Machine: Do you use all five fingers of one hand to operate? Yes /__/  No /__/

## EMPLOYMENT APPLICATION AND AGREEMENT (Cont'd.)

I understand and agree that:

1. Any deliberate misrepresentation or omission of facts in my application may be justification for refusal of, or if employed, termination from employment.

2. It is my understanding that _____ may make a review of my history to verify all data given in my application for employment, related papers, or oral interviews. I authorize such review and the giving and receiving of any information requested by _____ and I release from liability any person giving or receiving any such information. I understand that inability to verify data or derogatory information discovered as a result of this review may prevent my being hired, or if hired, may subject me to dismissal.

3. I agree that my employment may be terminated by this Company at any time without liability for wages or salary except such as may have been earned at the date of such termination. I authorize any physician or hospital to release information which may be necessary to determine my ability to perform the duties of a job I am being considered for prior to employment or in the future during my employment with _____ .

4. Although _____ make every effort to accommodate individual preferences, business needs may at times make the following conditions mandatory: overtime, a rotating work schedule, or a work schedule other than Monday through Friday. I understand and accept these as conditions of my continuing employment.

I understand that this is an application for employment and that no employment contract is being offered.

I understand that, if I am employed, such employment is for no definite period of time and that _____ can change wages, benefits, and conditions in the future.

I have read and understand the above.


Date: _____   Signature: _____


\* \* \* \* \* \* \* \* \* \* \* \*

# Employment Eligibility Verification

## Section 1. Instructions to Employee/Preparer for completing this form

### Instructions for the employee.

All employees, upon being hired, must complete Section 1 of this form. Any person hired after November 6, 1986 must complete this form. (For the purpose of completion of this form the term "hired" applies to those employed, recruited or referred for a fee.)

All employees must print or type their complete name, address, date of birth, and Social Security Number. The block which correctly indicates the employee's immigration status must be checked. If the second block is checked, the employee's Alien Registration Number must be provided. If the third block is checked, the employee's Alien Registration Number *or* Admission Number must be provided, as well as the date of expiration of that status, if it expires.

All employees whose present names differ from birth names, because of marriage or other reasons, must print or type their birth names in the appropriate space of Section 1. Also, employees whose names change after employment verification should report these changes to their employer.

All employees must sign and date the form.

### Instructions for the preparer of the form, if not the employee.

If a person assists the employee with completing this form, the preparer must certify the form by signing it and printing or typing his or her complete name and address.

## Section 2. Instructions to Employer for completing this form

(For the purpose of completion of this form, the term "employer" applies to employers and those who recruit or refer for a fee.)

Employers must complete this section by examining evidence of identity and employment eligibility, and:
- checking the appropriate box in List A *or* boxes in both Lists B and C;
- recording the document identification number and expiration date (if any);
- recording the type of form if not specifically identified in the list;
- signing the certification section.

**NOTE: Employers are responsible for reverifying employment eligibility of employees whose employment eligibility documents carry an expiration date.**

Copies of documentation presented by an individual for the purpose of establishing identity and employment eligibility may be copied and retained for the purpose of complying with the requirements of this form and no other purpose. Any copies of documentation made for this purpose should be maintained with this form.

Name changes of employees which occur after preparation of this form should be recorded on the form by lining through the old name, printing the new name and the reason (such as marriage), and dating and initialing the changes. Employers should not attempt to delete or erase the old name in any fashion.

### RETENTION OF RECORDS.

The completed form must be retained by the employer for:
- three years after the date of hiring; or
- one year after the date the employment is terminated, whichever is later.

Employers may photocopy or reprint this form as necessary.

U.S. Department of Justice
Immigration and Naturalization Service

OMB #1115-0136
Form I-9 (05/07/87)

# EMPLOYMENT ELIGIBILITY VERIFICATION (Form I-9)

**1** **EMPLOYEE INFORMATION AND VERIFICATION:** (To be completed and signed by employee.)

| Name: (Print or Type)   Last | First | Middle | Birth Name |
|---|---|---|---|
| Address: Street Name and Number | City | State | ZIP Code |
| Date of Birth (Month/Day/Year) | | Social Security Number | |

I attest, under penalty of perjury, that I am (check a box):

☐ 1. A citizen or national of the United States.

☐ 2. An alien lawfully admitted for permanent residence (Alien Number A _____ ).

☐ 3. An alien authorized by the Immigration and Naturalization Service to work in the United States (Alien Number A _____ , or Admission Number _____ , expiration of employment authorization, if any _____ ) .

I attest, under penalty of perjury, the documents that I have presented as evidence of identity and employment eligibility are genuine and relate to me. I am aware that federal law provides for imprisonment and/or fine for any false statements or use of false documents in connection with this certificate.

| Signature | Date (Month/Day/Year) |
|---|---|

**PREPARER/TRANSLATOR CERTIFICATION** (To be completed if prepared by person other than the employee). I attest, under penalty of perjury, that the above was prepared by me at the request of the named individual and is based on all information of which I have any knowledge.

| Signature | Name (Print or Type) | | |
|---|---|---|---|
| Address (Street Name and Number) | City | State | Zip Code |

**2** **EMPLOYER REVIEW AND VERIFICATION:** (To be completed and signed by employer.)

Instructions:

Examine one document from List A and check the appropriate box, **_OR_** examine one document from List B **_and_** one from List C and check the appropriate boxes. Provide the **_Document Identification Number_** and **_Expiration Date_** for the document checked.

| List A<br>Documents that Establish<br>Identity and Employment Eligibility | List B<br>Documents that Establish<br>Identity | **and** | List C<br>Documents that Establish<br>Employment Eligibility |
|---|---|---|---|
| ☐ 1. United States Passport | ☐ 1. A State-issued driver's license or a State-issued I.D. card with a photograph, or information, including name, sex, date of birth, height, weight, and color of eyes. (Specify State)_____ ) | | ☐ 1. Original Social Security Number Card (other than a card stating it is not valid for employment) |
| ☐ 2. Certificate of United States Citizenship | | | ☐ 2. A birth certificate issued by State, county, or municipal authority bearing a seal or other certification |
| ☐ 3. Certificate of Naturalization | ☐ 2. U.S. Military Card | | |
| ☐ 4. Unexpired foreign passport with attached Employment Authorization | ☐ 3. Other (Specify document and issuing authority) | | ☐ 3. Unexpired INS Employment Authorization Specify form # _____ |
| ☐ 5. Alien Registration Card with photograph | | | |
| **_Document Identification_** | **_Document Identification_** | | **_Document Identification_** |
| # _____ | # _____ | | # _____ |
| **_Expiration Date (if any)_** | **_Expiration Date (if any)_** | | **_Expiration Date (if any)_** |
| _____ | _____ | | _____ |

**CERTIFICATION: I attest, under penalty of perjury, that I have examined the documents presented by the above individual, that they appear to be genuine and to relate to the individual named, and that the individual, to the best of my knowledge, is eligible to work in the United States.**

| Signature | Name (Print or Type) | Title |
|---|---|---|
| Employer Name | Address | Date |

Form I-9 (05/07/87)
OMB No. 1115-0136

U.S. Department of Justice
Immigration and Naturalization Service

# EMPLOYMENT APPLICATION

## PERSONAL INFORMATION:

Date _____     Social Security Number _____

Name _____
        *Last*          *First*          *Middle*

Present Address _____
         *Street*          *City*          *State*          *Zip*

Permanent Address _____
         *Street*          *City*          *State*          *Zip*

Phone No. _____     Height _____     Weight _____

Relatives Already Employed By This Company _____

Referred by _____

Last

First

Middle

## EMPLOYMENT DESIRED:

Position _____     Date You Can Start _____     Salary Desired _____

Are You Employed Now? _____     If So – May We Inquire of Your Present Employer? _____

Ever Applied to this Company Before? _____     When? _____

## EDUCATION:

| | Name and Location of School | Circle Last Year completed | Did You Graduate? | Subjects Studied and Degree(s) Received |
|---|---|---|---|---|
| Grammar School | | 1 2 3 4 | [ ] Yes [ ] No | |
| High School | | 1 2 3 4 | [ ] Yes [ ] No | |
| College | | 1 2 3 4 5 6 | [ ] Yes [ ] No | |
| Trade, Business or Correspondence School | | 1 2 3 4 | [ ] Yes [ ] No | |

Subjects of Special Study or Research Work: _____

What Foreign Languages Do You Speak Fluenty? _____

Read? _____     Write? _____

List Activities Other Than Religious (Civic, Athletic, etc.) _____

EXCLUDE ORGANIZATIONS – THE NAME OR CHARACTER OF WHICH INDICATES THE RACE, CREED, COLOR OR NATIONAL ORIGIN OF ITS MEMBERS

(Continued)

## EMPLOYMENT APPLICATION *(Cont'd.)*

**FORMER EMPLOYERS:** List Below the Last Four Employers – Starting with Last One First

| Date Month and Year | Name and Address of Employer | Salary | Position | Reason for Leaving |
|---|---|---|---|---|
| From | | | | |
| To | | | | |
| From | | | | |
| To | | | | |
| From | | | | |
| To | | | | |
| From | | | | |
| To | | | | |

**REFERENCES:** List Below the Names of Three Persons, Not Related To You, Whom You Have Known At Least One Year.

| Name | Address | Business | Years Acquainted |
|---|---|---|---|
| 1. | | | |
| 2. | | | |
| 3. | | | |

**PHYSICAL RECORD:** Do you have any physical condition which may influence your particular position application?

In Case of
Emergency Notify

| Name | Address | Phone No. |
|---|---|---|

*I authorize investigation of all statements contained in this application. I understand that misrepresentation or omission of facts called for is cause for termination of further consideration or dismissal. I understand and agree that my employment is for no definite period and may be terminated at any time for good cause.*

Date _____ Signature _____

### DO NOT WRITE BELOW THIS LINE

Interviewed By _____ Date _____

REMARKS: _____

# EMPLOYEE EARNINGS RECORD

| Employee | | Employee No. | Social Security Number | Dependents | Salary/Wages |
|---|---|---|---|---|---|
| Position | | | Started On | | |

## FIRST QUARTER

| WEEK ENDING | HOURS | | DEDUCTIONS | | | | NET PAY |
|---|---|---|---|---|---|---|---|
| | REG. | O.T | FED. W/H | ST. W/H | FICA | | |
| | | | | | | | |
| | | | | | | | |
| | | | | | | | |
| | | | | | | | |
| | | | | | | | |
| | | | | | | | |
| | | | | | | | |
| | | | | | | | |
| | | | | | | | |
| | | | | | | | |
| | | | | | | | |
| | | | | | | | |
| | | | | | | | |
| TOTAL 1st QTR | | | | | | | |
| TOTAL 3 Mos. | | | | | | | |

## SECOND QUARTER

| WEEK ENDING | HOURS | | DEDUCTIONS | | | | NET PAY |
|---|---|---|---|---|---|---|---|
| | REG. | O.T | FED. W/H | ST. W/H | FICA | | |
| | | | | | | | |
| | | | | | | | |
| | | | | | | | |
| | | | | | | | |
| | | | | | | | |
| | | | | | | | |
| | | | | | | | |
| | | | | | | | |
| | | | | | | | |
| | | | | | | | |
| | | | | | | | |
| | | | | | | | |
| | | | | | | | |
| TOTAL 2nd QTR | | | | | | | |
| TOTAL 6 Mos. | | | | | | | |

## THIRD QUARTER

| WEEK ENDING | HOURS | | DEDUCTIONS | | | | NET PAY |
|---|---|---|---|---|---|---|---|
| | REG. | O.T | FED. W/H | ST. W/H | FICA | | |
| | | | | | | | |
| | | | | | | | |
| | | | | | | | |
| | | | | | | | |
| | | | | | | | |
| | | | | | | | |
| | | | | | | | |
| | | | | | | | |
| | | | | | | | |
| | | | | | | | |
| | | | | | | | |
| | | | | | | | |
| | | | | | | | |
| TOTAL 3rd QTR | | | | | | | |
| TOTAL 9 Mos. | | | | | | | |

## FOURTH QUARTER

| WEEK ENDING | HOURS | | DEDUCTIONS | | | | NET PAY |
|---|---|---|---|---|---|---|---|
| | REG. | O.T | FED. W/H | ST. W/H | FICA | | |
| | | | | | | | |
| | | | | | | | |
| | | | | | | | |
| | | | | | | | |
| | | | | | | | |
| | | | | | | | |
| | | | | | | | |
| | | | | | | | |
| | | | | | | | |
| | | | | | | | |
| | | | | | | | |
| | | | | | | | |
| | | | | | | | |
| TOTAL 4th QTR | | | | | | | |
| TOTAL 12 Mos. | | | | | | | |

# EMPLOYEE FLEXTIME SCHEDULE

Employee _____          Week of: _____

| DAY | A.M. TIME IN | LUNCH | | P.M. TIME OUT | EVENING | | HOURS FOR DAY |
| | | OUT | IN | | IN | OUT | |
|---|---|---|---|---|---|---|---|
| MONDAY | | | | | | | |
| TUESDAY | | | | | | | |
| WEDNESDAY | | | | | | | |
| THURSDAY | | | | | | | |
| FRIDAY | | | | | | | |
| SATURDAY | | | | | | | |
| SUNDAY | | | | | | | |

TOTAL HOURS FOR WEEK

# SALES EXPERIENCE—EMPLOYMENT HISTORY

*To be Completed by Applicant*

Name: _____

Address and Zip: _____

_____

_____

Phone: _____  Age: _____

Marital Status: _____ No. Dependents: _____

PHOTO

## EDUCATION AND TRAINING (SCHOOLS, YEARS GRADUATED, DEGREES)

## PERTINENT OUTSIDE ACTIVITIES AND ACCOMPLISHMENTS, PAST AND PRESENT

## SALES EXPERIENCE (MOST RECENT)

| Company | Supervisor |
|---|---|
| Address | |
| | Phone |
| Product or Service | |
| Employed From                                        To | |
| Monthly [ ]    or Annual [ ] | $ |
| Monthly [ ]    or Annual [ ] | $ |
| Compensation and Expense Plan | |
| | |
| Average Monthly Earnings    At Start:            $ | At End:            $ |
| Reason for Leaving | |
| | |

*If previous experience is pertinent, please continue on next sheet.*

# SALES EXPERIENCE–EMPLOYMENT HISTORY (Continued)

| Company | | Supervisor | |
|---|---|---|---|
| Address | | | |
| | | Phone | |
| Product or Service | | | |
| Employed From | To | | |
| Monthly [ ]    or Annual [ ] | | $ | |
| Monthly [ ]    or Annual [ ] | | $ | |
| Compensation and Expense Plan | | | |
| | | | |
| Average Monthly Earnings    At Start:    $ | | At End:    $ | |
| Reason for Leaving | | | |
| | | | |

| Company | | Supervisor | |
|---|---|---|---|
| Address | | | |
| | | Phone | |
| Product or Service | | | |
| Employed From | To | | |
| Monthly [ ]    or Annual [ ] | | $ | |
| Monthly [ ]    or Annual [ ] | | $ | |
| Compensation and Expense Plan | | | |
| | | | |
| Average Monthly Earnings    At Start:    $ | | At End:    $ | |
| Reason for Leaving | | | |
| | | | |

| Company | | Supervisor | |
|---|---|---|---|
| Address | | | |
| | | Phone | |
| Product or Service | | | |
| Employed From | To | | |
| Monthly [ ]    or Annual [ ] | | $ | |
| Monthly [ ]    or Annual [ ] | | $ | |
| Compensation and Expense Plan | | | |
| | | | |
| Average Monthly Earnings    At Start:    $ | | At End:    $ | |
| Reason for Leaving | | | |
| | | | |

## EMPLOYEE RECORD

| Employee Name | | Employment Date | Status |
|---|---|---|---|
| | | | [ ] Regular   [ ] Part   [ ] Temporary Time |
| Address | | | |

| Years of Service | 1 | 2 | 3 | 4 | 5 | 6 | 7 | 8 | 9 | 10 | 11 | 12 | 13 | 14 | 15 | 16 | 17 | 18 | 19 | 20 | 21 | 22 | 23 | 24 | 25 | 26 | Security Clearance/Bonding (Date) |
|---|---|---|---|---|---|---|---|---|---|---|---|---|---|---|---|---|---|---|---|---|---|---|---|---|---|---|---|
| | | | | | | | | | | | | | | | | | | | | | | | | | | | |

## PAYROLL DATA

| Birthday | Sex | Social Security No. | | | Marital Status | Name of Spouse | | | No. of Children | |
|---|---|---|---|---|---|---|---|---|---|---|
| | Exemptions Claimed | | | | | | | | | |
| Federal Withholding | Additonal Amount Withheld | | | | | | | | | |

| | Date Eligible | Date Joined | Date Withdrawn |
|---|---|---|---|
| Union Status | | | |
| Pension Plan | | | |
| Credit Union | | | |
| | | | |
| | | | |

| Insurance | Date Eligible | Date Joined | Date Withdrawn |
|---|---|---|---|
| Life | | | |
| Medical–Self | | | |
| Dependent(s) | | | |
| Maj. Med–Self | | | |
| Dependent(s) | | | |

## GENERAL INFORMATION

| In Emergency Notify | Relationship | City | State | Zip | Phone |
|---|---|---|---|---|---|
| | Relationship | City | State | Zip | Phone |
| | | | | | |

| RELATIVES OR FRIENDS EMPLOYED BY THIS COMPANY | Names | Relationship | Names | Relationship |
|---|---|---|---|---|
| | | | | |

| EDUCATION | ELEM. _____ J H S _____ S H S _____  COLLEGE 1 2 3 4 5 6 MAJOR _____  OTHER _____ | SPECIAL SKILLS OR TRAINING | |
|---|---|---|---|

## TERMINATION RECORD

| DATE | REASON |
|---|---|
| | |

43

# JOB DESCRIPTION WORKSHEET

**Position Title**

**Department or Office**

**Supervisor's Title**

**Nature of Position (Brief Description)**

**Complexity of Position (Data)**

**Complexity of Position (People)**

**Complexity of Position (Things)**

**Position Relationships**

**ENVIRONMENT**

**Physical Requirements**

**Work Environment**

# JOB DESCRIPTION WORKSHEET

## POSITION RESPONSIBILITIES

| |
|---|
| **Policy Formulation** |
| |
| |
| **Planning** |
| |
| |
| **Decision Authority** |
| |
| |
| **Budgetary** |
| |
| |
| **Directing Others** |
| |
| |

## MINIMUM QUALIFICATIONS REQUIRED

| |
|---|
| **Education/Training** |
| |
| |
| **Technical Skills** |
| |
| |
| **Relevant Experience** |
| |
| |

## DESIRABLE ADDITIONAL QUALIFICATIONS

| |
|---|
| |
| |
| |
| |
| |
| |

45

# PAYROLL RECORD

| PERIOD ENDING | NAME OF EMPLOYEE | SOCIAL SECURITY NUMBER | HOURS WORKED | | RATE PER HOUR | A. EARNINGS | | | | B. WITHHOLDING AND DEDUCTIONS | | | | | | | NET PAY (A–B) | STATE U/I COMP. |
|---|---|---|---|---|---|---|---|---|---|---|---|---|---|---|---|---|---|---|
| | | | REG | O.T. | | REGULAR | OVERTIME | OTHER | TOTAL A | FEDERAL TAX | F.I.C.A. | STATE | CITY | ADVANCE EIC | OTHER | TOTAL B | | |
| | | | | | | | | | | | | | | | | | | |
| | | | | | | | | | | | | | | | | | | |
| | | | | | | | | | | | | | | | | | | |
| | | | | | | | | | | | | | | | | | | |
| | | | | | | | | | | | | | | | | | | |
| | | | | | | | | | | | | | | | | | | |
| | | | | | | | | | | | | | | | | | | |
| | | | | | | | | | | | | | | | | | | |
| | | | | | | | | | | | | | | | | | | |
| **TOTAL FOR MONTH** | | | | | | | | | | | | | | | | | | |
| **BALANCE FORWARD** | | | | | | | | | | | | | | | | | | |
| **TOTAL TO DATE** | | | | | | | | | | | | | | | | | | |

## DEPOSIT INFORMATION: Federal Withholding and FUTA Tax

Deposited _____, 19___   Federal W/H: Income Tax $ _____   + FICA Tax $ _____   + Employer Contrib. FICA $ _____   – Advance EIC = Total _____

Deposited _____, 19___   Federal W/H: Income Tax $ _____   + FICA Tax $ _____   + Employer Contrib. FICA $ _____   – Advance EIC = Total _____

Deposited _____, 19___   Federal W/H: Income Tax $ _____   + FICA Tax $ _____   + Employer Contrib. FICA $ _____   – Advance EIC = Total _____

Deposited _____, 19___   Federal W/H: Income Tax $ _____   + FICA Tax $ _____   + Employer Contrib. FICA $ _____   – Advance EIC = Total _____

Quarterly State Unemployment Insurance Contributions paid: Deposited _____, 19___ ; Amount $ _____

For information about depositing taxes and filing Form 941, see IRS Circular E—Employers' Tax Guide.

# PAYROLL REGISTER

DATE:_____

| YEAR-TO-DATE | | EMPLOYEE | | NAME OF EMPLOYEE | HOURS WORKED | BASE RATE | EARNINGS | | | | TOTAL | DEDUCTIONS | | | | NET PAY |
| EARNINGS | WITH TAX | DEPT | NUMBER | | | | REGULAR | OT PREM | OTHER | | | FICA | WITH TAX | MISC | |
|---|---|---|---|---|---|---|---|---|---|---|---|---|---|---|---|
| | | | | | | | | | | | | | | | |
| | | | | | | | | | | | | | | | |
| | | | | | | | | | | | | | | | |
| | | | | | | | | | | | | | | | |
| | | | | | | | | | | | | | | | |
| | | | | | | | | | | | | | | | |
| | | | | | | | | | | | | | | | |
| | | | | | | | | | | | | | | | |
| | | | | | | | | | | | | | | | |
| | | | | | | | | | | | | | | | |
| | | | | | | | | | | | | | | | |
| | | | | | | | | | | | | | | | |
| | | | | | | | | | | | | | | | |
| | | | | | | | | | | | | | | | |
| | | | | | | | | | | | | | | | |
| | | | | | | | | | | | | | | | |
| | | | | | | | | | | | | | | | |
| | | | | | | | | | | | | | | | |
| | | | | | | | | | | | | | | | |
| | | | | | | | | | | | | | | | |
| | | | | | | | | | | | | | | | |
| | | | | | | | | | | | | | | | |

47

# WEEKLY PAYROLL SUMMARY

DEPARTMENT _____    WEEK ENDING _____

| EMPLOYEE NAME | HOURS WORK'D | RATE | TOTALS | | | DEDUCTIONS | | | | | NET PAY | CHECK NO. |
|---|---|---|---|---|---|---|---|---|---|---|---|---|
| | | | REG. WAGES | O.T. WAGES | GROSS WAGES | FED. TAXES | STATE TAXES | FICA | INS. | DUES | | |
| | | | | | | | | | | | | |
| | | | | | | | | | | | | |
| | | | | | | | | | | | | |
| | | | | | | | | | | | | |
| | | | | | | | | | | | | |
| | | | | | | | | | | | | |
| | | | | | | | | | | | | |
| | | | | | | | | | | | | |
| | | | | | | | | | | | | |
| | | | | | | | | | | | | |
| | | | | | | | | | | | | |
| | | | | | | | | | | | | |
| | | | | | | | | | | | | |
| | | | | | | | | | | | | |
| | | | | | | | | | | | | |
| | | | | | | | | | | | | |

# 3.

# FINANCIAL FORMS: BANKING, CREDIT, COLLECTIONS, AND PERSONAL

This group of forms presents a more sophisticated extension of bookkeeping and accounting forms. They will help entrepreneurs do what the title implies—control the business. Without these controls, running a business is like driving into uncharted territory without a road map, or building a house without blueprints. Most financial control forms serve three distinct and necessary purposes: (1) tell the business owner about his performance, where he has been and where he might be going; (2) prepare evidence that will enable the entrepreneur to borrow money if and when this becomes a necessity; and (3) provide a record that will help to determine tax obligations. Each one of these forms is extremely important and will be well to study, and to use those that are pertinent to the business's sound operation. The orderly and successful management of a business often depends on how thoroughly and accurately financial controls are implemented. These forms will help you do just that.

## ASSET DEPRECIATION SCHEDULE

Prepared By: _____     Date: _____

| | Date of Purchase | Item | Total Cost | No. Yrs. Useful Lifetime | Salvage Value | Total Depreciation | Annual Depreciation | Depreciation Years From | To |
|---|---|---|---|---|---|---|---|---|---|
| 1 | | | | | | | | | |
| 2 | | | | | | | | | |
| 3 | | | | | | | | | |
| 4 | | | | | | | | | |
| 5 | | | | | | | | | |
| 6 | | | | | | | | | |
| 7 | | | | | | | | | |
| 8 | | | | | | | | | |
| 9 | | | | | | | | | |
| 10 | | | | | | | | | |
| 11 | | | | | | | | | |
| 12 | | | | | | | | | |
| 13 | | | | | | | | | |
| 14 | | | | | | | | | |
| 15 | | | | | | | | | |
| 16 | | | | | | | | | |
| 17 | | | | | | | | | |
| 18 | | | | | | | | | |
| 19 | | | | | | | | | |
| 20 | | | | | | | | | |

TOTAL
ANNUAL FIXED ASSETS
DEPRECIATION:  _____

# BALANCE SHEET

Year Ending _____ , 19____
                 *($000)*

## ASSETS

**Current Assets**

Cash _____

Accounts Receivable _____

   Less: Allowance for

     doubtful accounts _____

       Net realizable value _____

Inventory _____

Temporary investment _____

Prepaid expenses _____

   **Total Current Assets** _____

**Long–Term Investments** _____

**Fixed Assets**

Land _____

Buildings _____ at

   cost, less accumulated depreciation

   of _____. Net book value _____

Equipment _____ at

   cost, less accumulated depreciation

   of _____. Net book value _____

Furniture/Fixtures _____ at

   cost, less accumulated depreciation

   of _____. Net book value _____

**Total Net Fixed Assets** _____

Other Assets _____

**TOTAL ASSETS** ════════

## LIABILITIES

**Current Liabilities**

Accounts payable _____

Short–term notes _____

Current portion of

   long–term notes _____

Interest payable _____

Taxes payable _____

Accrued payroll _____

   **Total Current Liabilities** _____

**Equity**

Total owner's equity (proprietorship) _____

*or*

_____equity _____

_____equity _____

   (partnership)

   Total partners' equity _____

*or*

Shareholders' equity (corporation) _____

Capital stock _____

Capital paid–in in excess of par _____

Retained earnings _____

   Total shareholders' equity _____

**TOTAL LIABILITIES
AND EQUITY** ════════

51

## CASH FLOW BUDGET

Year: _____

| | Jan | Feb. | Mar. | April | May | June | July | Aug. | Sept. | Oct. | Nov. | Dec. | Cumulative |
|---|---|---|---|---|---|---|---|---|---|---|---|---|---|
| Cash balance—beginning | | | | | | | | | | | | | |
| Cash from operations | | | | | | | | | | | | | |
| Total Available Cash | | | | | | | | | | | | | |
| Less: | | | | | | | | | | | | | |
| Captial expenditures | | | | | | | | | | | | | |
| Interest | | | | | | | | | | | | | |
| Dividends | | | | | | | | | | | | | |
| Debt retirement | | | | | | | | | | | | | |
| Other | | | | | | | | | | | | | |
| Total Cash Disbursements | | | | | | | | | | | | | |
| Cash Balance of (deficit) | | | | | | | | | | | | | |
| Add: | | | | | | | | | | | | | |
| Short—term loans | | | | | | | | | | | | | |
| Long—term loans | | | | | | | | | | | | | |
| Capital stock issues | | | | | | | | | | | | | |
| Cash Balance—end | | | | | | | | | | | | | |

# CASH REGISTER RECONCILIATION

NAME _____

HOUR _____
DATE _____

| | | |
|---|---|---|
| OPENING – CASH | | |
| OPENING – F/S | | |
| REGISTER READING | | |
| EXTRA CASH | | |
| REBATES | | |
| TOTAL | | |
| | TWENTIES | |
| | TENS | |
| | FIVES | |
| | ONES | |
| | HALVES | |
| | QUARTERS | |
| | DIMES | |
| | NICKELS | |
| | PENNIES | |
| | CHECKS | |
| | ENDING – CASH | |
| | ENDING – F/S | |
| | PAYOUTS | |
| | DEPOSITS | |
| | REFUNDS | |

TOTAL _____

OVER _____        SHORT _____

# DAILY CASH BALANCE

DATE: _____

CASH ON HAND            $ _____

CASH SALES – COUNTER    $ _____

CASH SALES – C.O.D.     $ _____

COLLECTIONS             $ _____

LESS: DEPOSITS          $ _____

_____        $ _____

## BALANCE                            $ _____

CASH                    $ _____

CHECKS                  $ _____

CASH PAYOUTS            $ _____

OUT TICKETS             $ _____

_____        $ _____

## BALANCE                            $ _____

REMARKS: _____

_____

_____

# DAILY CASH RECORD

Date: _____

CASH ON HAND—Beginning of Day                    $ [        |    ]

RECEIPTS:

| Accounts Receivable | $ | | |
|---|---|---|---|
| | | | |
| | | | |
| | | | |
| | | | |
| | | | |
| | | | |
| | | | |
| | | | |
| | | | |
| | | | |
| | | | |
| | | | |

Total Received on Account          $ [    |    ]

Sales:

| | $ | | |
|---|---|---|---|
| | | | |
| | | | |
| | | | |

Total Sales
Sales Tax
Other Cash Receipts: (Explain)     _____

Employer Advances
        TOTAL CASH RECEIPTS          $ [    |    ]
        CASH TO BE ACCOUNTED FOR     $ [    |    ]

DISBURSEMENTS:

Auto Expense                          $ [    |    ]
Bank Deposits
Discounts and Allowances
Employer Withdrawals
Freight
Merchandise
Office Expense
Postage
Repairs
Supplies
Wages:

| NAME | TOTAL WAGES | WITH-HOLDING TAX | F.I.C.A. | OTHER | NET |
|---|---|---|---|---|---|
| | | | | | |
| | | | | | |
| | | | | | |

Other Paid Outs: Explain Fully       _____
_____
_____

        TOTAL DISBURSEMENTS          $ [    |    ]
        Cash Balance Should Be:
CASH COUNT $_____  [ ] Cash Over $_____  [ ] Cash Short $_____

BALANCE AT END OF DAY (Carry Forward)       $ [    |    ]

# DEPRECIATION SCHEDULE

Name _____
Address _____

Year Ended _____ 19 ___
Social Security or Identification No. _____

| 1. Kind of Property | 2. Date Acquired | 3. Cost or Basis to Begin | 4. Investment Credit Reference | 5. Estimated Salvage Value | 6. Adjusted Cost or Basis at End | 7. Depreciation Allowed Prior Years | 8. Life (Years) | 9. Method Used | 10. Rate (%) | 11. DEPRECIATION THIS YEAR | |
|---|---|---|---|---|---|---|---|---|---|---|---|
| | | | | | | | | | | Special First Year | Regular Depreciation |
| | | | | | | | | | | | |

TOTALS......
TOTAL DEPRECIATION.....................

SL – Straight Line
DB – Declining Balance
SY – Sum of Years

56

# EXPENSE BUDGET

Month of: _____

|  | | Estimate | Actual | Difference $ | % |
|---|---|---|---|---|---|
| **PERSONNEL:** | Office: | | | | |
| | Store: | | | | |
| | Salespeople: | | | | |
| | Others (List): | | | | |
| | Shop: | | | | |
| | | | | | |
| **OPERATING:** | Advertising: | | | | |
| | Bad Debts: | | | | |
| | Cash Discounts: | | | | |
| | Delivery Costs: | | | | |
| | Depreciation: | | | | |
| | Dues and Subscriptions: | | | | |
| | Employee Benefits: | | | | |
| | Insurance: | | | | |
| | Interest: | | | | |
| | Legal and Auditing: | | | | |
| | Maintenance and Repairs: | | | | |
| | Office Supplies: | | | | |
| | Postage: | | | | |
| | Rent or Mortgage: | | | | |
| | Sales Expenses: | | | | |
| | Shipping and Storage: | | | | |
| | Supplies: | | | | |
| | Taxes: | | | | |
| | Telephone: | | | | |
| | Utilities: | | | | |
| | Other (List): | | | | |
| | | | | | |
| | **TOTAL:** | | | | |

# GENERAL & ADMINISTRATIVE EXPENSE BUDGET

| | Month Ending _____ 19__ | | | Year to Date | | |
|---|---|---|---|---|---|---|
| | Budget | Actual | ± Difference | Budget | Actual | ± Difference |
| **Fixed** | | | | | | |
| Executive Salaries | | | | | | |
| Office Salaries | | | | | | |
| Employee Benefits | | | | | | |
| Payroll Taxes | | | | | | |
| Pensions | | | | | | |
| Travel and Entertainment | | | | | | |
| Directors' Fees & Expenses | | | | | | |
| Insurance | | | | | | |
| Rent | | | | | | |
| Depreciation | | | | | | |
| Taxes | | | | | | |
| Legal | | | | | | |
| Audit | | | | | | |
| Telephone and Telegraph | | | | | | |
| Utilities | | | | | | |
| Contributions | | | | | | |
| Postage | | | | | | |
| Dues | | | | | | |
| Sundry | | | | | | |
| | | | | | | |
| **Variable** | | | | | | |
| Office Salaries | | | | | | |
| Employee Benefits | | | | | | |
| Payroll Taxes | | | | | | |
| Advertising & Promotion | | | | | | |
| Travel and Entertainment | | | | | | |
| Vehicle Operation | | | | | | |
| Telephone and Telegraph | | | | | | |
| Stationery and Office Supplies | | | | | | |
| Bad Debts | | | | | | |
| Postage | | | | | | |
| Contributions | | | | | | |
| Sundry | | | | | | |
| | | | | | | |
| **TOTAL** | | | | | | |

# PETTY CASH RECONCILIATION

Department: _____    Section: _____

Petty Cash Check: _____    Supervisor: _____

Last Audit Date: _____    Audited By: _____

| Date | Paid to or Received From | For | Cash Received Cash Disbursed | Balance |
|------|--------------------------|-----|------------------------------|---------|
| | Balance from Last Page | | | |
| | | | | |
| | | | | |
| | | | | |
| | | | | |
| | | | | |
| | | | | |
| | | | | |
| | | | | |
| | | | | |
| | | | | |
| | | | | |
| | | | | |
| | | | | |
| | | | | |
| | | | | |
| | | | | |

| | Summary | |
|---|---|---|
| Audit/Review:    Date: _____    by _____ | Cash on Hand | _____ |
| P.C. Reimbursement:    Date: _____    Amount _____ | Petty Cash Slips | _____ |
| By: _____    Ck. No. _____ | Total | _____ |
| Audited/Reconciled By | [ ] Over _____   Disposition: _____ | [ ] Short _____   Disposition: _____ |
| Supervisor Approval | | |

59

# RENTAL INCOME

Name _____

Social Security or
Identification No. _____

Address _____

Form _____ Year Ended _____ , 19____

|  | Property #1 | Property #2 | Property #3 | Property #4 | Property #5 | Property #6 | TOTAL |
|---|---|---|---|---|---|---|---|
| **GROSS INCOME** $ | | | | | | | |

**EXPENSES**

|  | Property #1 | Property #2 | Property #3 | Property #4 | Property #5 | Property #6 | TOTAL |
|---|---|---|---|---|---|---|---|
| Advertising | | | | | | | |
| Commissions | | | | | | | |
| Depreciation | | | | | | | |
| Fuel | | | | | | | |
| Garbage & Refuse | | | | | | | |
| Gas | | | | | | | |
| Insurance | | | | | | | |
| Interest | | | | | | | |
| Legal and Collection | | | | | | | |
| Licenses | | | | | | | |
| Light and Power | | | | | | | |
| Management Fees | | | | | | | |
| Office Supplies | | | | | | | |
| Painting & Decorating | | | | | | | |
| Plumbing | | | | | | | |
| Repairs – | | | | | | | |
| Repairs – | | | | | | | |
| Supplies – | | | | | | | |
| Supplies – | | | | | | | |
| Taxes – Property | | | | | | | |
| Taxes – Payroll | | | | | | | |
| Taxes – Other | | | | | | | |
| Wages | | | | | | | |
| Water | | | | | | | |
| | | | | | | | |
| | | | | | | | |
| | | | | | | | |
| | | | | | | | |
| **TOTAL EXPENSES** | | | | | | | |
| Less ____ % Occupancy by Taxpayer | | | | | | | |
| **NET EXPENSES** | | | | | | | |

| **NET RENTAL INCOME** | | | | | | | |
|---|---|---|---|---|---|---|---|

## DEPRECIATION SCHEDULE – Adaptable

| Kind of Property | Date Acquired | Cost or Other Basis | Previous Depreciation | Method | Rate (%) or Life (Yrs.) | Depreciation for this Year |
|---|---|---|---|---|---|---|
| | | | | | | |
| | | | | | | |
| | | | | | | |
| | | | | | | |
| | | | | | | |
| | | | | | | |
| | | | | | | |
| | | | | | | |
| **TOTAL DEPRECIATION** | | | | | | |

## FEASIBILITY FORMS

These forms help the business person determine the likelihood that a certain situation, promotion, product or product line, or development will fulfill the objectives set. It is a way of organizing an educated guess in a controlled format. Financial Feasibility will help you determine the cash flow needed for a specific period—how much to allocate, to shift, to borrow. A Marketing Feasibility will help determine whether a certain established product or service, or a new one, will be worth the effort, how much it might earn, how much of a market share it might garner, and how much it might return on investment. Feasibility studies can be applied to most all business situations. They must be done with honest realism and perhaps even with some degree of conservatism. It will usually be better to have your projections exceeded than to struggle with a shortfall and lame excuses. Feasibility forms will help you arrive at pragmatic conclusions.

# FINANCIAL FEASIBILITY

| PRO FORMA PROFIT AND LOSS, AND CASH FLOW SCHEDULE 19___ TO 19___ | 19___ | 19___ | 19___ | 19___ | 19___ |
|---|---|---|---|---|---|
| 1.  Total Gross Revenue | $ | $ | $ | $ | $ |
| 2.  Cost of Sales | | | | | $ |
| 3.  Gross Profit | | | | | |
| 4.  Cash Operating Expenses | | | | | |
| 5.  Interest--Term Loan | | | | | |
| 6.  Interest--Demand Loan | | | | | |
| 7.  Depreciation | | | | | |
| 8.  Total Expenses | | | | | |
| 9.  Net Profit before Taxes | | | | | |
| 10. Income Taxes (@ ___%) | | | | | |
| 11. Net Profit after Taxes | | | | | |
| 12. Depreciation | | | | | |
| 13. Cash Flow from Operations | | | | | |
| 14. Repayment of Principal | ( ) | ( ) | ( ) | ( ) | ( ) |
| 15. (Demand Loan)/Bank Balance | ( ) | | | | |
| 16. Actual Cash Flow | | | | | |

# FINANCIAL FEASIBILITY

| PRO FORMA PROFIT AND LOSS, AND CASH FLOW SCHEDULE 19___ TO 19___ | 19___ | 19___ | 19___ | 19___ | 19___ |
|---|---|---|---|---|---|
| 1. Total Gross Revenue | $160,700 | $176,200 | $184,200 | $193,800 | $203,700 |
| 2. Cost of Sales | 51,100 | 56,000 | 58,600 | 61,600 | 64,600 |
| 3. Gross Profit | 109,600 | 120,200 | 125,600 | 132,200 | 138,600 |
| 4. Cash Operating Expenses | 45,000 | 49,300 | 51,600 | 54,300 | 56,900 |
| 5. Interest--Term Loan | 15,000 | 12,600 | 10,000 | 7,000 | 3,700 |
| 6. Interest--Demand Loan | 3,000 | 500 | 0 | 0 | 0 |
| 7. Depreciation | 22,900 | 21,300 | 19,900 | 18,600 | 17,400 |
| 8. Total Expenses | 85,900 | 83,700 | 81,500 | 79,900 | 78,000 |
| 9. Net Profit before Taxes | 23,800 | 36,500 | 44,100 | 52,300 | 60,600 |
| 10. Income Taxes (@ ___%) | 5,950 | 9,125 | 11,025 | 13,075 | 15,150 |
| 11. Net Profit after Taxes | 17,850 | 27,375 | 33,075 | 39,225 | 45,450 |
| 12. Depreciation | 22,800 | 21,300 | 19,900 | 18,600 | 17,400 |
| 13. Cash Flow from Operations | 40,650 | 48,675 | 52,975 | 57,825 | 62,850 |
| 14. Repayment of Principal | (19,700) | (22,000) | (24,700) | (27,600) | (31,000) |
| 15. (Demand Loan)/Bank Balance | (25,000) | (4,050) | 22,625 | 50,900 | 81,125 |
| 16. Actual Cash Flow | $(4,050) | $22,625 | $50,900 | $81,125 | $112,975 |

(Worked Out Sample Schedule)

# FEASIBILITY STUDY, NEW BUSINESS

## (Note: A small hospitality industry project is used as an example)

### MARKET FEASIBILITY

| QUESTIONS | | ANSWERS |
|---|---|---|
| (planning a motel/hotel/resort in an area where facilities currently exist) | (planning a motel/hotel/resort in an area where no facilities currently exist) | TOTAL MARKET POTENTIAL: |
| 1. What is the current supply of motel/hotel/resort rooms in the area? | 1. What will the supply of rooms be over the next few years? | |
| 2. What will the supply of rooms be over the next few years? | | |
| 3. What percentage of these rooms is currently occupied on average for the area? | | |
| 4. How quickly will demand grow over the next few years? | 2. What is the demand likely to be over the next few years? | |
| 5. How many rooms will be needed to meet this demand? | | |
| 6. How big is the gap between supply and demand for rooms? How big should my motel be? | 3. How big is the gap between supply and demand for rooms? How big should my motel be? | MARKET SHARE |
| 7. What will my gross revenue be from the rental of rooms? | 4. What will my gross revenue be from the rental of rooms? | GROSS REVENUE |
| 5. What will my gross revenue be from the sale of food? | | |
| 6. What will my total gross revenue be from the overall operation? | | |

64

| OPERATING FEASIBILITY | |
|---|---|
| QUESTIONS | ANSWERS |
| 1. What type of building, equipment, and furnishings will I need? | Building, Equipment, and Furnishings Requirements |
| 2. How much will it cost me to run the room operation and the restaurant? | Direct Departmental Expenses |
| 3. What cash expenses will I have to meet other than those already worked out? | Calculation of Cash Operating Expenses |
| 4. What other expenses do I have to allow for? Will I have to borrow money? | Budgeting for Other Expenses |

| FINANCIAL FEASIBILITY | |
|---|---|
| QUESTIONS | ANSWERS |
| 1. After paying all expenses, how much do I make? | Sales Less Expenses |

| VENTURE FEASIBILITY | |
|---|---|
| QUESTIONS | ANSWERS |
| 1. Is it worthwhile? | Return on Investment |
| 2. Should I go ahead with the venture? | Final Decision |

65

# BANK LOAN FORM

|  | Customer | Joint Customer (where applicable) |
|---|---|---|
| Name | | |
| Occupation or Business | | |
| Address | | |
| Social Security Number | | |

**To The**      **Bank of**

The undersigned, for the purpose of procuring and maintaining credit from time to time in any form whatsoever with the above named Bank, for claims and demands against the undersigned, submit(s) the following as being a true and accurate statement of his/her/their financial condition on the .......... day of ...................................., 19......, and agree(s) that if any change occurs that materially reduces the means or ability of the undersigned to pay all claims or demands against him/her/them, the undersigned will immediately and without delay notify the said Bank, and unless the Bank is so notified it may continue to rely upon the statement herein given as a true and accurate statement of the financial condition of the undersigned. An individual should indicate any items that are jointly held or jointly owing, while joint customers should indicate any items that are not jointly held or jointly owing. In consideration of the granting of such credit, the undersigned agree(s) that if the undersigned at any time fail(s) or become(s) insolvent, or commit(s) an Act of Bankruptcy, or if any of the representations made below prove to be untrue, or if the undersigned fail(s) to notify you of any material change as before agreed; then and in either such case all obligations of the undersigned held by you shall, at your election, immediately become due and payable without demand or notice, and the same may be charged against the balance of any deposit of the undersigned with you, the undersigned hereby giving a continuing lien upon such balance of deposit account from time to time existing to secure all obligations of the undersigned held by you. If you are applying for individual credit in your own name and are relying on your own income or assets and not on the income or assets of another person as the basis for the repayment of the credit requested, you need not complete items referring to "joint customer."

| **Assets** | | | | **Liabilities** | | | |
|---|---|---|---|---|---|---|---|
| Cash in Bank | | | | Notes payable to banks (Itemize on Reverse) | | | |
| Notes Receivable (good) owing by customers | | | | Notes payable to others (Itemize on Reverse) | | | |
| Accounts Receivable (good) owing by customers | | | | Open accounts payable | | | |
| Cash Value Life Insurance | | | | Borrowed on Life Insurance | | | |
| Real Estate (Itemize below) | | | | Mortgages or liens on real estate | | | |
| Equipment used in business | | | | | | | |
| Stocks—(Itemize on Reverse) | | | | | | | |
| Bonds—(Itemize on Reverse) | | | | | | | |
| 1st Mortgages Owned (Itemize on Reverse) | | | | | | | |
| 2nd Mortgages Owned (Itemize on Reverse) | | | | | | | |
| | | | | Total Liabilities | | | |
| | | | | **NET WORTH** | | | |
| Total | | | | Total | | | |

**Real Estate**/Please Give Particulars on Each Parcel Owned

| Date Acquired | Street and Number | Title in Name of | Cost | Est. Value | Mortgages | Insurance |
|---|---|---|---|---|---|---|
| | | | $ | $ | $ | $ |
| | | | | | | |
| | | | | | | |
| | | | | | | |

| | Customer | Joint Customer (where applicable) |
|---|---|---|
| State annual **net** income from real estate and securities | $ | $ |
| State annual **net** income from business or profession | $ | $ |
| Salary per annum | $ | $ |

**Alimony, child support, or separate maintenance income need not be revealed if you do not wish to have it considered as a basis for repayment of the credit requested.**

Alimony, child support, separate maintenance received under: court order ☐      written agreement ☐      oral understanding ☐

Other income: $      per      Source(s) of other income:

Is any income listed in this Section likely to be reduced before the credit requested is paid off?

Amount of life insurance carried, $      Beneficiary:

Give details of contingent liability of any kind or nature, as endorser or guarantor, or accommodation endorser

Are any of your assets, other than real estate, pledged or hypothecated in any way?

Do you have a will?      Name of Executor:

Are you a partner in any firm?

Is there any other person interested in your business, either as a special or limited partner?

**Stocks:**

| Number of Shares | Name of Corporation | Class of Stock | Market Values |
|---|---|---|---|
| | | | $ |
| | | | |
| | | | |
| | | | |
| | | | |
| | | | |
| | | | |
| | | | |
| | | | |

**Bonds:**

| Par Values | Name of Corporation or Authority | Description and Maturity Date | Market Values |
|---|---|---|---|
| $ | | | $ |
| | | | |
| | | | |
| | | | |
| | | | |
| | | | |
| | | | |

**First Mortgages or Second Trusts Owned:**

| Property | Street and Number | Total First | Total Second | Amount Owned |
|---|---|---|---|---|
| | | $ | $ | $ |
| | | | | |
| | | | | |
| | | | | |
| | | | | |
| | | | | |

**Notes Payable to Banks and Others:** (Attach additional sheet if necessary)

| Lender | Address | Collateral | Original Amount | Balance | Payments |
|---|---|---|---|---|---|
| | | | $ | $ | $ |
| | | | | | |
| | | | | | |
| | | | | | |
| | | | | | |
| | | | | | |

Other Credit References: (Include Mortgage Holders)

I/We hereby certify that the above is a true and correct statement as of the date above stated and I/we understand that any credit now or hereafter given me/us is made upon the strength of the statements contained herein. I/we understand that you will retain this statement whether or not it is approved. You are authorized to check my/our credit and employment history and to answer questions about your credit experience with me/us.

_____ / _____    _____ / _____
Customer's Signature          Date      Joint Customer's Signature (where applicable)   Date

# BANK RECONCILIATION

Name _____     Month of _____ 19 ____

Bank _____     Prepared by _____

| GENERAL LEDGER ACCOUNT BALANCE | $ | | | BALANCE PER BANK STATEMENT AS OF _____ 19 ____ | $ | |
|---|---|---|---|---|---|---|
| ADD DEBITS | $ | | | ADD DEPOSITS IN TRANSIT | $ | |
| | | | | | | |
| | | | | | | |
| | | | | | | |
| Total Dr | $ | | | Total in Transit | $ | |
| Total | | $ | | Total | $ | |
| LESS CREDITS: | $ | | | LESS CHECKS OUTSTANDING (SEE LIST BELOW) | $ | |
| | | | | | | |
| | | | | | | |
| Total Cr | $ | | | Total | $ | |
| BANK BALANCE – Per General Ledger | | $ | | BANK BALANCE – Per Reconciliation | $ | |

### CHECKS OUTSTANDING

| NUMBER | AMOUNT | NUMBER | AMOUNT | NUMBER | AMOUNT | NUMBER | AMOUNT |
|---|---|---|---|---|---|---|---|
| | | | | | | | |
| | | | | | | | |
| | | | | | | | |
| | | | | | | | |
| | | | | | | | |
| | | | | | | | |
| | | | | | | | |
| | | | | | | | |
| | | | | | | | |
| | | | | | | | |
| | | | | | | | |
| | | | | | | | |
| | | | | | | | |
| | | | | | | | |
| | | | | | | | |
| | | | | | | | |
| | | | | | | | |
| | | | | | | | |
| | | | | | | | |
| | | | | | | | |
| | | | | | | | |
| | | | | | | | |
| | | | | | | | |
| | | | | | | | |
| | | | | | | TOTAL $ | |

# BANK STOP-CHECK PAYMENT

**Date**

**Address**

**Dear** _____

**re: Stop-Check Payment**

**Following up our telephone instructions of** _____ **you are hereby directed to stop payment on presentation of the following check:**

**Account number** _____
**Account name** _____
**Check number** _____
**Dated** _____
**Payable to** _____
**Amount $** _____

**If any additional information or explanation is required, kindly contact this writer. Thank you.**

**Very truly yours,**

_____

COMMERCIAL CREDIT APPLICATION

**NAME** _____

**ADDRESS** _____

**CITY/STATE/ZIP** _____

**CREDIT MANAGER** _____

**PHONE NUMBER** _____

**BUSINESS TYPE:** ☐ Sole Proprietorship ☐ Partnership ☐ Corporation – State of _____

**Number of years in business** _____ **D & B Number** _____

NAME AND ADDRESS OF INDIVIDUALS OR PARTNERS – NAME/TITLE/PHONE

_____

_____

_____

NAME OF PERSON TO CONTACT REGARDING PURCHASE ORDERS AND INVOICE PAYMENTS, TITLE, ADDRESS AND PHONE NUMBER

_____   _____

_____   _____

_____   _____

_____   _____

_____   _____

BANK REFERENCE                          BANK ACCOUNT NUMBER, CONTACT, TITLE AND PHONE NUMBER

_____   _____

_____   _____

_____   _____

_____   _____

_____   _____

TRADE REFERENCES: COMPANY NAME, ADDRESS, CONTACT AND TITLE, AND PHONE NUMBER

_____   _____   _____

_____   _____   _____

_____   _____   _____

_____   _____   _____

_____   _____   _____

| THE ABOVE INFORMATION IS HEREWITH SUBMITTED FOR THE PURPOSE OF OPENING AN ACCOUNT. I DO HEREBY CERTIFY THIS INFORMATION TO BE TRUE. | **SIGNED** _____<br><br>**TITLE** _____<br><br>**DATE** _____ |
| --- | --- |

# CREDIT APPLICATION (PERSONAL)

Legal name of applicant _____

Present address _____

_____

Home phone _____    Work phone _____

## HOME DATA

Do you rent or own your present address? (   ) rent     (   ) own

How long have you lived at your present address? _____

Previous addresses and periods when you lived there:

_____

_____

## WORK DATA

Are you employed?_____    In business?_____

If employed: _____

What is your present employment? _____

Name of employer and address: _____

_____

How long have you worked for this employer?

_____

## BUSINESS DATA

What type of business are you engaged in? _____

Name and address of business: _____

_____

How long have you owned this business? _____

What is the legal organization of this business? _____

If either employment or business has been of less than one (1) year duration, what was your prior working/business affiliation? _____

_____

## ANNUAL INCOME

Gross income from work or business? _____

Overtime or outside income? _____

Interest and/or dividends? _____

Commissions or fees? _____

Rentals from property? _____

Other income (specify)? _____

TOTAL ANNUAL INCOME _____

71

**ESTIMATED VALUE OF YOUR POSSESSIONS**

Equity in home _____

Equity in other property _____

Car(s) _____

Savings _____

Stocks/bonds _____

TOTAL ASSETS _____

**ESTIMATED DEBTS**

Mortgage bal. _____

Car loan _____

Bank loan _____

Credit card(s) _____

Other _____

TOTAL DEBTS _____

**BANKRUPTCY**

Have you ever found it necessary to declare bankruptcy during the past five (5) years?

(  ) yes     (  ) no

What was the date? _____

**CERTIFICATION**

I certify the aforegoing information to be accurate and complete to the best of my knowledge and hereby authorize the disclosure and release of any credit-related information based on this application to

_____

_____

Dated _____ 19_____     Signed _____

# CREDIT INFORMATION

| Trading Name | | | |
|---|---|---|---|
| Street Address | | | |
| City | | State | Zip |
| Type of Enterprise | | | |
| Affiliated With | | | |
| Rated with D&B | Rated with Others | | |
| Name of Proprietor | | Phone | |
| Name of Bank | | | |
| Bank Address | | | |
| Street Address | | | |
| City | | State | Zip |

REFERENCES

| NAME | ADDRESS | CITY, STATE, ZIP |
|---|---|---|
| | | |
| | | |
| | | |
| | | |
| | | |
| | | |

| Remarks | |
|---|---|
| | |
| | |
| | |
| | Date |

73

CREDIT INQUIRY

DATE _____

ON _____

ADDRESS _____

CITY,STATE,ZIP _____

CONTACT _____     PHONE NO. _____

IN ORDER THAT WE MIGHT PROCESS A CREDIT APPLICATION THAT WE HAVE RECEIVED ON THE ABOVE ACCOUNT, WE WOULD APPRECIATE YOUR PROVIDING US WITH THE INFORMATION REQUESTED BELOW. YOUR RESPONSE WILL BE TREATED WITH ABSOLUTE CONFIDENTIALITY.

DOLLAR SALES FROM _____ TO _____     TOTALED _____

TOTAL DOLLAR SALES IN YEAR ____ = $_____     IN YEAR ____ = $_____

TERMS _____     SPECIAL TERMS _____

LARGEST AMOUNT OWED _____ WHEN _____     CURRENT     [  ]  YES     [  ]  NO

TOTAL AMOUNT NOW OWED _____     CURRENT [ ] YES [ ] NO     AMT. PAST DUE _____

RECENT TRENDS     ) [ ] PROMPTNESS     [ ] FULL TERM     [ ] SLIGHTLY SLOW     [ ] VERY SLOW

MAKES UNJUST CLAIMS     _____

CREDIT [ ] HONORED   [ ] REFUSED–EXPLAIN     _____

[ ] CHECK MANNER OF PAYMENT

[ ] PROMPT & SATISFACTORY        [ ] SLOW BUT COLLECTIBLE        [ ] AN EXCELLENT ACCOUNT–
[ ] PROMPT TO ____ DAYS SLOW     [ ] SLOW AND UNSATISFACTORY          BEST RECOMMENDATION
[ ] PROMPT TO ____ DAYS SLOW     [ ] ACCEPTS C.O.D.'S PROMPTLY   [ ] WE DO NOT RECOMMEND
[ ] MAKES PARTIAL PAYMENTS       [ ] COLLECTED BY AN ATTORNEY        EXTENDING CREDIT TO
[ ] ASKS FOR ADDITIONAL TIME     [ ] IN HANDS OF ATTORNEY            THIS ACCOUNT

SPECIAL COMMENTS

WE WILL GLADLY SHARE ANY INFORMATION WE HAVE THAT WILL ASSIST IN YOUR CREDIT DECISIONS. THANK YOU FOR YOUR ASSISTANCE.

NAME _____

TITLE _____

# CREDIT INFORMATION REQUEST

## GENERAL INFORMATION – APPLICANT

| First | Middle | Last | | |
|---|---|---|---|---|
| | | | | |

| Street | | City | State | Zip |
|---|---|---|---|---|
| | | | | |

| Home Telephone Number | Office Telephone Number | | Date of Birth | |
|---|---|---|---|---|
| | | | | |

| Employer's Name | How Long | Position | Annual Salary | |
|---|---|---|---|---|
| | | | | |

| Employer's Address | | City | State | Zip |
|---|---|---|---|---|
| | | | | |

| Other Income (Annual) | No. of Children and Ages | |
|---|---|---|
| | | |

## GENERAL INFORMATION – CO-APPLICANT

| First | Middle | Last | | |
|---|---|---|---|---|
| | | | | |

| Street | | City | State | Zip |
|---|---|---|---|---|
| | | | | |

| Home Telephone Number | Office Telephone Number | | Date of Birth | |
|---|---|---|---|---|
| | | | | |

| Employer's Name | How Long | Position | Annual Salary | |
|---|---|---|---|---|
| | | | | |

| Employer's Address | | City | State | Zip |
|---|---|---|---|---|
| | | | | |

## LIABILITIES

| Creditor | Address | Purpose | Mo. Payment | Balance Owing |
|---|---|---|---|---|
| | | | | |
| | | | | |
| | | | | |

## ASSETS

| Checking | Savings | Stocks – Bonds | Home Equity |
|---|---|---|---|
| | | | |

## PRESENT HOUSING STATUS

| [ ] Own | [ ] Rent | [ ] Other |
|---|---|---|

| Lender/Management Co. | Address | Yearly Taxes | Mo. Payment | How Long |
|---|---|---|---|---|
| | | | | |

## PERSONAL REFERENCES

| Name | Address | Occupation |
|---|---|---|
| | | |
| | | |
| | | |

The above information is to the best of my (our) knowledge a true and accurate statement.
I (we) give my (our) permission for the examination of my (our) credit files with the necessary credit bureau.

_____         _____
Applicant                                Co-Applicant

_____         _____
Date                                     Date

## COLLECTION LETTERS

American business is done primarily on credit. If you use credit cards, then you will be paid quickly by the credit card purveyor, usually a bank, American Express, Choice, or any of the other credit card companies. However, many charges go directly to the customer or client and it is then that collection problems may arise. Collections for extended credit should be billed immediately and collections should be effected within 60 days. In the medical field it has been found that billing patients at the end of the month results in a 65 percent collection rate. Obviously, the job of collecting money is a sensitive one. The way a collection letter is worded—firm yet friendly—and the speed and persistency with which one, two, or three letters are mailed, will impact the results. Here are some sample letters that vary in intent and intensity. Turning a collection over to an attorney or collection agency is a last resort—and it is costly, because the collector keeps from 25 to 50 percent of the amount collected. On top of that you will invariably have lost the customer anyway. We have included several professional samples. Use them as is or adapt them to your particular situations and tastes. Whichever you use, put yourself into the shoes of the recipient and decide whether you want to continue doing business with the client.

# COLLECTION LETTER (to Attorneys)

**Date**

**Attorney(s)**
**Address**

**Dear**

re: <u>Institution of Collection Proceedings</u>

Please accept this letter as your instructions to commence collection proceedings on our behalf against the following debtor:

Full name _____

Full address _____

Full description of debt _____

In the amount of $ _____

We enclose copies of relevant documents for your file, keeping original documents on file in case these are required in court:

_____ Purchase order     _____ Bad check

_____ Invoice             _____ Notice of return

_____ Statement           _____ Correspondence

If you need further documentation or information, please contact this writer.

Please keep us informed periodically of any progress and consult us if and when our legal bills approach $_____.

Very truly yours,

Encs.

## COLLECTION LETTER (general)

Dear

This is a reminder that your payment of $_____ is being awaited. Perhaps your check and this reminder are crossing each other in the mail. Perhaps the missing payment is due to an oversight or other pressing matters. If there are vital reasons why you cannot make the full payment at this time, please give us the courtesy of an explanation and reply today.

Credit, whether personally or in business, is a precious commodity for all of us. It is an especially American institution. It helps all of us live better and satisfy our gratifications more quickly.

But like any delicate commodity, good credit needs to be nurtured. One slight and credit can be damaged. May we suggest that you check on this missing payment and either send us a check for the amount due or a reason for being unable to make full payment today. We are, after all, as anxious to keep your business as you are, we hope, to do business with us.

Cordially,

# COLLECTION LETTER (last resort)

(This letter is a 60-day version. It goes out 60 days after the sale and prior to turning it over to a collection agency. Chances of collection are diminished quickly after 60 days past due. The averages are that after the receipt of a letter such as the sample below, 25 percent of recipients will pay up, 30 percent will propose a repayment plan, 35 percent will demur and stronger collection efforts will be required, and 10 percent will never pay.)


Dear

re: PAST DUE BALANCE $_____
The choice of placing your past due account with a collection agency is one we do not take lightly especially in the case of a good customer like you. Your goodwill is important to us, as is your continued business.

However, since we did our part, we expect you to do yours. If we need to resort to actions that might jeopardize your credit standing and cause you embarrassment, we would both suffer.

We are hopeful that you will act promptly and forward us your check immediately and in full. We will suspend further action until _____. It is important that we receive a positive response from you by then. We would very much regret having to make a decision that neither of us wants.

Very truly yours,


File No. _____

## COLLECTION LETTER (Professional)

Dear

When we do business together for our mutual benefit, it is called a symbiosis. When one of us reneges on our promises, it could be due to

_____ an embarrassing shortfall of funds
_____ a big check we had expected did not come in
_____ an unexpected emergency came up for which we had to have the funds earmarked for you
_____ we weren't entirely happy with what we received from you and want to discuss it with you
_____ we are awaiting adjustment of a questioned invoice
_____ oops, we plain overlooked your bill and we promise to send it in the next few days

And then, of course, there is the best solution of all:
send us a check for the amount now past due and let's continue to do more business together. As we said before, that's what's called a symbiosis—and it'll make both of us happy. If this is not possible today, please check off one of the six possible excuses above, or jot down any additional comments below, and return this note to us.

Thanks for taking care of this matter!

Cordially,

# PAST DUE NOTICE (Version 1)

**Date** _____

**First invoice sent to you** _____

**Statement sent to you** _____

Any problems? Can we help? Perhaps the lack of payment is a temporary situation or an oversight. Communication is the first step in keeping your credit reputation clean.

We would be grateful for your prompt attention to this PAST DUE item and your immediate remittance. If there are any questions or problems with this billing, please let us know immediately!

Thank you.

**(signature)**

# PAST DUE NOTICE (Version 2)

DATE
BALANCE DUE TODAY


TO:

We are very pleased with the friendly relationship that exists between us and the people with whom we do business. It is evidence of the fact that this relationship is beneficial to both. To encourage and promote such amicable relationships we extend credit in order for our customers/clients to more easily budget their expenditures.

The attached invoice from us to you is now more than past due. Our limited financial resources and the high cost of borrowing working capital do not allow us the resources to extend credit any further.

The fact that we do business together, to the benefit of each other, indicates that the attached invoice needs to be satisfied immediately. It would be greatly appreciated if you would put this invoice at the top of your list of bills to pay this week.

Thank you.


Encl.: Past Due Balance

# PAST DUE NOTICE (Version 3)

**Past Due Balance:   $** _____

_____ **Duplicate statement enclosed**

_____ **Stamped, self-addressed envelope enclosed**

_____ **If there are troubling circumstances, please tell us now. A reply form is enclosed.**

**Date** _____

# RETURNED CHECK NOTICE

Dear Customer:

Outlined below is information regarding your check which was returned to us as uncollectible.

The complexity of keeping accurate bank balances sometimes creates such embarrassing situations and we know that you will want to correct this matter immediately. We appreciate your business and are sorry for this mutual inconvenience.

## RETURNED CHECK INFORMATION

You are hereby notified that your check dated _____, 19_____, for $_____ has been presented to the bank for payment and has been returned to us unpaid. As state laws and/or penal codes prohibit the issuance of checks without adequate deposits to cover them, we ask you to arrange to pay the amount of this check within ten (10) business days from the date you first receive this notice. Thank you.

Date _____

Company _____

Address _____

_____

Phone _____

Signed _____

## PERSONAL INFORMATION FORMS

There are many choices in information forms for employment and loan applications. Here are three versions: a brief one-page document that might be used by an employer or personnel department; a Personal Financial Statement required by the Small Business Administration and banks; and a Sample Personal Financial Statement used in making application for credit or an equipment loan.

# PERSONAL DATA FORM

_____ (Date)

Name: _____, _____
      Last Name                    First Name and Middle Initial

1. Date Employed: _____ 2. Date of Birth: _____

3. Marital Status: _____

4. Spouse's Name: _____

5. Spouse Is Employed By: _____

   Address: _____
            _____

6. Children's Names: _____    Date of Birth: _____
                     _____                    _____
                     _____                    _____
                     _____                    _____
                     _____                    _____

7. Do you own a car?: _____

8. Form of transportation for commuting to/from work: _____

9. CPA examination, etc.:

   **Date taken**                    **Parts passed**
   _____                   _____
   _____                   _____
   _____                   _____

                                                    State    Cert. #
10. States from which certificates have been granted:  _____   _____
                                                       _____   _____
11. Professional Memberships:                          _____          _____
                                                       _____   Other
                                                       _____
                                                       _____
                                                       _____

12. Other Licenses:                     _____
                                        _____
                                        _____

13. Outside Activities Including Club Memberships:  _____
    _____

14. In Case of Emergency: Parents' Names: _____
                          Address: _____
                          Telephone #: _____

86

# PERSONAL FINANCIAL STATEMENT

**IMPORTANT: Read these directions before completing this Statement.**

☐ If you are applying for individual credit in your own name and are relying on your own income or assets and not the income or assets of another person as the basis for repayment of the credit requested, complete only Sections 1 and 3.

☐ If you are applying for joint credit with another person, complete all Sections providing information in Section 2 about the joint applicant.

☐ If you are applying for individual credit, but are relying on income from alimony, child support, or separate maintenance or on the income or assets of another person as a basis for repayment of the credit requested, complete all Sections, providing information in Section 2 about the person whose alimony, support or maintenance payments or income or assets you are relying.

☐ If this statement relates to your guaranty of the indebteness of other person(s), firm(s) or corporation(s), complete Sections 1 and 3.

TO:

| SECTION 1—INDIVIDUAL INFORMATION (Type or Print) | SECTION 2—OTHER PARTY INFORMATION (Type or Print) |
|---|---|
| Name | Name |
| Residence Address | Residence Address |
| City, State & Zip | City, State & Zip |
| Position or Occupation | Position or Occupation |
| Business Name | Business Name |
| Business Address | Business Address |
| City, State & Zip | City, State & Zip |
| Res. Phone          Bus. Phone | Res. Phone          Bus. Phone |

**SECTION 3—STATEMENT OF FINANCIAL CONDITION AS OF _____ 19_____**

| ASSETS (Do not include Assets of doubtful value) | In Dollars (Omit cents) | | LIABILITIES | In Dollars (Omit cents) | |
|---|---|---|---|---|---|
| Cash on hand and in banks | | | Notes payable to banks—secured | | |
| U.S. Gov't. & Marketable Securities—see Schedule A | | | Notes payable to banks—unsecured | | |
| Non-Marketable Securities—See Schedule B | | | Due to brokers | | |
| Securities held by broker in margin accounts | | | Amounts payable to others—secured | | |
| Restricted or control stocks | | | Amounts payable to others—unsecured | | |
| Partial interest in Real Estate Equities | | | Accounts and bills due | | |
| see Schedule C | | | Unpaid income tax | | |
| Real Estate Owned—see Schedule D | | | Other unpaid taxes and interest | | |
| Loans Receivable | | | Real estate mortgages payable | | |
| Automobiles and other personal property | | | see Schedule D | | |
| Cash value-life insurance—see Schedule E | | | Other debts—itemize | | |
| Other assets—itemize | | | | | |
| | | | | | |
| | | | | | |
| | | | | | |
| | | | TOTAL LIABILITIES | | |
| | | | NET WORTH | | |
| TOTAL ASSETS | | | TOTAL LIAB. AND NET WORTH | | |

| SOURCES OF INCOME FOR YEAR ENDED _____, 19_____ | PERSONAL INFORMATION |
|---|---|
| Salary, bonuses & commissions          $ | Do you have a will?_____If so, name of executor. |
| Dividends | |
| Real estate income | Are you a partner or officer in any other venture? If so, describe. |
| Other income (Alimony, child support, or separate maintenance | |
| income need not be revealed if you do not wish to have it | Are you obligated to pay alimony, child support or separate |
| considered as a basis for repaying this obligation) | maintenance payments? If so, describe. |
| | Are any assets pledged other than as described on schedules? If |
| TOTAL          $ | so, describe. |

| CONTINGENT LIABILITIES | |
|---|---|
| Do you have any contingent liabilities? If so, describe. | Income tax settled through (date)_____ |
| | Are you a defendant in any suits or legal actions? |
| As indorser, co-maker or guarantor?          $ | Personal bank accounts carried at: |
| On leases or contracts?          $ | |
| Legal claims          $ | |
| Other special debt          $ | Have you ever been declared bankrupt? If so, describe. |
| Amount of contested income tax liens          $ | |

# SCHEDULE A—U.S. GOVERNMENTS & MARKETABLE SECURITIES

| Number of shares or Face Value (Bonds) | Description | In Name Of | Are These Pledged? | Market Value |
|---|---|---|---|---|
| | | | | |
| | | | | |
| | | | | |
| | | | | |

# SCHEDULE B—NON-MARKETABLE SECURITIES

| Number of Shares | Description | In Name Of | Are These Pledged? | Source of Value | Value |
|---|---|---|---|---|---|
| | | | | | |
| | | | | | |
| | | | | | |
| | | | | | |

# SCHEDULE C—PARTIAL INTEREST IN REAL ESTATE EQUITIES

| Address & Type Of Property | Title In Name Of | % Of Ownership | Date Acquired | Cost | Market Value | Mortgage Maturity | Mortgage Amount |
|---|---|---|---|---|---|---|---|
| | | | | | | | |
| | | | | | | | |
| | | | | | | | |
| | | | | | | | |

# SCHEDULE D—REAL ESTATE OWNED

| Address & Type Of Property | Title In Name Of | Date Acquired | Cost | Market Value | Mortgage Maturity | Mortgage Amount |
|---|---|---|---|---|---|---|
| | | | | | | |
| | | | | | | |
| | | | | | | |
| | | | | | | |

# SCHEDULE E—LIFE INSURANCE CARRIED, INCLUDING N.S.L.I. AND GROUP INSURANCE

| Name Of Insurance Company | Owner Of Policy | Beneficiary | Face Amount | Policy Loans | Cash Surrender Value |
|---|---|---|---|---|---|
| | | | | | |
| | | | | | |
| | | | | | |
| | | | | | |

# SCHEDULE F—BANKS OR FINANCE COMPANIES WHERE CREDIT HAS BEEN OBTAINED

| Name & Address Of Lender | Credit In The Name Of | Secured Or Unsecured? | Original Date | High Credit | Current Balance |
|---|---|---|---|---|---|
| | | | | | |
| | | | | | |
| | | | | | |
| | | | | | |

The information contained in this statement is provided for the purpose of obtaining, or maintaining credit with you on behalf of the undersigned, or persons, firms or corporations in whose behalf the undersigned may either severally or jointly with others, execute a guaranty in your favor. Each undersigned understands that you are relying on the information provided herein (including the designation made as to ownership of property) in deciding to grant or continue credit. Each undersigned represents and warrants that *the information provided is true and complete* and that you may consider this statement as continuing to be true and correct until a written notice of change is given to you by the undersigned. You are authorized to make all inquiries you deem necessary to verify the accuracy of the statements made herein, and to determine my/our credit-worthiness. You are authorized to answer questions about your credit experience with me/us.

Signature (individual) _____

S.S. No. _____ Date of Birth _____

Signature (Other Party) _____

S.S. No. _____ Date of Birth _____

Date Signed _____ 19 _____

(USE ADDITIONAL SCHEDULES IF NECESSARY)

# SAMPLE PERSONAL FINANCIAL STATEMENT

Name _____

Address _____

For the purpose of causing you to grant credit to me from time to time either directly or indirectly, or to persons, firms, or corporations for whom I may be an endorser or guarantor, I submit the following statement of my financial condition on _____, 19_____; I agree that if any change occurs which materially reduces my means or ability to pay obligations I will give you prompt notification unless I am not indebted to you in any way at the time of the change; so long as I am indebted to you or whenever I apply for credit either directly or indirectly, you may rely upon this statement as a continuing statement of my financial standing until you are given written notification of a change.

| ASSETS | Indiv. | Joint | If joint w/whom | LIABILITIES | Indiv. | Joint | If joint w/whom |
|---|---|---|---|---|---|---|---|
| Cash on hand and in banks ...... | | | | Notes payable to banks—secured | | | |
| U.S. Government securities ...... | | | | —unsecured | | | |
| Listed securities ............... | | | | Notes payable to relatives ...... | | | |
| Unlisted securities ............. | | | | Notes payable to others ......... | | | |
| Mortgages owned ............. | | | | Accounts and bills due .......... | | | |
| Accounts and notes receivable due from relatives and friends .. | | | | Accrued interest, etc. ........... | | | |
| | | | | Taxes unpaid or accrued ........ | | | |
| Accounts and notes receivable due from others—good ........ | | | | Mortgages payable on real estate . | | | |
| —doubtful ........ | | | | Chattel mortages and other liens payable ................... | | | |
| Real estate owned ............. | | | | Other debts—itemize .......... | | | |
| Cash value life insurance ........ | | | | | | | |
| Automobiles .................. | | | | | | | |
| Personal property ............. | | | | | | | |
| Other assets—itemize.......... | | | | | | | |
| | | | | TOTAL LIABILITIES ............. | | | |
| | | | | Net Worth ................... | | | |
| | | | | TOTAL LIABILITIES AND NET WORTH ............. | | | |
| TOTAL ASSETS ............... | | | | | | | |

## SOURCE OF INCOME

Alimony, child support or maintenance income need not be revealed if you do not wish it to be considered as a basis for repaying this obligation.

| | Indiv. | Joint | If joint w/whom |
|---|---|---|---|
| Salary ...................... | | | |
| Bonds and commissions ........ | | | |
| Dividends and bond interest...... | | | |
| Real estate income ............ | | | |
| Other income—itemize ......... | | | |
| TOTAL...................... | | | |

## PERSONAL INFORMATION

If you are applying for individual credit, information about your spouse or ex-spouse need not be revealed unless you are relying on income from alimony, child support or maintenance or on the income or assets of another person as a basis for repaying this obligation:

_____

Business or occupation:

Partner or officer in other venture:

| MARITAL STATUS (Do not complete if this is submitted for individual unsecured credit.) | No. of Dependents |
|---|---|
| ☐ Married ☐ Separated ☐ Unmarried (including single, divorced or widowed) | |

## CONTINGENT LIABILITIES

| | Indiv. | Joint | If joint w/whom |
|---|---|---|---|
| As endorser or co-maker ........ | | | |
| On leases or contracts .......... | | | |
| Legal claims ................. | | | |
| Taxes not shown above: Income taxes ................ | | | |
| Delinquent or contested taxes ............. | | | |
| OTHER SPECIAL DEBTS ........ | | | |

## GENERAL INFORMATION

Are any assets pledged? _____

Are you defendant in any suit or legal action?

_____

Personal bank accounts carried at:

Individual: _____

Joint: _____

If joint, with whom: _____

Have you ever taken bankruptcy? If yes, explain: _____

## LIST OF BANKS AND FINANCE COMPANIES WHERE CREDIT HAS BEEN OBTAINED

| NAME(S) IN WHICH OBTAINED | NAME OF BANK OR COMPANY | HIGH CREDIT | PRESENT BALANCE | TYPE OF LOAN |
|---|---|---|---|---|
| | | | | |
| | | | | |
| | | | | |
| | | | | |

REMARKS _____
_____
_____
_____

## U.S. GOVERNMENT AND LISTED STOCKS AND BONDS

| HELD IN NAME(S) OF | DESCRIPTION | COST | MARKET VALUE |
|---|---|---|---|
| | | | |
| | | | |
| | | | |
| | | | |

## MORTGAGES, UNLISTED SECURITIES AND OTHER INVESTMENTS

| HELD IN NAME(S) OF | DESCRIPTION, INCLUDING MATURITIES | COST | MARKET VALUE |
|---|---|---|---|
| | | | |
| | | | |
| | | | |
| | | | |
| | | | |
| | | | |

## REAL ESTATE OWNED

| DESCRIPTION AND LOCATION | TITLE IN NAME(S) OF | MARKET VALUE | MORTGAGES | TAXES PAID TO |
|---|---|---|---|---|
| | | | | |
| | | | | |
| | | | | |
| | | | | |

## LIFE INSURANCE

| OWNER | NAME OF COMPANY | BENEFICIARY | AMOUNT | CASH VALUE | LOANS |
|---|---|---|---|---|---|
| | | | | | |
| | | | | | |
| | | | | | |
| | | | | | |
| | | | | | |

## ACCOUNTS AND NOTES RECEIVABLES

| OWNER(S) | DEBTOR AND ADDRESS | PRESENT BALANCE DUE |
|---|---|---|
| | | |
| | | |
| | | |

## PERSONAL PROPERTY AND VEHICLES

| DESCRIPTION AND LOCATION | OWNER(S) | | MORTGAGES |
|---|---|---|---|
| | | | |
| | | | |
| | | | |

The foregoing financial statement and explanations have been fairly and correctly presented according to the best of my knowledge and belief.

Date signed: _____, 19 _____   Signature _____

Date signed: _____, 19 _____   Signature _____

# STATEMENT OF NET WORTH

## DECEMBER 31, 19___

### ASSETS

**CURRENT ASSETS:**

| | | |
|---|---|---|
| Cash in Bank | $_____ | |
| Cash on Hand | _____ | |
| Accounts Receivable | _____ | |
|    Less—Reserve for Bad Debts | _____ | _____ |
| Loans Receivable | | _____ |
| Merchandise Inventory | | _____ |
| Prepaid Expense | | _____ |
| _____ | | _____ |
| _____ | | _____ |
|    Total Current Assets | | $_____ |

**FIXED ASSETS:**

| | | |
|---|---|---|
| Machinery and Equipment (cost) | $_____ | |
| Autos and Trucks (cost) | _____ | |
| Office Equipment (cost) | _____ | |
| Buildings (cost) | _____ | |
|    Total | _____ | |
| Less—Accumulated Depreciation | _____ | |
|    Net Total | _____ | |
| Add—Land (cost) | _____ | |
|    Total Fixed Assets | | $_____ |

**OTHER ASSETS:**

| | |
|---|---|
| _____ | _____ |
| _____ | _____ |

**TOTAL**   $_____

## LIABILITIES AND NET WORTH/STOCKHOLDERS EQUITY

**CURRENT LIABILITIES:**

| | | |
|---|---|---|
| Accounts Payable | $_____ | |
| Taxes Accrued, Payroll, Etc. | _____ | |
| Notes Payable | _____ | |
| Loans Payable | _____ | |
| Federal Income Taxes | _____ | |
| _____ | _____ | |
|    Total Current Liabilities | | $_____ |

**FIXED LIABILITIES:**

| | | |
|---|---|---|
| Mortgage Payable | $_____ | |
| Long Term Debt | _____ | |
|    Total Fixed Liabilities | | $_____ |

**CAPITAL STOCK (Corporation)** _____

**STOCKHOLDERS EQUITY (Corporation)** _____

**NET WORTH (Partnership/Sole Proprietorship)** _____

**TOTAL**   $_____

# 4.

# GOVERNMENT FORMS

## IRS TAX FORMS

The Internal Revenue Service produces in excess of 700 forms and 106 publications. As it is impossible to reproduce all forms here because of their quantity and because changes are made almost annually, we want to point out some of the currently available forms and brochures that are of particular interest to small business. Some of these also are translated into Spanish.

Tax Calendars for 1992 (Publication 509), 16 pg.

Guide to Free Tax Services (Publication 910), 30 pg.

Tax Guide for Small Business (Publication 334), 8 parts

Taxpayers Starting a Business (Publication 583), for sole proprietors

All IRS publications are free "to make your taxes less taxing," according to Publication 910. These may be ordered by calling the tollfree hotline—1-800-829-3676, or from a local IRS office, or one of the regional Forms Distribution Centers:

P.O. Box 25866, Richmond, VA 23289

P.O. Box 9903, Bloomington, IL 61799

Rancho Cordova, CA 95743-0001

Many major libraries and post offices also stock these and other common IRS forms, or originals that can be photocopied. Small business tax assistance can also be obtained during tax season through the IRS's Small Business Tax Education Program and through many local branches of the American Association of Retired Persons (AARP). Both of these services are free.

# TAX PLANNING WORKSHEET

|                                                                              | CURRENT YEAR | PROJECTED YEAR |
|------------------------------------------------------------------------------|--------------|----------------|
| **INCOME**                                                                   |              |                |
| *Wages, salary, etc.*                                                        | $ _____   | $ _____     |
| *Interest and dividends*                                                     | _____     | _____       |
| *Net capital gain (loss)*                                                    | _____     | _____       |
| *Income (loss) from a business*                                              | _____     | _____       |
| *Passive income (or 40% of net loss, usually)*                               | _____     | _____       |
| *Taxable social security income*                                             | _____     | _____       |
| *Other income*                                                               | _____     | _____       |
| **TOTAL INCOME**                                                             | _____     | _____       |
|                                                                              |              |                |
| **ADJUSTMENTS**                                                              |              |                |
| *Keogh payments and alimony paid*                                            | ( _____ ) | ( _____ )   |
| *IRA, as modified*                                                           | ( _____ ) | ( _____ )   |
|                                                                              |              |                |
| **ADJUSTED GROSS INCOME (AGI)**                                              | _____     | _____       |
|                                                                              |              |                |
| **ITEMIZED DEDUCTIONS**                                                      |              |                |
| *Medical and dental (amount above 7.5% of AGI)*                              | _____     | _____       |
| *Certain state taxes*                                                        | _____     | _____       |
| *Interest*                                                                   |              |                |
|    First and second homes                                     | _____     | _____       |
|    Allowed investment interest                                | _____     | _____       |
| *Miscellaneous and employee business expense allowed*                        |              |                |
|    *(amount exceeding 2% of AGI)*                             | _____     | _____       |
| **TOTAL ITEMIZED DEDUCTIONS**                                                | _____     | _____       |
|                                                                              |              |                |
| **TOTAL DEDUCTIONS (larger of standard or itemized)**                        | ( _____ ) | ( _____ )   |
|                                                                              |              |                |
| **PERSONAL EXEMPTIONS**                                                      | ( _____ ) | ( _____ )   |
|                                                                              |              |                |
| **TAXABLE INCOME**                                                           | _____     | _____       |
| *Tax from tables*                                                            | _____     | _____       |
| *Credits*                                                                    | ( _____ ) | ( _____ )   |
|                                                                              |              |                |
| **TOTAL TAX**                                                                | $ _____   | $ _____     |

# FEDERAL INCOME TAX PLANNING WORKSHEET

NAME: _____

|  | Current Year Actual | Next Year Projected |
|---|---|---|

### Income

| | Current Year Actual | Next Year Projected |
|---|---|---|
| Wages and Salaries | $ | $ |
| Taxable Interest Income | $ | $ |
| Dividend Income | $ | $ |
| State Tax Refund | $ | $ |
| Alimony Received | $ | $ |
| Business Income | $ | $ |
| Net Short–Term Capital Gain/Loss | $ | $ |
| Net Long–Term Capital Gain/Loss | $ | $ |
| Ordinary Gain From 4797 | $ | $ |
| Pension and Annuity Income | $ | $ |
| Rent and Royalty Income | $ | $ |
| Farm Rental Income | $ | $ |
| Partnership Income | $ | $ |
| Estate and Trust Income | $ | $ |
| S Corporation Income | $ | $ |
| Farm Income | $ | $ |
| Unemployment Compensation | $ | $ |
| Social Security Benefits | $ | $ |
| Miscellaneous Income | $ | $ |
| Gross Income | $ | $ |

### Adjustments to Income

| | Current Year Actual | Next Year Projected |
|---|---|---|
| Reimbursed Employee Business Expenses | $ | $ |
| Payments to IRA | $ | $ |
| Self–Employed Health Insurance Deduction | $ | $ |
| Payments to Keogh/SEP | $ | $ |
| Penalty on Early Withdrawal of Savings | $ | $ |
| Alimony Paid | $ | $ |
| Foreign Housing Deduction | $ | $ |
| Adjusted Gross Income | $ | $ |

95

|  | Current Year Actual | Next Year Projected |
|---|---|---|
| Adjusted Gross Income | $ | $ |

**Itemized Deductions**

|  | Current Year Actual | Next Year Projected |
|---|---|---|
| Medical and Dental Expense Deduction | $ | $ |
| Tax Expense | $ | $ |
| Interest Expense | $ | $ |
| Contributions | $ | $ |
| Casualty/Theft Losses | $ | $ |
| Moving Expenses | $ | $ |
| Miscellaneous | $ | $ |
| Total Itemized Deductions | $ | $ |
| Standard Deduction | $ | $ |
| Personal and Dependant Exemptions | $ | $ |
| Taxable Income | $ | $ |
| Income Tax | $ | $ |

**Additional Taxes**

|  | Current Year Actual | Next Year Projected |
|---|---|---|
| Self–Employment Tax | $ | $ |
| Alternative Minimum Tax | $ | $ |
| Other Taxes | $ | $ |
| Total Tax | $ | $ |

**Credits**

|  | Current Year Actual | Next Year Projected |
|---|---|---|
| Credit For the Elderly | $ | $ |
| Child Care Credit | $ | $ |
| Foreign Tax Credit | $ | $ |
| General Business Credit | $ | $ |
| Gas Tax Credit | $ | $ |
| Earned Income Credit | $ | $ |
| Other Credits | $ | $ |
| Net Income Tax | $ | $ |

**Payments, Interest and Penalties**

|  | Current Year Actual | Next Year Projected |
|---|---|---|
| Less Withholding | $ | $ |
| Less Estimated Tax Payments | $ | $ |
| Less Other Payments | $ | $ |
| Plus Interest and Penalties | $ | $ |
| Total Balance Due (Overpayment) | $ | $ |

**FEDERAL TAX FORMS CHECKLIST**

The Internal Revenue Service issues several dozen tax forms. Forms for each type of business are different and the requirements as well as some details in each form may change from year to year. The following checklist is only for your guidance. You will want to use it in order to obtain the correct forms from your nearest IRS office or to prepare pertinent information for your accountant. All IRS forms come to you free of charge and postage prepaid.

Forms You Need for Each of the Four Legal Business Formations

CORPORATION

_____ 1120 income tax return

_____ Schedule D capital gains and losses

_____ 3468 investment and energy credits

_____ 4562 depreciation

_____ 5884 jobs credit

_____ 7004 (6 months) application for extension

_____ 1139 application for tax refund based on carryback

_____ 1096 annual summary of U.S. information return

_____ 1099-DIV payment of dividends

_____ 1099-INT payment of interest

_____ 1099-MISC payment of rents, royalties, commissions, et al.

_____ 5500 (or C or R) return/report of employee benefit plan

_____ 1120X amended return

S CORPORATION

_____ 1120S income tax return

_____ Schedule K-1 share of income/loss passed through from business

_____ Schedule D capital gains and losses

_____ 3468 investment and energy credits

_____ 4562 depreciation

_____ 5884 jobs credit

_____ 2553 election as S corporation

_____ 7004 application for extension

_____ 1096 annual summary of U.S. information return

_____ Payment of Dividends

_____ 1099-DIV payment of dividends

_____ 1099-INT payment of interest

_____ 1099-MISC payment of rents, royalties, commissions, et al.

_____ 5500 or 5500-C or R return/report of employee benefit plan

_____ 1120S amended return

## PARTNERSHIP

_____ 1065 informational return

_____ Sched K-1 (with 1065)

_____ Sched D (with 1065)

_____ 3468 (with 1065)

_____ 4562 (with 1065)

_____ 5884 (with 1065)

_____ 2758 (extension application)

_____ 1096 (annual summary)

_____ 1099-INT payment of interest

_____ 1099-MISC payment of rents, royalties, commissions, et al.

_____ 5500 report of employee benefit plan

_____ 1065 amended return

## SOLE PROPRIETORSHIP

_____ 1040 income tax return

_____ Sched C income or profit passed through from business

_____ Sched D capital gains and losses

_____ 3468 investment and energy credits

_____ 4562 depreciation

_____ 5884 jobs credit

_____ 4868 application for extension

_____ 1045 application for tax refund

_____ Scheduled SE Social Security self-employment tax

_____ 1096 annual summary of U.S. Information return

_____ 1099-INT payment of interest

_____ 1099-MISC payment of rents, royalties, commissions, and other compensations

_____ 5500 employee benefit plan

_____ 1040X amended return

Note: the law requires a Form 1099 to be prepared for all payments to unincorporated entities or individuals totalling more than $599 in any calendar year for services performed in the course of a trade or business.

Above checklist is based on information supplied by Arthur Andersen & Co., Baltimore (MD) office.

# Your Business Tax Kit

Department of the Treasury
**Internal Revenue Service**
Publication 454-A (Rev. 2-90)
Cat. No. 465255

Here's *Your Business Tax Kit* (YBTK) to help make your taxes less taxing. You have the right to know all you can about your Federal tax benefits and responsibilities. The forms and publications enclosed apply solely to Federal taxes, therefore, you should consult with state or local taxing authorities for their requirements. In your kit you'll find Publication 334, Tax Guide for Small Business, an easy-to-read business tax reference which explains situations that apply to a small business.

To find out about educational programs for small businesses, complete the interest form on the enclosed Publication 1057, Small Business Tax Education (SBTE) Program Brochure, and mail it to the nearest IRS office listed for your state. Through a unique partnership between IRS and many community and junior colleges, universities and business associations across the country, small business owners (sole-proprietors, partnerships and corporations) have an opportunity to learn what they need to know about taxes. Often educational programs are offered in conjunction with a variety of Federal and State agencies providing you with one-stop assistance. Contact your local Taxpayer Education Coordinator to find out about other IRS tax services available for small businesses, such as Community Outreach Tax Education. For more information, review the enclosed Publication 910, Guide to Free Tax Services.

## THE FOLLOWING ITEMS ARE INCLUDED IN YBTK

*Form SS-4*, Application for Employer Identification Number
*Form 1040ES*, Estimated Tax for Individuals

*Publication 334*, Tax Guide for Small Business
*Publication 454-A*, YBTK Content Sheet
*Publication 509*, Tax Calendars for 1990
*Publication 583*, Taxpayers Starting a Business

*Publication 910*, Guide to Free Tax Services
*Publication 937*, Business Reporting
*Publication 1057*, Small Business Tax Education Program Brochure

If a tax form, instruction or publication you want is not included in your kit, you may call the IRS toll-free number (1–800–424–3676) to order the item(s); or you may use the order blank provided below.

We will send you two (2) copies of each form and one (1) copy of each set of instructions or publication you circle. Please cut the order blank on the dotted line and be sure to print or type your name and address accurately on the bottom portion. Enclose this order blank in your own envelope and address your envelope to the IRS address shown on reverse for your state. Be sure to allow two (2) weeks for delivery.

## YBTK ORDER BLANK

| | | | | |
|---|---|---|---|---|
| Form W-4 | Form 1040 Sch SE | Form 1120 | Inst 1120-S Sch D | Pub 15 |
| Form 940 | Form 1065 | Form 1120 Sch D | Form 1120-W | Pub 393 |
| Form 941 | Inst 1065 | Inst 1120/1120-A | Form 2553 | Pub 505 |
| Form 1040 | Form 1065 Sch D | Form 1120-A | Inst 2553 | Pub 541 |
| Inst 1040 | Form 1065 Sch D | Form 1120-S | Form 4562 | Pub 542 |
| Form 1040 Sch C | Form 1065 Sch K-1 | Inst 1120-S | Inst 4562 | Pub 589 |
| Form 1040 Sch E | Inst 1065 Sch K-1 | Form 1120-S Sch D | | |

**Internal Revenue Service**                                                                                                    **YBTK**

**Name**

**Number and Street**

**City, State, and ZIP Code**

**THE FOLLOWING ITEMS MAY BE ORDERED ON THE ORDER BLANK PROVIDED**

### Sole Proprietorships

*Form 1040* U.S. Individual Income Tax Return and Instructions
*Schedule C* (Form 1040) Profit or Loss From Business
*Schedule SE* (Form 1040) Social Security Self-Employment Tax
*Form 4562* Depreciation and Amortization and Instructions

*Publication 505* Tax Withholding and Estimated Tax
*Publication 533* Self-Employment Tax

### Corporations

*Form 1120* U.S. Corporation Income Tax Return and Instructions
*Schedule D* (Form 1120) Capital Gains and Losses
*Form 1120-A* U.S. Income Tax Return and Instructions
*Form 1120-S* U.S. Income Tax for an S Corporation and Instructions
*Schedule D* (Form 1120S) Capital Gains and Losses and Built-In Gains and Instructions
*Form 1120-W* Corporation Estimated Tax
*Form 2553* Election by a Small Business Corporation and Instructions
*Form 4562* Depreciation and Amortization and Instructions

*Publication 542* Tax Information on Corporations
*Publication 589* Tax Information on S Corporations

### Partnerships

*Form 1065* U.S. Partnership Return of Income and Instructions
*Schedule D* (Form 1065) Capital Gains and Losses and Instructions
*Schedule K-1* (Form 1065) Partner's Share of Income Credits Seductions, etc. and Instructions
*Schedule E* (Form 1040) Supplemental Income and Loss
*Schedule SE* (Form 1040) Social Security Self-Employment Tax
*Form 4562* Depreciation and Amortization and Instructions

*Publication 505* Tax Withholding and Estimated Tax
*Publication 541* Tax Information on Partnerships

### Employment Taxes

*Form W-4* Employee's Withholding Allowance Certificate
*Form 940* Employer's Annual Federal Unemployment (FUTA) Tax Return
*Form 941* Employer's Quarterly Federal Tax Return

*Publication 15* (Circular E) Employer's Tax Guide
*Publication 393* Federal Employment Tax Forms

| If you are located in: | Send to "Forms Distribution Center" for your state |
|---|---|
| | |

| | |
|---|---|
| Alabama, Arkansas, Illinois, Indiana, Iowa, Kansas, Kentucky, Louisiana, Michigan, Minnesota, Mississippi, Missouri, Nebraska, North Dakota, Ohio, Oklahoma, South Dakota, Tennessee, Texas, Wisconsin | P.O. Box 9903 Bloomington, IL 61799 |
| Alaska, Arizona, California, Colorado, Hawaii, Idaho, Montana, Nevada, New Mexico, Oregon, Utah, Washington, Wyoming | Rancho Cordova CA 95743–0001 |
| Connecticut, Delaware, District of Columbia, Florida, Georgia, Maine, Maryland, Massachusetts, New Hampshire, New Jersey, New York, North Carolina, Pennsylvania, Rhode Island, South Carolina, Vermont, Virginia, West Virginia | P.O. Box 25866 Richmond, VA 23289 |

**Foreign Addresses** — Taxpayers with mailing addresses in foreign countries should send their requests for forms and publications to: Forms Distribution Center, P.O. Box 25866, Richmond, VA 23289; Forms Distribution Center, Rancho Cordova, CA 95743–0001, whichever is closer.

**Puerto Rico** — Forms Distribution Center, P.O. Box 25866, Richmond, VA 23289

**Virgin Islands** — V.I. Bureau of Internal Revenue, Lockharts Garden, No. 1A, Charlotte Amalie, St. Thomas, VI 00802

✩U.S. Government Printing Office: 1990-262-164/04343

# FINANCIAL STATEMENT SPREAD SHEET

| Name | | Business | | | | | | | | SIC # | | |
|---|---|---|---|---|---|---|---|---|---|---|---|---|
| Type Statement | | Review | | Review | | | | | | | | |
| Statement Date | | | % | | % | | % | | % | | | % |
| Cash | 1 | | | | | | | | | | | |
| Marketable Securities | 2 | | | | | | | | | | | |
| Receivables - Trade | 3 | | | | | | | | | | | |
| Less: Allow for Bad Debts | 4 | | | | | | | | | | | |
| Notes Receivable | 5 | | | | | | | | | | | |
| Inventories | 6 | | | | | | | | | | | |
| | 7 | | | | | | | | | | | |
| | 8 | | | | | | | | | | | |
| All Other Current | 9 | | | | | | | | | | | |
| TOTAL CURRENT ASSETS | 10 | | | | | | | | | | | |
| Fixed Assets - Net | 11 | | | | | | | | | | | |
| Due From Officers/Affiliates | 12 | | | | | | | | | | | |
| Investments/Inv. In Affiliates | 13 | | | | | | | | | | | |
| | 14 | | | | | | | | | | | |
| All Other Noncurrent | 15 | | | | | | | | | | | |
| TOTAL NONCURRENT ASSETS | 16 | | | | | | | | | | | |
| Intangible Assets | 17 | | | | | | | | | | | |
| TOTAL ASSETS | 18 | | 100 | | 100 | | 100 | | 100 | | | 100 |
| Notes Payable - Banks | 19 | | | | | | | | | | | |
| | 20 | | | | | | | | | | | |
| Due Officers/Affiliates | 21 | | | | | | | | | | | |
| Accounts Payable - Trade | 22 | | | | | | | | | | | |
| Taxes | 23 | | | | | | | | | | | |
| Current Maturities of L.T. Debt | 24 | | | | | | | | | | | |
| | 25 | | | | | | | | | | | |
| All Other Current | 26 | | | | | | | | | | | |
| TOTAL CURRENT DEBT | 27 | | | | | | | | | | | |
| Long Term Debt | 28 | | | | | | | | | | | |
| | 29 | | | | | | | | | | | |
| All Other Noncurrent | 30 | | | | | | | | | | | |
| TOTAL NONCURRENT DEBT | 31 | | | | | | | | | | | |
| | 32 | | | | | | | | | | | |
| Deferred Income Taxes | 33 | | | | | | | | | | | |
| Subordinated Debt | 34 | | | | | | | | | | | |
| TOTAL LIABILITIES | 35 | | | | | | | | | | | |
| | 36 | | | | | | | | | | | |
| Capital - Preferred Stock | 37 | | | | | | | | | | | |
| Capital - Common Stock | 38 | | | | | | | | | | | |
| Paid-In (Capital) Surplus | 39 | | | | | | | | | | | |
| Retained Earnings | 40 | | | | | | | | | | | |
| NET WORTH | 41 | | | | | | | | | | | |
| TOTAL LIABILITIES & NET WORTH | 42 | | 100 | | 100 | | 100 | | 100 | 100 | | |
| WORKING CAPITAL (10-27) | 43 | | | | | | | | | | | |
| TANGIBLE NET WORTH (41-17) | 44 | | | | | | | | | | | |
| Ratios:    Current | 45 | | | | | | | | | | | |
| Quick | 46 | | | | | | | | | | | |
| (Days)    Sales to Receivables | 47 | | | | | | | | | | | |
| (Days)    Cost of Sales to Inv. | 48 | | | | | | | | | | | |
| Sales to Working Capital | 49 | | | | | | | | | | | |
| E.B.I.T. to Interest | 50 | | | | | | | | | | | |
| Cash Flow to Cur. Mat. L.T.D. | 51 | | | | | | | | | | | |
| Total Debt to T.N.W. | 52 | | | | | | | | | | | |
| % Profit Before Taxes to Sales | 53 | | | | | | | | | | | |
| % Profit Before Taxes to T.N.W. | 54 | | | | | | | | | | | |
| % Profit Before Taxes to T.A. | 55 | | | | | | | | | | | |
| Sales to Total Assets | 56 | | | | | | | | | | | |
| CONTINGENT LIABILITIES | 57 | | | | | | | | | | | |

| | | | 100 | | 100 | | 100 | | 100 | | 100 |
|---|---|---|---|---|---|---|---|---|---|---|---|
| Date of Statement | | | | | | | | | | | |
| Operations Period | | | | | | | | | | | |
| NET SALES | 58 | | | | | | | | | | |
| Materials Used | 59 | | | | | | | | | | |
| Labor | 60 | | | | | | | | | | |
| Manufacturing Expenses | 61 | | | | | | | | | | |
| | 62 | | | | | | | | | | |
| COST OF GOODS SOLD | 63 | | | | | | | | | | |
| GROSS PROFIT | 64 | | | | | | | | | | |
| Selling Expenses | 65 | | | | | | | | | | |
| General & Adm. Expenses | 66 | | | | | | | | | | |
| | 67 | | | | | | | | | | |
| TOTAL OPERATING EXPENSES | 68 | | | | | | | | | | |
| OPERATING PROFIT | 69 | | | | | | | | | | |
| Other Income | 70 | | | | | | | | | | |
| | 71 | | | | | | | | | | |
| Other Expense | 72 | | | | | | | | | | |
| | 73 | | | | | | | | | | |
| NET PROFIT BEFORE TAX | 74 | | | | | | | | | | |
| Income Taxes | 75 | | | | | | | | | | |
| | 76 | | | | | | | | | | |
| NET PROFIT AFTER TAX | 77 | | | | | | | | | | |
| Depreciation & Amortization | 78 | | | | | | | | | | |
| | 79 | | | | | | | | | | |
| Gross Cash Flow (77 + 78 + 79) | 80 | | | | | | | | | | |
| | 81 | | | | | | | | | | |
| RECONCILIATION OF NET WORTH | | | | | | | | | | | |
| Net Worth - Beginning | 82 | | | | | | | | | | |
| Add: Net Profit Less: (Net Loss) | 83 | | | | | | | | | | |
| Less: Dividends | 84 | | | | | | | | | | |
| | 85 | | | | | | | | | | |
| | 86 | | | | | | | | | | |
| | 87 | | | | | | | | | | |
| | 88 | | | | | | | | | | |
| Net Worth - Ending | 89 | | | | | | | | | | |
| Change In Net Worth (89 - 82) | 90 | | | | | | | | | | |
| SOURCE & APPLICATION OF FUNDS | | | | | | | | | | | |
| Sources of Funds: | | | | | | | | | | | |
| Net Profit After Tax | 91 | | | | | | | | | | |
| Depr., Amort., Depletion | 92 | | | | | | | | | | |
| | 93 | | | | | | | | | | |
| | 94 | | | | | | | | | | |
| Increase-Noncurrent Debt | 95 | | | | | | | | | | |
| | 96 | | | | | | | | | | |
| | 97 | | | | | | | | | | |
| | 98 | | | | | | | | | | |
| | 99 | | | | | | | | | | |
| Other Accounts - Net | 100 | | | | | | | | | | |
| Decrease Net Working Capital | 101 | | | | | | | | | | |
| TOTAL SOURCES | 102 | | | | | | | | | | |
| Applications of Funds: | | | | | | | | | | | |
| Dividends Paid | 103 | | | | | | | | | | |
| | 104 | | | | | | | | | | |
| | 105 | | | | | | | | | | |
| Purchase of Fixed Assets | 106 | | | | | | | | | | |
| Decrease - Noncurrent Debt | 107 | | | | | | | | | | |
| | 108 | | | | | | | | | | |
| | 109 | | | | | | | | | | |
| | 110 | | | | | | | | | | |
| | 111 | | | | | | | | | | |
| Other Accounts - Net | 112 | | | | | | | | | | |
| Increase in Working Capital | 113 | | | | | | | | | | |
| TOTAL APPLICATIONS | 114 | | | | | | | | | | |

# U.S. GOVERNMENT PRINTING OFFICE

**BEFORE USING THIS FORM, READ IMPORTANT INFORMATION ON REVERSE SIDE
PLEASE PRINT OR TYPE ALL INFORMATION**

## S057

# ORDER FORM

**Customer's Telephone No.'s**

| | | | |
|---|---|---|---|
| Area Code | Home | Area Code | Office |

MasterCard VISA

**Credit Card No.**

**Date.......................... Your Order Number..........................**

**Customer's Name and Address**

**Expiration Date
Month/Year**

**ZIP**

### MAIL TO:

**Superintendent of Documents
U. S. Government Printing Office
Washington, D. C. 20402**

### FOR OFFICE USE ONLY

| QUANTITY | CHARGES |
|---|---|
| _____ Publications _____ | |
| _____ Subscriptions _____ | |
| Special shipping charges _____ | |
| International handling .. _____ | |
| Special charges ........ _____ | |
| OPNR .................. _____ | |
| _____ UPNS | |
| _____ Balance Due | |
| _____ Discount | |
| _____ Refund | |

### Deposit Account Number

| | | | | | | | — | |
|---|---|---|---|---|---|---|---|---|

Charge orders may be telephoned to the GPO order desk at (202)783-3238 from 8 00 a m to 4 00 p m eastern time, Monday-Friday (except holidays)

| Stock No. | Quantity | Unit of Issue | List ID | ☐ Publication | Title of | ☐ Subscription | Unit Price | Total |
|---|---|---|---|---|---|---|---|---|
| | | | | | | | | |
| | | | | | | | | |
| | | | | | | | | |
| | | | | | | | | |
| | | | | | | | | |
| | | | | | | | | |
| | | | | | | | | |
| | | | | | | | | |
| | | | | | | | | |
| | | | | | | | | |
| | | | | | | | | |
| | | | | | | | | |
| | | | | | | | | |

**TOTAL ENCLOSED $**

**SHIP TO: (If different from above)**

**ZIP**

| Unit of issue | Explanation |
|---|---|
| EA | Each - single copy |
| KT | Kit of multiple items in a special container |
| PD | Pad containing multiple sheets |
| PK | Package containing multiple copies |
| SE | Set of multiple items |
| SU | Subscription |

103

# U.S. GOVERNMENT PRINTING OFFICE (Cont'd.)

INFORMATION CONCERNING YOUR ORDER

Payment is required in advance of shipment of publications. You may order using check or money order drawn on a bank located in Canada, the United States, or United States possessions, in U.S. dollars. (NOTE: In accordance with U.S. Department of the Treasury regulations, we cannot accept checks drawn on Canadian banks or Candian money orders for amounts of less than four U.S. dollars ($4.00). If your order totals less than $4.00, we suggest that you use your MasterCard or VISA account.) Make checks/money orders payable to the Superintendent of Documents. Checks returned by the bank as uncollectible are subject to a penalty of up to 10 percent of the amount of the check, with a minimum charge of five dollars ($5.00). You may also order by using your VISA, MasterCard, or Superintendent of Documents Prepaid Deposit Account. Do not send currency (bills or coins) or postage stamps.

Shipping is by non-priority mail or United Parcel Service (UPS). First class and airmail services are available for an additional charge if requested. Please contact us in advance for rates if you desire this service (202-783-3238) and indicate on your order if you desire special postage.

## DISCOUNTS:

With the exception of certain publications and subscriptions, a discount of 25% from the domestic price is allowed on orders of 100 or more units of issue mailed to a single address. A discount of 25% from the domestic price is also applicable on orders from bookdealers, for orders of any quantity, mailed to the dealer's business address. (The maximum discount allowable is 25%).

## INTERNATIONAL CUSTOMERS:

Mailing regulations require special handling for orders mailed to addresses outside the United States or its possessions for which we charge an additional 25% of the domestic price. Payment is required in advance by one of the methods stated above. You may also remit by UNESCO coupons or by International Postal Money Order, made payable to the Superintendent of Documents. Foreign currency and foreign checks will not be accepted. All orders must be in English. International customers are allowed the same discounts stated above.

Orders are sent via surface mail unless otherwise requested. Should you desire airmail service, please contact us in advance by letter, telephone (202-783-3238), or Telex (#710-822-9413;ANSWERBACK USGPO WSH) for the total cost of your order.

### To Order, Use Form On Reverse Side

1. A separate order form must be used for ordering publications and subscriptions.

2. Type or print your complete name and address, home and office telephone numbers, date, order number (if any), Deposit Account Number (if applicable), VISA or MasterCard number and expiration date (if applicable), in proper places at the top of the form. If order is to be shipped to another location, enter address at bottom of form. All prices include postage and handling.

3. When ordering publications, type or print the stock number, unit of issue (see front), quantity, title, price, and total payment enclosed. Allow 4 weeks for delivery (longer for International Orders).

4. When ordering a subscription service, type or print the quantity, title, price, List ID (when available), and total payment enclosed. Allow 2-6 weeks, plus mailing time, for processing. All subscriptions are for one year, unless otherwise noted. Subscribers will be notified by mail in ample time to renew.

5. Mail your order form to Superintendent of Documents, U.S. Government Printing Office, Washington, D.C. 20402.

6. Orders and inquiries can be placed with our order/information desk (202-783-3238) from 8:00 a.m. to 4:00 p.m., Eastern Time.

7. This form may be reproduced.

U.S. GOVERNMENT PRINTING OFFICE: 1990 O—944-921

## TAX INFORMATION REPORTING GUIDE

Of the nearly 700 tax forms that could bedevil the small business person, the following 76 were selected by John C. Zimmerman, JD, CPA, an accounting professor at the University of Nevada (Las Vegas), and reprinted with permission from the CP JOURNAL, October 1990, (c) 1990. (See pages 106–113.)

| FORM | FORM'S PURPOSE | ISSUER AND TO WHOM ISSUED | FILING DATE |
|---|---|---|---|
| | **REAL ESTATE TRANSACTIONS**\*\* | | |
| 1099-A | To report information about the acquisition or abandonment of property that is security for a debt. | Filed by secured lender with the IRS and borrower. | File with the IRS by February 28. |
| 1099-S | Gross proceeds from the sale or exchange of certain real estate transactions. | Filed by the person closing the real estate transaction with the IRS and recipient. | File with the IRS by February 28. File with the recipient by January 31. |
| \*\*Note: *The IRS has proposed Form 8824 (not yet available) to report Sec. 1031 tax free exchanges.* | | | |
| | **SECURITIES TRANSACTIONS** | | |
| 1099-B | To report the sales or redemptions of securities, futures transactions, commodities and barter exchange transactions. | Filed by the broker with the IRS and recipient. | File with the IRS by February 28. File with the recipient by January 31. |
| | **TIPS** | | |
| 4070 | To report an employee's tips to an employer if $20 or more during the month. | Filed by the employee with the employer. | File by the 10th day of the month following the month the tips were received. |
| 8027 | To report on receipts from food or beverage operations and tips received by employees. | Filed by large food or beverage establishment (see instructions for definition) with the IRS in Andover, Mass. | File by February 28. |

| FORM | FORM'S PURPOSE | ISSUER AND TO WHOM ISSUED | FILING DATE |
|---|---|---|---|
| | **IINTEREST, ORIGINAL ISSUE DISCOUNT AND CERTIFIED INDEBTEDNESS** *(continued from previous page)* | | |
| 8329 | To report by lenders of certified indebtedness loans on the issuance of mortgage credit certificates. | Filed by the lender with the IRS in Philadelphia. | File on or before the 31st day of January following the year the loan was made. |
| 8330 | To provide information on mortgage credit certificates required by Sec. 25. | Filed by the issuer of MCCs with the IRS in Philadelphia. | File on the last day of the month following the month of the quarter ending March 31, June 30, September 30 and December 31. |
| | **JOBS CREDIT INFORMATION** | | |
| 6199 | To report youth who qualify as participating in a qualified cooperative education program for purposes of the jobs credit taken by the employer of the youth. | Filed by the qualified school with the employer. | No date specified. |
| | **LENDER LIABILITY FOR WITHHOLDING TAXES** | | |
| 4219 | To report the payment of wages by a lender to another's employees to insure that the proper taxes have been withheld. | Filed by the lender with the IRS office where the employer files employment tax returns. | File by the quarterly date when the employer's employment tax return would be due. |
| | **MOVING EXPENSE REIMBURSEMENT** | | |
| 4782 | To provide employees with a breakdown of moving expense reimbursements made by an employer. | Filed by the employer with the employee. | File by January 31. |
| | **PASS-THROUGH ENTITIES** | | |
| 2439 | To inform shareholders of a regulated investment company of gains reported and taxes paid by the RIC which shareholders report on their tax return. | Filed by the RIC with the shareholder; and all forms 2439 to the IRS. | File with the IRS with form 1120-RIC. File with the shareholder by 60th day after the close of the RIC tax year. |
| 8082 | To report items treated differently by a partner, S corporation holder and holder of a REMIC interest than the treatment by the pass-through entity. | Filed by the holder of the pass-through interest with the IRS. | Due with tax return. |
| 8271 | To report information relating to tax shelter investments. | Filed by the investor with the IRS. | Due with the tax return. |
| 8308 | To report the sale or exchange of a partnership interest with Sec. 751(a) unrealized receivables, Sec. 1245 depreciation and appreciated inventory items. | Filed by the partnership with the IRS. | Due with form 1065. |
| 8811 | To report information by a REMIC and issuers of Collateralized Debt Obligations that can be published in Publication 938. | Filed by REMIC and CDO issuers with the IRS in Philadelphia. | See instructions. |

107

| FORM | FORM'S PURPOSE | ISSUER AND TO WHOM ISSUED | FILING DATE |
|---|---|---|---|
| **INDEBTEDNESS DISCHARGE** | | | |
| 982 | To report reduction of tax attributes due to discharge of indebtedness. | Filed by the party discharged | Due with tax return with the IRS. |
| **INDIVIDUAL RETIREMENT ARRANGEMENTS** | | | |
| 5498 | To report IRA contributions and rollovers and the value of IRAs and SEPs. | Filed by the plan's trustee or issuer to the IRS and plan participants. | File with the IRS by May 31. File with the participants by January 31 for value of account and May 31 for contributions. |
| **INDIVIDUAL STATUS AND INCOME** | | | |
| SS-8 | To ask the IRS to determine whether the individual is an employee or independent contractor by providing the IRS with certain information. | Filed by the employer with the IRS. | File whenever the employer needs this information. |
| W-2P | To report annual retirement payments other than lump sum distributions. | Filed by the payer to the Social Security Administration and recipient. | File with the SSA by February 28. File with the recipient by January 31. |
| 1099 Misc. | To report payments of $600 or more made from a trade or business or for prizes and awards that are not made for services; $10 or more for royalties and substitute dividends. | Filed by the payer with the IRS and recipient. | File with the IRS by February 28. File with the recipient by January 31. |
| 1099R | To report total distributions from pension and profit sharing plans, IRAs, SEPs and insurance contracts. | Filed by the payer with the IRS and recipient. | File with the IRS by February 28. File with the recipient by January 31. |
| **INSURANCE COMPANY REPORTING** | | | |
| 8390 | To report information by certain insurance companies that will be used to compute the "differential earnings rate" which will affect the tax liability of all mutual life insurance companies. | Filed by the insurance company with the IRS. | See form. |
| **INTEREST, ORIGINAL ISSUE DISCOUNT AND CERTIFIED INDEBTEDNESS** | | | |
| 1098 | To report mortgage interest received by a person or financial institution of $600 or more. | Filed by the lender with the IRS and borrower. | File with IRS by February 28. File with the borrower by January 31. |
| 1099 INT | To report interest income of $10 or more paid to a recipient. | Filed by the payer with the IRS and recipient. | File with IRS by February 28. File with recipient by January 31. |
| 1099 OID | To report original issue discount to the recipient of $10 or more. | Filed by the OID issuer with the recipient and IRS. | File with the IRS by February 28. File with recipient by January 31. |
| 8281 | To report information by an issuer of publicly offered original issue discount debt instruments. | Filed by the issuer with the IRS in Detroit. | File within 30 days of the issuance of the OID instrument. |

108

| FORM | FORM'S PURPOSE | ISSUER AND TO WHOM ISSUED | FILING DATE |
|---|---|---|---|
| **FOREIGN AND INTERNATIONAL TAXATION** *(continued from previous page)* | | | |
| 8644-A | To report a U.S. shareholder's pro rata share of ordinary earnings and net capital gain in a qualified electing fund (QEF). | Filed by the QEF with the IRS in in Philadelphia. | File by the 15th day of the ninth month following the QEF's tax year. |
| 8709 | To claim an exemption from withholding by a foreign government or international organization. | Filed by the foreign government or international organization with the withholding agent. | No date specified. |
| 8804 | To annually report the withholding liability and payments made for all foreign partners' effectively connected taxable income. | By the partnership or properly designated person with the IRS in Philadelphia. | 15th day of the fourth month following the close of the partnership tax year. |
| 8805 | To annually report the withholding liability and payments made for an individual foreign partner's effectively connected taxable income. | By the partnership or properly designated person with the IRS in Philadelphia. | 15th day of the fourth month following the close of the partnership tax year. |
| 8813 | To report each payment of foreign withholding tax made by a partnership. | By the partnership with the IRS in Philadelphia. | On or before the 15th day of the fourth, sixth, ninth and twelfth month of the partnership tax year. |
| **FOREST AND TIMBER** | | | |
| T | To report timber acquisitions if certain deductions are taken or elections made. | Filed by the taxpayer with the IRS. | Due with tax return. |
| **GAMBLING WINNINGS** | | | |
| W-2G | To report gambling winnings from certain activities generally $600 or more; $1,200 or more from bingo or slot machines; $1,500 or more from Keno. | Filed by the payer with the IRS and recipient. | File with IRS by February 28. File with the recipient by January 31. |
| 5754 | To report gambling winnings received by someone for another or as a member of a group. | Filed by the payee with the payer. | File before payer sends the W-2G. |
| **GOVERNMENT PAYMENTS AND GRANTS** | | | |
| 1099-G | To report taxable payments of $10 or more made by state and local governments to individuals. | Filed by the government agency with IRS and recipient. | File with IRS by February 28. File with recipient by January 31. |
| 6497 | To report non-taxable energy grants or subsidized energy financing under a government program. | Filed by administrator of government program with the IRS. | File on last day of February following the calendar year of payment. |

## FOREIGN AND INTERNATIONAL TAXATION (continued from previous page)

| FORM | FORM'S PURPOSE | ISSUER AND TO WHOM ISSUED | FILING DATE |
|---|---|---|---|
| 926 | To report transfers of property to foreign entities. | Filed by the domestic transferor with the IRS. | Filed the day of the transfer. |
| 1001 | To report to a withholding agent both the ownership of the income and reduced or exempt rate of the tax under tax conventions or treaties. | Filed by the foreign owner of the income with the withholding agent. | Depends upon the type of income to which the form applies. |
| 1042S | To report income subject to withholding under Secs.1441, 1442 and Reg. 1.1445-8T. | Filed by the withholding agent with the IRS in Philadelphia and the income recipient. | File by March 15 with the IRS and recipient. |
| 1042 | To summarize transactions reported on form1042S. | Filed by the withholding agent with the IRS in Philadelphia. | File by March 15. |
| 2952 | To report information on controlled foreigncorporations. | Filed by the person or entity who owns more than 50% of a CFC for an uninterrupted period of 30 days or more during the annual accounting period with the IRS. | Due with the tax return. |
| 3206 | To report dividends paid by a United States corporation to a nominee with a United Kingdom address. | Filed by the United Kingdom withholding agent with the IRS in Philadelphia. | No date specified. |
| 3520 | To report the creation of or transfers to a foreign trust. | Filed by grantor of an inter-vivos trust or trustee of testamentary trust with the IRS in Philadelphia. | File by 90th day after the creation of the trust or transfer of property to the trust. |
| 4224 | To obtain an exemption from withholding of tax on income effectively connected with a trade or business for non-residant aliens and foreign entities. | Filed by the owner of income with the withholding agent. | File before payment of any income to which form applies. |
| 5471 | To report information on owners' earnings, profits and operations of a controlled foreign corporation. | Filed by the owner with the IRS in Philadelphia. | Due with the tax return. |
| 5713 | To report on operations in boycotting countries by United States persons and entities. | Filed by the individual or entity with the IRS in Philadelphia. | Due with the tax return. |
| 8233 | To obtain an exemption from withholding for independent personal services by a non-resident alien individual under a tax treaty or personal exemption amount. | Filed by the non-resident alien with the withholding agent, who certifies the form and sends it to the IRS in Washington D.C. | File with IRS within five days of the withholding agent's acceptance. |
| 8288 | To report the amount of withholding tax imposed on the foreign seller of a U.S. real property interest. | Filed by the withholding agent with the IRS in Philadelphia. | File by the 20th day after the transfer. |
| 8288-A | Withholding statement attached to form 8288. | Filed by the withholding agent with the IRS in Philadelphia. | Due with form 8288. |

| FORM | FORM'S PURPOSE | ISSUER AND TO WHOM ISSUED | FILING DATE |
|------|----------------|---------------------------|-------------|
| **EXEMPT ORGANIZATIONS AND TAXPAYERS** *(continued from previous page)* | | | |
| 8038T | To report an arbitrage rebate on a state or local bond issue to the U.S. | Issuers of tax exempt bonds to the IRS in Philadelphia. | 60 days after the end of every fifth bond year during the term of the issue. |
| 8282 | To report by a donee charitable organization and successor donees who dispose of charitable deduction property within two years after receiving the property if the property's value exceeds $500. | Filed by the donee organization with the IRS in Cincinnati. | Filed within 125 days after the disposition of the property. |
| **FIDUCIARIES** | | | |
| 56 | To report the creation or termination of a fiduciary relationship for an individual, estate, trust, or terminating entities. | Filed by the trustee with the IRS. | Filed within 10 days from the date the fiduciary is appointed. |
| 706-B(1) | To report distributions of a generation skipping trust to younger generation beneficiaries, charities; and all GST terminations. | Filed by the trustee with the IRS. | See form instructions. |
| 706-B(2) | To notify beneficiaries of a generation skipping trust that they must file form 706-B. | Filed by the trustee with the generation skipping beneficiary. | Due date for filing form 706-B(1) with the IRS. |
| 706 CE | To report foreign death taxes paid so that credit may be taken on the form 706. See listed countries which have death tax conventions with the U.S. | Filed by the estate's executor with the foreign government. The foreign government certifies the form and sends it to the IRS. | No due date given. Due before the Form 706 is filed. |
| 1041-A | To report charitable information required by Sec. 6034 and the related regulations concerning trust accumulations of charitable amounts. | Filed by the trustee with the IRS. | Filed on the 15th day of the fourth month following the close of the tax year. |
| 5227 | To report on charitable activities of split interest trusts created after May 26, 1969. | Filed by the trustee with the IRS. | Filed on the 15th day of the fourth month following the close of the year. |
| **FOREIGN AND INTERNATIONAL TAXATION** | | | |
| TDF 90-22.1 | To report foreign bank, securities or other financial account in excess of $10,000. | Filed by the person having a financial interest in or authority over the account with the Department of the Treasury. | Filed by June 30 of succeeding year. |
| W-8 | To report an exemption by a non-resident alien or foreign entity from information return reporting or backup withholding or to notify the withholding agent that the foreign taxpayer no longer qualifies for the exemption. | Filed by the foreign taxpayer with the middle-man, broker or barter exchange agent. | Filed during the calendar year unless the statement has been filed within the two preceding calendar years. |

111

# TAX INFORMATION REPORTING GUIDE

| FORM | FORM'S PURPOSE | ISSUER AND TO WHOM ISSUED | FILING DATE |
|---|---|---|---|
| | **ASSET ACQUISITIONS** | | |
| 8594 | To show asset acquisitions after May 6, 1986 if going concern value or goodwill could attach and if the buyer's basis in the assets is determined by the amount paid. | Filed by the buyer and seller of the assets with the IRS. | Date of tax return of buyer and seller. |
| | **CHARITABLE DONATIONS** | | |
| 8283 | To report certain information about non-cash charitable gifts that exceed $500 | Filed by the taxpayer with the IRS. | Due date of tax return. |
| | **CORPORATIONS*** *(See also DIVIDENDS)* | | |
| 851 | To report affiliations of corporations filing consolidated tax returns. | Filed by the parent of the consolidated group with the IRS. | Due date of tax return. |
| 964-A | To determine f the corporation is a qualified corporation for purposes of complete liquidation, and if the corporation qualifies to determine taxable income. A qualified corporation is defined in the form. | Filed by the qualified corporation with the IRS. | Due within 30 days after adopting a plan of complete liquidation and with the final income tax return. |
| 966 | To inform the RS of a corporation's liquidation plan. | Filed by the liquidating corporation with the IRS. | Due within 30 days after a plan of liquidation is adopted. |

* Note: *The IRS has proposed form 8820 (not yet available) for reporting corporate acquisitions and recapitalization of $10 million or more.*

| FORM | FORM'S PURPOSE | ISSUER AND TO WHOM ISSUED | FILING DATE |
|---|---|---|---|
| | **CURRENCY TRANSACTIONS** | | |
| 4789 | To report any currency transaction with a financial institution, other than a casino, that involves more than $10,000. | Filed by the financial institution with the IRS in Detroit. | Due within 15 days after the date of the transaction. |
| 8300 | To report cash payments of more than $10,000 received in a trade or business. | Filed by the business with the IRS in Detroit and to the payer. | Due to the IRS within 15 days after the transaction. Due to the payer by January 31 of the year following payment. |
| 8362 | To report a currency transaction with a casino with gross annual gaming revenues in excess of $1 million that involves cash transactions of more than $10,000. | Filed by the casino with the IRS in Detroit. | Due within 15 days after the date of the transaction. |

112

| FORM | FORM'S PURPOSE | ISSUER AND TO WHOM ISSUED | FILING DATE |
|------|----------------|---------------------------|-------------|
| **DEPENDENT CARE INFORMATION** | | | |
| W-10 | To report the correct name, address and I.D. number of the dependent care provider on the Form 2441. | Filed by the dependent care provider with the individual taking the child care credit on Form 2441. | No date given. Presumably due before the individual files his or her tax return. |
| **DIVIDENDS** | | | |
| 1099 Div. | To report amount of dividends from the paying corporation during the year for $10 or more. | Filed by the paying corporation with the IRS and dividend recipient. | Filed with the IRS by February 28. Filed with the recipient by January 31. |
| 1099 Part. | To report dividend distributions from cooperatives for $10 or more. | Filed by the paying cooperative with the IRS and recipient. | Filed with the IRS by February 28. Filed with the recipient by January 31. |
| 5452 | To report non-taxable dividend distributions. | Filed by the paying corporation with the IRS in Washington, D.C. | Filed by February 28 after the close of the calendar year. |
| **EXEMPT ORGANIZATIONS AND TAXPAYERS** | | | |
| 990 BL | To report on a Black Lung Benefit Trust. | Filed by the trust with the IRS in Cincinnati. | Filed by the 15th day of 5th month following the end of the taxpayer's year. |
| 1000 | To exempt from withholding the owner of bonds which have a tax free covenant issued before 1934. | Filed by the owner of the bonds with the withholding agent. | No time specified. |
| 8038 | To report by the issuers of tax exempt private activity bonds, issued after December 31, 1986, the information required by Sec. 149. | Filed by the issuer of the bonds with the IRS in Philadelphia. | Filed on or before the 15th day of the second calendar month after the close of the calendar quarter that contains the issue date. |
| 8038G | To report by the issuers of tax exempt governmental bonds, issued after December 31, 1986, information required by Sec. 149(e) if the issue price is $100,000 or more. | Filed by the issuer of the bonds with the IRS in Philadelphia. | Filed on or before the 15th day of the second calendar month after the close of the calendar quarter in which the bond issue is issued. |
| 8038GC | To report by the issuers of tax exempt governmental bonds, issued after December 31, 1986, information required by Sec. 149(e) if the issue price is less than $100,000. | Filed by the issuer with the IRS in Philadelphia. | Filed on or before February 15 after the close of the calendar year in which the issue is issued. |

# 5.

# INVENTORY RECORDKEEPING FORMS

## INVENTORY FORMS

Inventory in a company's possession is cash in the bank. Unless periods of shortages develop, inventory usually does not garner interest or appreciation. The key to profits, therefore, is to turn over the inventory as often as possible in order to maximize profits. These forms will help you keep track of your inventory and a frequent analysis of your forms will help you avoid obsolescence and increase profits.

Forms/checklist for official Record Retention can be found in this section, too, which might eliminate need for inventory space.

## INVENTORY DISCOUNT SCHEDULE

[ ] Retail      [ ] Wholesale      Valid From _____ To _____

| Item | Retail Price | Quantity | % – Amount Of Discount | Net Unit Price |
|------|------|------|------|------|
| | | | | |
| | | | | |
| | | | | |
| | | | | |
| | | | | |
| | | | | |
| | | | | |
| | | | | |
| | | | | |
| | | | | |
| | | | | |
| | | | | |
| | | | | |
| | | | | |
| | | | | |
| | | | | |
| | | | | |
| | | | | |
| | | | | |
| | | | | |
| | | | | |
| | | | | |
| | | | | |
| | | | | |
| | | | | |
| | | | | |
| | | | | |
| | | | | |
| | | | | |
| | | | | |
| | | | | |
| | | | | |
| | | | | |
| | | | | |
| | | | | |
| | | | | |

# INVENTORY JOURNAL

*Beginning Inventory* _____ *(Date)*

| Date | INVENTORY PURCHASED | | | | | | | | | |
|------|------|------|------|------|------|------|------|------|------|------|
| | Cash Purchases | | Credit Purchases | | Paid on Account | | Removed for Personal Use | | Returns/ Allowances | |
| 1 | | | | | | | | | | |
| 2 | | | | | | | | | | |
| 3 | | | | | | | | | | |
| 4 | | | | | | | | | | |
| 5 | | | | | | | | | | |
| 6 | | | | | | | | | | |
| 7 | | | | | | | | | | |
| 8 | | | | | | | | | | |
| 9 | | | | | | | | | | |
| 10 | | | | | | | | | | |
| 11 | | | | | | | | | | |
| 12 | | | | | | | | | | |
| 13 | | | | | | | | | | |
| 14 | | | | | | | | | | |
| 15 | | | | | | | | | | |
| 16 | | | | | | | | | | |
| 17 | | | | | | | | | | |
| 18 | | | | | | | | | | |
| 19 | | | | | | | | | | |
| 20 | | | | | | | | | | |
| 21 | | | | | | | | | | |
| 22 | | | | | | | | | | |
| 23 | | | | | | | | | | |
| 24 | | | | | | | | | | |
| 25 | | | | | | | | | | |
| 26 | | | | | | | | | | |
| 27 | | | | | | | | | | |
| 28 | | | | | | | | | | |
| 29 | | | | | | | | | | |
| 30 | | | | | | | | | | |
| 31 | | | | | | | | | | |
| Total for Month | | | | | | | | | | |
| Balance Forward | | | | | | | | | | |
| TOTAL | | | | | | | | | | |

*Ending Inventory* _____ *(Date)*

# INVENTORY LEDGER

Unit: _____

Article: _____

Minimum: _____

Location: _____

| Date | Description | Received | | | Disbursed | | Balance on Hand | |
|------|-------------|----------|--------|-----------|-----------|--------|-----------------|--------|
| | | Quantity | Amount | Unit Cost | Quantity | Amount | Quantity | Amount |
| | | | | | | | | |
| | | | | | | | | |
| | | | | | | | | |
| | | | | | | | | |
| | | | | | | | | |
| | | | | | | | | |
| | | | | | | | | |
| | | | | | | | | |
| | | | | | | | | |
| | | | | | | | | |
| | | | | | | | | |
| | | | | | | | | |
| | | | | | | | | |
| | | | | | | | | |
| | | | | | | | | |
| | | | | | | | | |
| | | | | | | | | |
| | | | | | | | | |
| | | | | | | | | |
| | | | | | | | | |

118

# INVENTORY RECORD

| Department | Location |
|---|---|
| Called By | Date |
| Entered By | Date |

| Date | | | |
|---|---|---|---|
| Sheet Number | Folio Number | This Sheet Completed – Date/T | |
| Priced By | | | Date |
| Examined By | | | Date |

| Item No. | Description | X | Quantity | Unit | Price | Unit | Extensions |
|---|---|---|---|---|---|---|---|
| | | | | | | | |
| | | | | | | | |
| | | | | | | | |
| | | | | | | | |
| | | | | | | | |
| | | | | | | | |
| | | | | | | | |
| | | | | | | | |
| | | | | | | | |
| | | | | | | | |
| | | | | | | | |
| | | | | | | | |
| | | | | | | | |
| | | | | | | | |
| | | | | | | | |
| | | | | | | | |
| | | | | | | | |
| | | | | | | | |
| | | | | | | | |
| | | | | | | | |
| | | | | | | | |
| | | | | | | | |
| | | | | | | | |
| | | | | | | | |
| | | | | | | | |
| | | | | | | | |
| | | | | | | | |
| | | | | | | | |
| | | | | | | | |
| | | | | | | | |
| | | | | | | | |
| | | | | | | | |
| | | | | | | | |
| | | | | | | | |
| | | | | | | | |
| | | | | | | | |
| | | Amount Forward | | | | | |

# PARTS INVENTORY

Bin Number _____

Date _____

Page _____ of _____

| Part Number | Quantity | Unit Price | Extension | Part Number | Quantity | Unit Price | Extension |
|---|---|---|---|---|---|---|---|
| | | | | | | | |
| | | | | | | | |
| | | | | | | | |
| | | | | | | | |
| | | | | | | | |
| | | | | | | | |
| | | | | | | | |
| | | | | | | | |
| | | | | | | | |
| | | | | | | | |
| | | | | | | | |
| | | | | | | | |
| | | | | | | | |
| | | | | | | | |
| | | | | | | | |
| | | | | | | | |
| | | | | | | | |
| | | | | | | | |
| | | | | | | | |
| | | | | | | | |
| | | | | | | | |
| | | | | | | | |
| | | | | | | | |
| | | | | | | | |
| | | | | | | | |
| | | | | | | | |
| | | | | | | | |

Subtotal Column 1 _____

Subtotal Column 2 _____

Subtotal Column 1 _____

TOTAL _____

# PERPETUAL INVENTORY CONTROL

Item: _____  Item Number: _____  Sheet Number: _____

| Ordered | | | |
| --- | --- | --- | --- |
| Date | Order No. | Quantity | Due Date |
| | | | |
| | | | |
| | | | |
| | | | |
| | | | |
| | | | |
| | | | |
| | | | |
| | | | |
| | | | |
| | | | |
| | | | |
| | | | |
| | | | |
| | | | |
| | | | |
| | | | |

| Received | | |
| --- | --- | --- |
| Date | Order No. | Quantity |
| | | |
| | | |
| | | |
| | | |
| | | |
| | | |
| | | |
| | | |
| | | |
| | | |
| | | |
| | | |
| | | |
| | | |
| | | |
| | | |
| | | |

| Sold | | | | |
| --- | --- | --- | --- | --- |
| Date | Order No. | Quantity | Balance | Comments |
| | | | | |
| | | | | |
| | | | | |
| | | | | |
| | | | | |
| | | | | |
| | | | | |
| | | | | |
| | | | | |
| | | | | |
| | | | | |
| | | | | |
| | | | | |
| | | | | |
| | | | | |
| | | | | |
| | | | | |
| | | | | |
| | | | | |
| | | | | |
| | | | | |
| | | | | |
| | | | | |
| | | | | |
| | | | | |
| | | | | |

## RECORD RETENTION

Keeping records, whether for personal or business reasons, is a requirement necessitated primarily by tax authorities and contract obligations. Here is a checklist of 45 different types of forms and documents that most of us might utilize and the lengths of time they should be kept before they become legally obsolete. With storage space usually at a premium, it is good to know that you do not need to keep all forms and documents longer than necessary.

# RECORDS RETENTION CHECKLIST

| Description | How Long to Keep (years) |
|---|---|
| Accident Reports and Claims | 7 |
| Accounts Payable Ledgers/Schedules | 7 |
| Accounts Receivables Ledgers/Schedules | 7 |
| Audit Reports | Permanently |
| Bank Reconciliations | 1 |
| Capital Bond/Stock Records | Permanently |
| Cash Books | Permanently |
| Checks* | 7 |
| Contracts and Leases (expired) | 7 |
| Contracts and Leases (current) | Permanently |
| Correspondence (routine) | 1 |
| Correspondence (legal) | Permanently |
| Deeds/Mortgages/Bills of Sale | Permanently |
| Depreciation Schedules | Permanently |
| Duplicate Deposit Receipts | 1 |
| Employee Personnel Records (past) | 3 |
| Employment Applications | 3 |
| Expense Analyses | 7 |
| Financial Statements | Permanently |
| General/Private Ledgers | Permanently |
| Insurance Policies (expired) | 3 |
| Insurance Policies/Records/Claims | Permanently |
| Internal Audit Reports | 3 or more |
| Inventory Schedules | 7 |
| Invoices (customers) | 7 |
| Invoices (from vendors) | 7 |
| Journals | Permanently |
| Minute Books, By-Laws, Charter | Permanently |
| Payroll Records | 7 |
| Pension Payment Records | 7 |
| Petty Cash Vouchers | 3 |
| Plant Cost Ledgers | 7 |
| Property Appraisals | Permanently |
| Property Records/Blueprints/Plans | Permanently |
| Purchase Orders | 1 |
| Receiving Records | 1 |
| Requisitions | 1 |

| | |
|---|---|
| **Sales Records** | 7 |
| **Scrap/Salvage/Recycling Records** | 7 |
| **Stock/Bond Certificates (canceled)** | 1 |
| **Subsidiary (secondary) Ledgers** | 7 |
| **Tax Returns/Worksheets/Reports** | Permanently |
| **Time Books** | 7 |
| **Trademark Registrations** | Permanently |
| **Vouchers (vendors, employees, officers)** | 7 |

**\*Canceled checks for tax, property, contractual, and other important payments should be kept permanently.**

# 6.

# MARKETING FORMS: ADVERTISING, SALES

## ADVERTISING FORMS

Virtually all businesses make consistent investments in advertising. Even former traditional non-advertisers like the Hershey Company and *Reader's Digest* have succumbed to competitive pressures and made advertising a part of their companies' operation and growth. Most companies invest or budget between less than one percent to 10 percent of gross sales. Some luxury products, like perfumes and precious jewelry, might go even higher. Obviously, with such a major budget item as a part of the entrepreneur's business operation, some form of control needs to be exercised. The controls are at least two: (1) the proper selection of media that produce optimum results, and (2) timing the advertising to attract the most prospects and sales. The forms proposed here will help in the research and analysis, as well as tracking and allocation, of advertising the year around. There are usually distinct fluctuations in the sales response of most products and services. Keeping track of advertising results, by media and by month, is one way entrepreneurs can properly analyze where and when to invest their advertising budget. Sometimes direct results are difficult to determine. For instance, a soft-sell or institutional advertisement might have only long-range goodwill effect, but its impact can last longer and be more helpful during downturns than hard-hitting sale ads. Billboards can have this public relations impact, as does publicity. Forms are a start in giving entrepreneurs the best value for their advertising investment—when supplemented with informed analysis and selection.

# ADVERTISING PLAN

Product Line/Department _____

## Dollar Amount By Month

| | | January | February | March | April | May | June | July | August | September | October | November | December |
|---|---|---|---|---|---|---|---|---|---|---|---|---|---|
| Yellow Pages | LY | | | | | | | | | | | | |
| | P | | | | | | | | | | | | |
| Television - Regional | LY | | | | | | | | | | | | |
| | P | | | | | | | | | | | | |
| Television - Local | LY | | | | | | | | | | | | |
| | P | | | | | | | | | | | | |
| Radio - Local | LY | | | | | | | | | | | | |
| | P | | | | | | | | | | | | |
| Newspaper | LY | | | | | | | | | | | | |
| | P | | | | | | | | | | | | |
| Magazines - Regional | LY | | | | | | | | | | | | |
| | P | | | | | | | | | | | | |
| Direct Mail | LY | | | | | | | | | | | | |
| | P | | | | | | | | | | | | |

LY = Last Year    P = Plan

126

# COMPARATIVE ADVERTISING PLAN

DATE _____

## MEDIA

| | TELEVISION | | RADIO | | MAGAZINE | | NEWSPAPER | | DIRECT MAIL | | BILLBOARD | | TOTAL | |
|---|---|---|---|---|---|---|---|---|---|---|---|---|---|---|
| | SPENT LAST YEAR | FORECAST THIS YEAR | SPENT LAST YEAR | FORECAST THIS YEAR | SPENT LAST YEAR | FORECAST THIS YEAR | SPENT LAST YEAR | FORECAST THIS YEAR | SPENT LAST YEAR | FORECAST THIS YEAR | SPENT LAST YEAR | FORECAST THIS YEAR | SPENT LAST YEAR | FORECAST THIS YEAR |
| JANUARY | | | | | | | | | | | | | | |
| FEBRUARY | | | | | | | | | | | | | | |
| MARCH | | | | | | | | | | | | | | |
| APRIL | | | | | | | | | | | | | | |
| MAY | | | | | | | | | | | | | | |
| JUNE | | | | | | | | | | | | | | |
| JULY | | | | | | | | | | | | | | |
| AUGUST | | | | | | | | | | | | | | |
| SEPTEMBER | | | | | | | | | | | | | | |
| OCTOBER | | | | | | | | | | | | | | |
| NOVEMBER | | | | | | | | | | | | | | |
| DECEMBER | | | | | | | | | | | | | | |
| YEAR | | | | | | | | | | | | | | |

# COMMISSION REPORT

Name: _____    Period From: _____  To: _____

| Order Date | Order Number | Account | Invoice Amount | Commission Rate | Amount |
|---|---|---|---|---|---|
|  |  |  |  |  |  |
|  |  |  |  |  |  |
|  |  |  |  |  |  |
|  |  |  |  |  |  |
|  |  |  |  |  |  |
|  |  |  |  |  |  |
|  |  |  |  |  |  |
|  |  |  |  |  |  |
|  |  |  |  |  |  |
|  |  |  |  |  |  |
|  |  |  |  |  |  |
|  |  |  |  |  |  |
|  |  |  |  |  |  |
|  |  |  |  |  |  |
|  |  |  |  |  |  |
|  |  |  |  |  |  |
|  |  |  |  |  |  |
|  |  |  |  |  |  |
|  |  |  |  |  |  |
|  |  |  |  |  |  |
|  |  |  |  |  |  |

Total Sales [_____]

Total Commission Earned _____

Less Advance/Credit _____

Commission Payable _____

_____        _____
      Date                                 Signed

## HOMEWORKER FORMS

Some industries have traditionally employed workers who work at home rather than in a shop or factory. Knitting and textile companies are two such categories. In this age of computer communication, working from home is becoming and will continue to be increasingly important. How do you compensate homeworkers? One way is to have the homeworker keep his or her own time schedule, such as on the form herewith, and submit it weekly to the sponsor or company for payment. If the homeworker is employed as a piece-worker, then of course he or she is paid by the finished item that is brought back to the company. Employers who utilize several homeworkers must obtain appropriate forms from the Department of Labor, as homeworkers are covered under certain federal labor laws.

# HOMEWORKER RECORD FORM

Workweek Ending Date:

**Article**
**Style or lot number and number of pieces of each**
**Other activities (travel, packing, etc.)**

| | Start | Stop | Hours | |
|---|---|---|---|---|
| Day1 | | | | |
| Day2 | | | | |
| Day3 | | | | |
| Day4 | | | | |
| Day5 | | | | |
| Day6 | | | | |
| Day7 | | | | |
| | | | **Total Hours** | **Expenses (description/amount)** |

# SALES SECTION

# CHART OF MONTHLY SALES

_____,19____ to ____,19____

| Jan. | Feb. | Mar. | Apr. | May | June | July | Aug. | Sept. | Oct. | Nov. | Dec. |
|------|------|------|------|-----|------|------|------|-------|------|------|------|
|      |      |      |      |     |      |      |      |       |      |      |      |
|      |      |      |      |     |      |      |      |       |      |      |      |
|      |      |      |      |     |      |      |      |       |      |      |      |
|      |      |      |      |     |      |      |      |       |      |      |      |
|      |      |      |      |     |      |      |      |       |      |      |      |
|      |      |      |      |     |      |      |      |       |      |      |      |
|      |      |      |      |     |      |      |      |       |      |      |      |
|      |      |      |      |     |      |      |      |       |      |      |      |
|      |      |      |      |     |      |      |      |       |      |      |      |
|      |      |      |      |     |      |      |      |       |      |      |      |

Month by month, 19____

# PURCHASE ORDER

Your Company Logo and Address Here

ALL PRICES GUARANTEED THROUGH _____

## BILL TO:

Name

Company

Street Address

City _____ State _____ Zip Code

Your Business Phone Number is Required

Person Ordering _____ Title _____

## SHIPPING INFORMATION

SHIP TO: (If different from Bill To)

Name

Company

Street Address

City _____ State _____ Zip Code

**SHIPPING METHOD:** *(Please check one)*

[ ] Regular Delivery (Usually UPS, except for bulky items)

[ ] Emergency Next-Day Delivery     *(Please call in your order 1 800-555-1212 by 1:00 P.M. CST)*

[ ] UPS 2nd Day Air Service

[ ] Request Inside Delivery (Additional Charge)

[ ] Other _____

## PAYMENT METHODS

**CREDIT PURCHASES**          If you've bought from _____
before, but your account number isn't listed above your name,
please enter it here:

D&B# _____

If you're listed with Dun & Bradstreet, please give us your D&B#

We'll process your order as quickly as possible. If anything
additional is required, we will contact you.

## PAYMENT METHOD     (TERMS: PAYABLE UPON RECEIPT OF INVOICE - NO C.O.D.'S) CHECK ONE:

[ ] Check or Money Order Enclosed

[ ] Open Account – new customers, please fill in credit purchase information to the left.

[ ] Company Purchase Order (required on orders over $_____     Purchase Order No. _____

[ ] Visa

[ ] MasterCard

[ ] American Express

Account Number _____

Credit Card Expiration Date _____

Authorized Signature _____

Print Name _____

## ORDER YOUR SUPPLIES HERE

| Quantity | Catalog Number | Item Description | Unit Price (ea., dz., etc.) | Total Amount |
|---|---|---|---|---|
|  |  |  |  |  |
|  |  |  |  |  |
|  |  |  |  |  |

Shipping charges will be added to your invoice.

Sales Tax _____

Total $ _____

Note Regarding State and Local Tax:
If you are tax exempt, please forward a copy of your tax exemption or re-sale certificate.

133

# QUOTATION FORM

**QUOTATION TO**

**DATE** _____

**F.O.B.** _____

**REQUESTED BY** _____

**REFER INQUIRIES TO** _____

| ITEM NO. | DESCRIPTION | QUANTITY | UNIT PRICE | TOTAL PRICE | DELIVERY DAYS FROM 'GO-AHEAD' |
|---|---|---|---|---|---|
|  |  |  |  |  |  |

**QUOTED PRICES AND CONDITIONS FIRM FOR 30 DAYS**

**AUTHORIZED SIGNATURE** _____

**TITLE** _____

134

# REQUEST FOR SAMPLE

Date: _____

Name: _____ Title: _____ Address: _____

Company _____ City: _____

Telephone _____ State: _____ Zip: _____

| [ ] New Account | [ ] Previous Customer | [ ] Charge | [ ] No Charge |
|---|---|---|---|
| Quantity | Description | | Total |
| | | | |
| | | | |
| | | | |
| | | | |
| | | | |
| | | | |
| | | | |
| | | | |
| | | | |
| | | | |
| | | | |
| | | | |
| | | | |
| | | | |

Ship Via: _____

Signed: _____ Authorized: _____

# SALES CALL SUMMARY REPORT

Sales Representative _____

| Date | Company | Individual Seen | Comments |
|------|---------|-----------------|----------|
| | Firm<br>Address<br>City & State | | |
| | Firm<br>Address<br>City & State | | |
| | Firm<br>Address<br>City & State | | |
| | Firm<br>Address<br>City & State | | |
| | Firm<br>Address<br>City & State | | |
| | Firm<br>Address<br>City & State | | |
| | Firm<br>Address<br>City & State | | |
| | Firm<br>Address<br>City & State | | |

136

# SALES COMMISSION REPORT

Sales Representative _____

Month of _____

| ACCOUNTS | GROSS SALES | LESS RETURNS | LESS DISCOUNT | NET SALES | GROSS COMMISSION | LESS DRAW | NET COMMISSION |
|---|---|---|---|---|---|---|---|
| | | | | | | | |
| | | | | | | | |
| | | | | | | | |
| | | | | | | | |
| | | | | | | | |
| | | | | | | | |
| | | | | | | | |
| | | | | | | | |
| | | | | | | | |
| | | | | | | | |
| | | | | | | | |
| | | | | | | | |
| | | | | | | | |
| | | | | | | | |
| | | | | | | | |
| | | | | | | | |
| TOTALS | | | | | | | |

137

# SALES CONTACT REPORT

Contact's Name _____

| Business |  |
|---|---|
| Address |  |
|  | Phone |
| Home Address |  |
|  | Phone |
| Spouse's Name |  |
| Children |  |
| Hobbies and Interests |  |

Personal Background

Civic Activities

# SALES FORECAST

For Period _____ , 19____

Department _____

Completed By _____

| Product(s) | Quarter 1 | Quarter 2 | Quarter 3 | Quarter 4 | Annual |
|---|---|---|---|---|---|
| | | | | | |
| | | | | | |
| | | | | | |
| | | | | | |
| | | | | | |
| | | | | | |
| | | | | | |
| | | | | | |
| | | | | | |
| | | | | | |
| | | | | | |
| | | | | | |
| | | | | | |
| | | | | | |
| | | | | | |
| | | | | | |
| TOTALS | | | | | |

# SALES LEAD

APPOINTMENT DATE

Day _____ Date _____ Time _____ [ ] A.M.
[ ] P.M.

SOURCE OF LEAD

Date _____

Name _____

Address _____

Phone No. _____

Interested in _____

_____

_____

_____

_____

Remarks: _____

_____

_____

_____

_____

# SALES ORDER (1)

SHIP TO _____

SALES ORDER NO. _____

INVOICE NO. _____  DATE _____

TERMS: NET 30 DAYS _____

CUSTOMER P.O. AND DATE _____

BILL TO _____

SALES REPRESENTATIVE _____

SHIP VIA _____

| ITEM | QUANTITY | DESCRIPTION | UNIT PRICE | TOTAL PRICE |
|------|----------|-------------|------------|-------------|
|      |          |             |            |             |
|      |          |             |            |             |
|      |          |             |            |             |
|      |          |             |            |             |
|      |          |             |            |             |
|      |          |             |            |             |
|      |          |             |            |             |
|      |          |             |            |             |
|      |          |             |            |             |

141

# SALES ORDER (2)

**DATE:**

| CUSTOMER | SALESPERSON |
|---|---|
| ADDRESS | OFFICE & PHONE |
| CITY   STATE   ZIP | PHONE QUOTE   O   WRITTEN QUOTE   O |
| CONTACT | CONTACTS PHONE |
| ORDERED BY | PURCHASE ORDER NO.   DATE |

| ITEM NO. | QUANTITY | DESCRIPTION | UNIT PRICE | TOTAL PRICE |
|---|---|---|---|---|
|  |  |  |  |  |
|  |  |  |  |  |
|  |  |  |  |  |
|  |  |  |  |  |
|  |  |  |  |  |
|  |  |  |  |  |
|  |  |  |  |  |
|  |  |  |  |  |
|  |  |  |  |  |
|  |  |  |  |  |
|  |  |  |  |  |
|  |  |  |  |  |

| PRICE VERIFIED BY | DATE |
|---|---|

| SOLD TO | SHIP TO |
|---|---|
| ATTN. | ATTN. |

# SALES PROSPECT FILE

New [ ]     Update [ ]     Follow-up date: _____

Company name: _____

Contact: _____ Title: _____

Address: _____

_____

Telephone: _____

Call-in [ ]     Referral [ ]     Referred by: _____

Current supplier: _____

Approximate volume (monthly): _____

Form letters sent: _____

Material sent: _____

Sales calls (date and summary): _____

_____

_____

_____

Date and summary of last discussion: _____

_____

_____

Desirability as client:     Very high [ ]     High [ ]     Medium [ ]     Low [ ]

Possibility of closing:     100% [ ]     90% [ ]     70% [ ]     50% [ ]     30% [ ]     None [ ]

General comments: _____

_____

_____

# MONTHLY SALES TREND ANALYSIS

|  | $ LAST YEAR | $ GOAL THIS YR | $ ACTUAL THIS YR | % | $ LAST YEAR | $ GOAL THIS YR | $ ACTUAL THIS YR | % | $ LAST YEAR | $ GOAL THIS YR | $ ACTUAL THIS YR | % |
|---|---|---|---|---|---|---|---|---|---|---|---|---|
| JAN |  |  |  |  |  |  |  |  |  |  |  |  |
| FEB |  |  |  |  |  |  |  |  |  |  |  |  |
| MAR |  |  |  |  |  |  |  |  |  |  |  |  |
| APR |  |  |  |  |  |  |  |  |  |  |  |  |
| MAY |  |  |  |  |  |  |  |  |  |  |  |  |
| JUN |  |  |  |  |  |  |  |  |  |  |  |  |
| JUL |  |  |  |  |  |  |  |  |  |  |  |  |
| AUG |  |  |  |  |  |  |  |  |  |  |  |  |
| SEP |  |  |  |  |  |  |  |  |  |  |  |  |
| OCT |  |  |  |  |  |  |  |  |  |  |  |  |
| NOV |  |  |  |  |  |  |  |  |  |  |  |  |
| DEC |  |  |  |  |  |  |  |  |  |  |  |  |
| YEAR |  |  |  |  |  |  |  |  |  |  |  |  |

PREPARED BY: _____

# SERVICE CONTRACT

**Customer's Name** _____

**Address** _____

**Phone** _____

**Date** _____

| ADDRESS(ES) OF WORK TO BE PERFORMED | ESTIMATE LABOR | ESTIMATE PARTS |
|---|---|---|
| | | |
| | | |
| | | |
| | | |
| | | |
| | | |
| | | |

**Services to be Performed** _____

_____

_____

_____

_____

_____

**Terms** _____

_____

_____
**CUSTOMER'S SIGNATURE**

_____
**DATE**

*While the company makes every attempt to adher to prices quoted at this time, changes beyond our control can occur. Should these changes be beyond our capacity to absorb them, or should other problems arise that were not foreseen, customer will be informed of any changes prior to proceeding with work.*

# SERVICE RECORD

| Date Order Sold | Client Name | | | Area Code | Customer Phone No. |
|---|---|---|---|---|---|
| Who Purchased | Street Address | | | Type of Business | |
| Who is Using | City | | County | State | Zip |
| Customer Number | Due | Received | Due | Received | Due | Received | Serial No. |
| | Down Payment | | Second Payment | | Final Payment | | |
| Salesman | New Order [ ] | | Reorder [ ] | | Product Name | | |

| MO. | DATE Serviced | BY Phone | IN Person | TIME Spent | Income for Month from Acct. | – COMMENTS – |
|---|---|---|---|---|---|---|
| 1 st Mo. | | | | | | |
| 2 nd Mo. | | | | | | |
| 3 rd Mo. | | | | | | |
| 4 th Mo. | | | | | | |
| 5 th Mo. | | | | | | |
| 6 th Mo. | | | | | | |
| 7 th Mo. | | | | | | |
| 8 th Mo. | | | | | | |
| 9 th Mo. | | | | | | |
| 10 th Mo. | | | | | | |
| 11 th Mo. | | | | | | |
| 12 th Mo. | | | | | | |
| 13 th Mo. | | | | | | |
| 14 th Mo. | | | | | | |
| 15 th Mo. | | | | | | |
| 16 th Mo. | | | | | | |
| 17 th Mo. | | | | | | |
| 18 th Mo. | | | | | | |
| 19 th Mo. | | | | | | |
| 20 th Mo. | | | | | | |
| 21 st Mo. | | | | | | |
| 22 nd Mo. | | | | | | |
| 23 rd Mo. | | | | | | |
| 24 th Mo. | | | | | | |

146

## TELEMARKETING REPORT

**REPORT FROM:**

**PROGESS REPORT FOR WEEK OF:**

| | NUMBER OF CALLS COMPLETED | | | NUMBER OF ORDERS PLACED | | |
|---|---|---|---|---|---|---|
| | TO CLIENTS | TO PROSPECTS | GOAL | FROM CLIENTS | FROM PROSPECTS | GOAL |
| MONDAY | | | | | | |
| TUESDAY | | | | | | |
| WEDNESDAY | | | | | | |
| THURSDAY | | | | | | |
| FRIDAY | | | | | | |
| THIS WEEK'S TOTAL | | | | | | |
| LAST WEEK'S TOTAL | | | | | | |
| NEXT WEEK'S TOTAL | | | | | | |

*Notes:*

_____

_____

_____

_____

_____

_____

_____

_____

_____

_____

_____

_____

_____

_____

# 7.

# OFFICE AND OPERATIONS FORMS

Managing a company, office, or store requires a great many records for efficient operation. More than two dozen forms suggested here can flag the entrepreneur as to his forms needs. Among the functions covered are:

Appointments
Auto Expenses and Repairs
Checklists
Community Directory
Fax Cover Form
Franchise Application
Plans and Project Forms
Receipt for Merchandise
Reminder Memos
Speed Memos
Telephone Reports
Time Logs
Vacation Schedule
Weekly Schedule

All forms can be duplicated and used as is or altered to suit individual needs.

# SEVEN DAY APPOINTMENTS

| | SUNDAY | MONDAY | TUESDAY | WEDNESDAY | THURSDAY | FRIDAY | SATURDAY | |
|---|---|---|---|---|---|---|---|---|
| 8:00 | | | | | | | | 8:00 |
| 8:30 | | | | | | | | 8:30 |
| 9:00 | | | | | | | | 9:00 |
| 9:30 | | | | | | | | 9:30 |
| 10:00 | | | | | | | | 10:00 |
| 10:30 | | | | | | | | 10:30 |
| 11:00 | | | | | | | | 11:00 |
| 11:30 | | | | | | | | 11:30 |
| 12:00 | | | | | | | | 12:00 |
| 12:30 | | | | | | | | 12:30 |
| 1:00 | | | | | | | | 1:00 |
| 1:30 | | | | | | | | 1:30 |
| 2:00 | | | | | | | | 2:00 |
| 2:30 | | | | | | | | 2:30 |
| 3:00 | | | | | | | | 3:00 |
| 3:30 | | | | | | | | 3:30 |
| 4:00 | | | | | | | | 4:00 |
| 4:30 | | | | | | | | 4:30 |
| 5:00 | | | | | | | | 5:00 |
| 5:30 | | | | | | | | 5:30 |

# AUTO EXPENSE RECORD

Prepared by _____     Month of _____

Company Charge Card _____     Company/Department _____

Card Number _____     Address _____

City _____

State _____ Zip _____

| Date | Odometer Reading | | Mileage | Gas/Oil | Parking/ Tolls | Misc. | Payment Method | | | Daily Totals |
| | Start | Stop | | | | | Company Charge | Employee Charge | Cash | |
|---|---|---|---|---|---|---|---|---|---|---|
| | | | | | | | | | | |
| | | | | | | | | | | |
| | | | | | | | | | | |
| | | | | | | | | | | |
| | | | | | | | | | | |
| | | | | | | | | | | |
| | | | | | | | | | | |
| | | | | | | | | | | |
| | | | | | | | | | | |
| | | | | | | | | | | |
| | | | | | | | | | | |
| | | | | | | | | | | |
| | | | | | | | | | | |
| | | | | | | | | | | |
| | | | | | | | | | | |
| | | | | | | | | | | |
| | | | | | | | | | | |
| | | | | | | | | | | |
| | | | | | | | | | | |
| | | | | | | | | | | |
| | | | | | | | | | | |
| | | | | | | | | | | |
| | | | | | | | | | | |
| | | | | | | | | | | |
| | | | | | | | | | | |
| | | | | | | | | | | |
| | | | | | | | | | | |
| | | | | | | | | | | |
| | | | | | | | | | | |
| | | | | | | | | | | |
| | | | | | | | | | | |
| | | | | | | | | | | |
| | | | | | | | | | | |
| Totals | | | | | | | | | | |

| Signed | Date |
|---|---|
| Approval | Date |

# ESTIMATE OF AUTO REPAIR COSTS

| Name | Address | | Phone No. | Phone Ext. | Date |
|---|---|---|---|---|---|

| Make of Car | Type | State | License Number | Job No. | Inspector |
|---|---|---|---|---|---|

| Year | Mileage | Motor No. | Serial No. | Insurance | Assured | Adjuster |
|---|---|---|---|---|---|---|

| Quantity | Work to be Done | Parts No. | Parts | Labor |
|---|---|---|---|---|
| | | | | |
| | | | | |
| | | | | |
| | | | | |
| | | | | |
| | | | | |
| | | | | |
| | | | | |
| | | | | |
| | | | | |
| | | | | |
| | | | | |
| | | | | |
| | | | | |
| | | | | |
| | | | | |
| | | | | |
| | | | | |
| | | | | |
| | | | | |
| | | | | |
| | | | | |
| | | | | |
| | | | | |
| | | | | |
| | | | | |

**TOTAL LABOR**

**TOTAL PARTS**

**TAX ON PARTS**

**TOTAL OF ESTIMATE**

*The above is an estimate based on our inspection and does not cover any additional parts or labor which may be required after the work has been opened up. Occassionally after the work has started, worn or damaged parts are discovered which are not evicdent on the first inspection. Because of this the above prices are not guaranteed, and are for immediate acceptance only. Should additional work and parts be needed, we will call you prior to completing such work.*

_____

*Customer Acceptance*

**52 WEEK CHECKLIST**

**YEAR** _____

| | 1 | 2 | 3 | 4 | 5 | 6 | 7 | 8 | 9 | 10 | 11 | 12 | 13 | 14 | 15 | 16 | 17 | 18 | 19 | 20 | 21 | 22 | 23 | 24 | 25 | 26 | 27 | 28 | 29 | 30 | 31 | 32 | 33 | 34 | 35 | 36 | 37 | 38 | 39 | 40 | 41 | 42 | 43 | 44 | 45 | 46 | 47 | 48 | 49 | 50 | 51 | 52 |
|---|---|---|---|---|---|---|---|---|---|---|---|---|---|---|---|---|---|---|---|---|---|---|---|---|---|---|---|---|---|---|---|---|---|---|---|---|---|---|---|---|---|---|---|---|---|---|---|---|---|---|---|---|
| | | | | | | | | | | | | | | | | | | | | | | | | | | | | | | | | | | | | | | | | | | | | | | | | | | | | |

**COMMUNITY DIRECTORY**

This form is primarily a suggestive or inspirational form that any business person should complete and keep visibly on hand. Every business, not being an island, will have contact with official and private organizations in the community. Some of them are needed in an emergency. Individuals you might want to contact should also be listed and sufficient room should be left to make the changes that inevitably arise periodically.

# COMPANY'S COMMUNITY ASSISTANCE DIRECTORY

| NAME | NAME | PHONE |
|------|------|-------|
| Nearest SBA Office | | |
| Management Assistance | | |
| Financial Assistance | | |
| Procurement Assistance | | |

| NAME | ADDRESS | PHONE |
|------|---------|-------|
| Banker | | |
| Lawyer | | |
| Accountant | | |
| Insurance Agent | | |
| Chamber of Commerce | | |
| Better Business Bureau | | |
| US Dept. of Labor. Wage/Hour/Public Contract Division | | |
| Local Office, Internal Revenue Service for Employers' ID Number, "Tax Guide for Small Business" | | |
| Social Security Office (Employee Withholding Tax) | | |
| State Dept. of Business Development | | |
| Trade Association and Journal | | |
| City Office of Licenses & Permits | | |
| Adult Education Dept., Local College or High School | | |
| | | |
| Business Section, Public Library | | |
| Business Owners I Know | | |
| | | |
| Potential Suppliers | | |
| | | |

FAX COVER SHEET FORM          DATE: _____

TO: _____   FOR INFO CALL: _____

FROM: _____   AT: _____

PAGES: _____   FAX NUMBER: _____
  (INCL. COVER SHEET)

# FRANCHISE APPLICATION
## PERSONAL DATA AND BUSINESS HISTORY

NAME _____ AGE _____

HOME ADDRESS _____ NO. OF YEARS IN AREA _____

CITY _____ STATE _____ ZIP _____

SOCIAL SECURITY # _____ DATE OF BIRTH _____

IF MARRIED: SPOUSE'S FIRST NAME _____ # OF DEPENDENTS _____

HOME PHONE (_____) _____-_____     BUSINESS PHONE (_____) _____-_____

BUSINESS ADDRESS _____

OTHER BUSINESS CONNECTIONS (OFFICER, DIRECTOR, OWNER, PARTNER, ETC.)

_____
_____
_____
_____

|  | FROM | TO | FIRM | POSITION | ANNUAL INCOME |
|---|---|---|---|---|---|
| **BUSINESS EXPERIENCE** | | | | | |
| | | | | | |
| | | | | | |
| | | | | | |

EXACT NATURE OF EXECUTIVE EXPERIENCE (including self-employment) _____

_____
_____
_____
_____
_____

DO YOU NOW OWN ANY FRANCHISE? (describe) _____
_____

HAVE YOU EVER FAILED IN BUSINESS OF COMPROMISED WITH CREDITORS? IF YOU HAVE, WHEN, WHERE, CIRCUMSTANCES. (including any

remaining liabilities) _____
_____
_____

ARE ANY LAWSUITS PENDING AGAINST YOU? (if yes—give particulars) _____
_____

HAVE YOU EVER BEEN CONVICTED OF A CRIME (except traffic misdemeanors)? If yes—give particulars. _____
_____

| EDUCATION | DEGREE ATTAINED | YEAR GRADUATED | MILITARY SERVICE | DATE & RANK |
|---|---|---|---|---|
| 1. | | | | |
| 2. | | | | |
| 3. | | | | |

HOW IS YOUR HEALTH? _____ U.S. CITIZEN _____

WHAT PROFESSIONAL MAGAZINES AND TRADE JOURNALS DO YOU READ? _____
_____

DO YOU OWN ANY PATENTS OR COPYRIGHTS? _____

HOBBIES? _____
_____

BUSINESS REFERENCES:
_____

| INDIVIDUAL | TITLE | COMPANY | CITY | PHONE |
|---|---|---|---|---|
| 1. | | | | |
| 2. | | | | |
| 3. | | | | |

CHARACTER REFERENCES:

1. _____ ADDRESS _____ PHONE _____
2. _____ ADDRESS _____ PHONE _____
3. _____ ADDRESS _____ PHONE _____

MEMBERSHIPS (Civic, business, professional): _____
_____
_____
_____

FINANCIAL DATA:

YOUR PERSONAL BANK _____ CONTACT _____
ADDRESS _____ CITY _____ PHONE _____
YOUR BUSINESS BANK _____ CONTACT _____
ADDRESS _____ CITY _____ PHONE _____

ASSETS

CASH _____ _____ $ _____
SECURITIES-READILY NEGOTIABLE _____ _____ $ _____
REAL ESTATE-FAIR MARKET VALUE, RESIDENCE _____ _____ $ _____
REAL ESTATE-FAIR MARKET VALUE, OTHER _____ _____ $ _____
NOTES RECEIVABLE _____ _____ $ _____
BUSINESS VENTURES-LIQUID _____ _____ $ _____
BUSINESS VENTURES-NON-LIQUID _____ _____ $ _____
LIFE INSURANCE CASH VALUE _____ _____ $ _____
RETIREMENT FUND _____ _____ $ _____
INCOME TAX REFUND _____ _____ $ _____
OTHER _____ _____ $ _____
    TOTAL ASSETS _____ $ _____

  LIABILITIES

MORTGAGES 1ST _____ _____ $ _____
MORTGAGES 2ND _____ _____ $ _____
ALL OTHER _____ _____ $ _____
    TOTAL ASSETS _____ $ _____

NET WORTH _____ _____ $ _____
                                                                  =================

**MANAGEMENT PLANS:**

If you were approved, when could you begin training? _____

Territory in which you are interested? (1st choice) _____
(2nd choice) _____

Are there any investor-associates who would join you in this venture? (Please have each fill out one of these forms.)

Names: _____

_____

_____

_____

**COMMENTS:**

Please use this space to tell us anything else you think is relevant, i.e., your present business objectives, and as I consider my experiences and abilities, I am confident that I can operate a successful _____ primarily because:

_____

_____

_____

_____

_____

_____

_____

_____

_____

_____

_____

_____

_____

_____

To the best of my knowledge and ability the information I have submitted is correct. I understand that the information I am receiving from the
_____ Corp. dba _____, its employees, agents, or franchisee is highly
confidential, has been developed with a great deal of effort and expense to _____, is being made available to me because of this application, and will be held in strictest confidence.

I will not divulge or use, for a period of two years from the date hereof, any data, techniques, methods, advertising materials, forms, of other information of whatever kind used in connection with _____ without _____ consent.

I also understand that _____ will keep my personal and business information contained herein in strictest confidence.

Signed _____ Date _____

# WEEKLY PROJECTS

WEEK OF _____

| CHECK DAY PLANNED | | | | | | | | DATE NEEDED | FOLLOW-UP NEEDED | FOLLOW-UP DATE | X |
|---|---|---|---|---|---|---|---|---|---|---|---|
| S | M | T | W | T | F | S | | | | | |
| | | | | | | | | | | | |
| | | | | | | | | | | | |
| | | | | | | | | | | | |
| | | | | | | | | | | | |
| | | | | | | | | | | | |
| | | | | | | | | | | | |
| | | | | | | | | | | | |
| | | | | | | | | | | | |
| | | | | | | | | | | | |
| | | | | | | | | | | | |
| | | | | | | | | | | | |
| | | | | | | | | | | | |
| | | | | | | | | | | | |
| | | | | | | | | | | | |
| | | | | | | | | | | | |
| | | | | | | | | | | | |
| | | | | | | | | | | | |
| | | | | | | | | | | | |
| | | | | | | | | | | | |

THIS MONTH'S PLANS

| SUNDAY | MONDAY | TUESDAY | WEDNESDAY | THURSDAY | FRIDAY | SATURDAY |
|--------|--------|---------|-----------|----------|--------|----------|
|        |        |         |           |          |        |          |
|        |        |         |           |          |        |          |
|        |        |         |           |          |        |          |
|        |        |         |           |          |        |          |
|        |        |         |           |          |        |          |

# SIX MONTH PROJECT PROGRESS

PROJECT: _____

START DATE: _____

| PHASE DESCRIPTION | PERSON/DEPT. RESPONSIBLE | WEEKS | | | | | | | | | | | | | | | | | | | | | | |
|---|---|---|---|---|---|---|---|---|---|---|---|---|---|---|---|---|---|---|---|---|---|---|---|---|---|
| | | 01 | 02 | 03 | 04 | 05 | 06 | 07 | 08 | 09 | 10 | 11 | 12 | 13 | 14 | 15 | 16 | 17 | 18 | 19 | 20 | 21 | 22 | 23 | 24 |
| | | | | | | | | | | | | | | | | | | | | | | | | | |
| | | | | | | | | | | | | | | | | | | | | | | | | | |
| | | | | | | | | | | | | | | | | | | | | | | | | | |
| | | | | | | | | | | | | | | | | | | | | | | | | | |
| | | | | | | | | | | | | | | | | | | | | | | | | | |
| | | | | | | | | | | | | | | | | | | | | | | | | | |
| | | | | | | | | | | | | | | | | | | | | | | | | | |
| | | | | | | | | | | | | | | | | | | | | | | | | | |
| | | | | | | | | | | | | | | | | | | | | | | | | | |
| | | | | | | | | | | | | | | | | | | | | | | | | | |
| | | | | | | | | | | | | | | | | | | | | | | | | | |
| | | | | | | | | | | | | | | | | | | | | | | | | | |
| | | | | | | | | | | | | | | | | | | | | | | | | | |

# ONE YEAR PROGRESS SHEET

| | | | | | | | | | | | | |
|---|---|---|---|---|---|---|---|---|---|---|---|---|
| Jan. | | | | | | | | | | | | Jan. |
| Feb. | | | | | | | | | | | | Feb. |
| Mar. | | | | | | | | | | | | Mar. |
| Apr. | | | | | | | | | | | | Apr. |
| May | | | | | | | | | | | | May |
| Jun. | | | | | | | | | | | | Jun. |
| Jul. | | | | | | | | | | | | Jul. |
| Aug. | | | | | | | | | | | | Aug. |
| Sept. | | | | | | | | | | | | Sept. |
| Oct. | | | | | | | | | | | | Oct. |
| Nov. | | | | | | | | | | | | Nov. |
| Dec. | | | | | | | | | | | | Dec. |

# ONE YEAR PROJECT PROGRESS

PROJECT: _____

START DATE: _____

| PHASE DESCRIPTION | PERSON/DEPT. RESPONSIBLE | Fill in 12 months, starting with first month of project | | | | | | | | | | | |
|---|---|---|---|---|---|---|---|---|---|---|---|---|---|
| | | | | | | | | | | | | | |
| | | | | | | | | | | | | | |
| | | | | | | | | | | | | | |
| | | | | | | | | | | | | | |
| | | | | | | | | | | | | | |
| | | | | | | | | | | | | | |
| | | | | | | | | | | | | | |
| | | | | | | | | | | | | | |
| | | | | | | | | | | | | | |
| | | | | | | | | | | | | | |
| | | | | | | | | | | | | | |
| | | | | | | | | | | | | | |
| | | | | | | | | | | | | | |

164

# RECEIPT

Date of Sale _____

Customer Name _____

Address _____

Phone Number _____

Product Sold _____

Quantity _____

Unit Price _____

Total Price _____

Sales Representative _____

## FOR OFFICE USE ONLY

Profit Per Unit (PPU) _____

Type of Customer (TOC) _____

Purpose of Product (POP)* _____

Referred By _____

*(POP = To discover unusual applications of product, secondary use, etc.)

# REMINDERS

| SUNDAY | MONDAY | TUESDAY | WEDNESDAY | THURSDAY | FRIDAY | SATURDAY |
|--------|--------|---------|-----------|----------|--------|----------|
|  |  |  |  |  |  |  |
|  |  |  |  |  |  |  |
|  |  |  |  |  |  |  |
|  |  |  |  |  |  |  |
|  |  |  |  |  |  |  |
|  |  |  |  |  |  |  |
|  |  |  |  |  |  |  |
|  |  |  |  |  |  |  |
|  |  |  |  |  |  |  |
|  |  |  |  |  |  |  |
|  |  |  |  |  |  |  |
|  |  |  |  |  |  |  |
|  |  |  |  |  |  |  |
|  |  |  |  |  |  |  |
|  |  |  |  |  |  |  |
|  |  |  |  |  |  |  |
|  |  |  |  |  |  |  |
|  |  |  |  |  |  |  |
|  |  |  |  |  |  |  |
|  |  |  |  |  |  |  |
|  |  |  |  |  |  |  |
|  |  |  |  |  |  |  |
|  |  |  |  |  |  |  |
|  |  |  |  |  |  |  |

**NOTES**

# SPEED MEMO

REFER TO: ☐ YOUR ☐ MY ☐ BELOW ☐ ATTACHED
☐ LETTER ☐ PHONE CALL ☐ ORDER ☐ INQUIRY ☐ MEMO ☐ TELEGRAM ☐ _____

DATED: _____

| TO: | FROM: |
|---|---|
| | |

DATE: _____

_____

_____

_____

_____

_____

_____

_____

_____

_____

_____

_____

_____

_____

**SIGNATURE/TITLE/LOCATION/PHONE**

## REPLY

DATE: _____

_____

_____

_____

_____

_____

_____

_____

_____

**SIGNATURE/TITLE/LOCATION/PHONE**

# TELEPHONE LOG

REPORT FROM: _____     DATE: _____     TIME PERIOD: _____

| TIME | LENGTH OF CALL | CALLED (check) | RECEIVED (check) | SPOKE TO | REASON | PERSONAL (check) | BUSINESS (check) | RESULT |
|---|---|---|---|---|---|---|---|---|
| | | | | | | | | |
| | | | | | | | | |
| | | | | | | | | |
| | | | | | | | | |
| | | | | | | | | |
| | | | | | | | | |
| | | | | | | | | |
| | | | | | | | | |
| | | | | | | | | |
| | | | | | | | | |
| | | | | | | | | |
| | | | | | | | | |
| | | | | | | | | |
| | | | | | | | | |
| | | | | | | | | |
| | | | | | | | | |
| | | | | | | | | |
| | | | | | | | | |

# TELEPHONE SALES ANALYSIS

Date: _____

Requested By: _____

| PROSPECT NAME | TELEPHONE NO. | TIME CALLED | COMMENTS |
|---|---|---|---|
| | | | |
| | | | |
| | | | |
| | | | |
| | | | |
| | | | |
| | | | |
| | | | |
| | | | |
| | | | |
| | | | |
| | | | |
| | | | |
| | | | |

# RECORD OF OUTGOING SALES PHONE CALLS

| DATE | PROSPECT/CLIENT | SUBJECT | CONCLUSIONS | CALLBACK |
|------|-----------------|---------|-------------|----------|
|      |                 |         |             |          |
|      |                 |         |             |          |
|      |                 |         |             |          |
|      |                 |         |             |          |
|      |                 |         |             |          |
|      |                 |         |             |          |
|      |                 |         |             |          |
|      |                 |         |             |          |
|      |                 |         |             |          |
|      |                 |         |             |          |
|      |                 |         |             |          |
|      |                 |         |             |          |
|      |                 |         |             |          |
|      |                 |         |             |          |
|      |                 |         |             |          |
|      |                 |         |             |          |
|      |                 |         |             |          |

# TELEPHONE SALES SUMMARIES

| Date | Person Inquiring/Called | Phone/Area Code | Purpose of Call | Result | Follow–Up Date |
|------|------------------------|-----------------|-----------------|--------|----------------|
|      |                        |                 |                 |        |                |
|      |                        |                 |                 |        |                |
|      |                        |                 |                 |        |                |
|      |                        |                 |                 |        |                |
|      |                        |                 |                 |        |                |

# DAILY TELEPHONE SALES REPORT

SALES: _____

ADDRESS: _____

CITY/STATE/ZIP: _____

PRODUCT: _____

DATE: _____

REPORTING PERIOD:

FROM : _____ TO: _____

DATE SUBMITTED: _____

| FIRM NAME AND ADDRESS | PARTY INTERVIEWED AND TITLE | PRODUCTS PRESENTED/SOLD/REMARKS |
|---|---|---|
| | | |
| | | |
| | | |
| | | |
| | | |
| | | |
| | | |
| | | |

SIGNATURE _____

TITLE _____

# 30 MINUTE TIME LOG

|  |  |
|---|---|
| 7:00 | |
| 7:30 | |
| 8:00 | |
| 8:30 | |
| 9:00 | |
| 9:30 | |
| 10:00 | |
| 10:30 | |
| 11:00 | |
| 11:30 | |
| 12:00 | |
| 12:30 | |
| 1:00 | |
| 1:30 | |
| 2:00 | |
| 2:30 | |
| 3:00 | |
| 3:30 | |
| 4:00 | |
| 4:30 | |
| 5:00 | |
| 5:30 | |

# DAILY TIME REPORT

DATE _____

| JOB ARRIVAL | JOB DEPART. | DATE | JOB # | JOB ADDRESS | TYPE OF WORK | NUMBER OF HOURS |
|---|---|---|---|---|---|---|
| | | | | | | |
| | | | | | | |
| | | | | | | |
| | | | | | | |
| | | | | | | |
| | | | | | | |
| | | | | | | |
| | | | | | | |
| | | | | | | |
| | | | | | | |
| | | | | | | |
| | | | | | | |
| | | | | | | |
| | | | | | | |
| | | | | | | |
| | | | | | | |
| | | | | | | |
| | | | | | | |
| | | | | | | |
| | | | | | | |
| | | | | | | |
| | | | | | | |
| | | | | | | |
| | | | | | | |
| | | | | | | |

_____
*Employee Signature*

174

# DAILY TIME AND EXPENSE LOG

DATE _____

| SERVICES RENDERED | TIME | |
|---|---|---|
| | HRS. | MIN. |
| | | |
| | | |
| | | |
| | | |
| | | |
| | | |
| | | |
| | | |
| | | |
| | | |
| | | |
| | | |
| | | |
| | | |
| | | |
| | | |

| EXPENSE | AMOUNT | COMMENTS |
|---|---|---|
| Travel | | |
| Breakfast | | |
| Lunch | | |
| Dinner | | |
| Lodging | | |
| Tips | | |
| Auto | | |
| Tolls/Parking | | |
| Telephone | | |
| Entertainment | | |
| . | | |
| | | |
| | | |
| TOTAL | | |

# WEEKLY TIME SHEETS

For week ending _____

| EMPLOYEE | Mon | Tues | Wed | Thurs | Fri | Sat | Sun | Total | Gross Pay | Ded | Net Pay |
|----------|-----|------|-----|-------|-----|-----|-----|-------|-----------|-----|---------|
|          |     |      |     |       |     |     |     |       |           |     |         |
|          |     |      |     |       |     |     |     |       |           |     |         |
|          |     |      |     |       |     |     |     |       |           |     |         |
|          |     |      |     |       |     |     |     |       |           |     |         |
|          |     |      |     |       |     |     |     |       |           |     |         |
|          |     |      |     |       |     |     |     |       |           |     |         |
|          |     |      |     |       |     |     |     |       |           |     |         |
|          |     |      |     |       |     |     |     |       |           |     |         |
|          |     |      |     |       |     |     |     |       |           |     |         |
|          |     |      |     |       |     |     |     |       |           |     |         |
|          |     |      |     |       |     |     |     |       |           |     |         |
| Totals   |     |      |     |       |     |     |     |       |           |     |         |

# VACATION SCHEDULE

Department _____

| EMPLOYEE ON VACATION | ALTERNATE TO COVER JOB | APRIL | MAY | JUNE | JULY | AUGUST | OTHER WEEKS |
|---|---|---|---|---|---|---|---|
| | | | | | | | |
| | | | | | | | |
| | | | | | | | |
| | | | | | | | |
| | | | | | | | |
| | | | | | | | |
| | | | | | | | |
| | | | | | | | |
| | | | | | | | |
| | | | | | | | |
| | | | | | | | |
| | | | | | | | |
| | | | | | | | |

WEEK BEGINNING:

# WEEKLY SCHEDULE

Week of _____

| EMPLOYEE | HOURS | | | | | | |
|---|---|---|---|---|---|---|---|
| | SUN | MON | TUE | WED | THU | FRI | SAT |
| | | | | | | | |
| | | | | | | | |
| | | | | | | | |
| | | | | | | | |
| | | | | | | | |
| | | | | | | | |
| | | | | | | | |
| | | | | | | | |
| | | | | | | | |
| | | | | | | | |
| | | | | | | | |
| | | | | | | | |
| | | | | | | | |
| | | | | | | | |
| | | | | | | | |
| | | | | | | | |
| | | | | | | | |
| | | | | | | | |
| | | | | | | | |
| | | | | | | | |
| | | | | | | | |
| | | | | | | | |
| | | | | | | | |
| | | | | | | | |
| | | | | | | | |
| | | | | | | | |
| | | | | | | | |
| | | | | | | | |
| | | | | | | | |
| | | | | | | | |
| | | | | | | | |
| | | | | | | | |

# SECTION TWO

# Legal Agreements and Documents

This comprehensive section covers the gamut of the most popular and needed agreements and contracts that are likely to be used in small business operation. These forms are typical of those used across the country and usually suffice. However, some legal agreements and forms are subject to the peculiarities and idyosyncracies of state and parochial laws. It still would be desirable to consult local counsel in such cases or if any doubt exists. Still, the agreements offered here will give users basic information and preparation, and even if a local attorney is consulted, such preparation can materially reduce the need for costly legal time.

It is further advisable that the section on forms by the United States Small Business Administration (SBA) be used as advance information and for preparatory purposes. Such forms are usually used for loan applications and might be changed occasionally. More than 100 local SBA offices and 385 SCORE offices will have up-to-date forms for final submission.

179

# THE SEVEN MOST POPULAR LEGAL DOCUMENTS

According to the 168-office legal firm of Hyatt Legal Services, of the thousands of documents drawn up for clients, the seven most requested ones are:

wills

leases

bills of sale

promissory notes

employment agreements

collection letters

credit reporting request

Samples of these documents are offered here on the following pages, in alphabetical sequence. For small business operators with computer capabilities, the computer program called Home Lawyer contains the above forms as well as others. It is produced by Meca Ventures of Westport, CT. for $99.95.

## ARTICLES OF INCORPORATION

The general legal agreements required to incorporate a business vary. There is the general corporation, the S corporation, and the non-profit corporation. Examples of the variations follow. To incorporate a business, profit or non-profit, is vital if any liabilities could arise from the activities of the company. Incorporating is not without its problems, of course. It is just a little cumbersome. It costs a little money. It imposes some restrictions as the company needs to operate under numerous federal and state regulations. It also means that if you have stockholders, you have responsibilities toward them that must be fulfilled. You have to operate your business within these legal limitations, renew your corporate existence annually, hold meetings, elect officers, and communicate with stockholders, usually with an annual report and financial statements. On the other hand, you have several important advantages. The corporation is a separate entity and if any liabilities arise, financial or operational, it is unlikely that you can be held liable in the same manner as you would if you were operating as a proprietorship. A corporation can raise money and borrow funds easier than an individual, and use its assets to back loans, rather than pledging personal assets of the owner(s). It is easier to operate as a branch and under absentee ownership. It is also easier to sell its assets when this becomes necessary or desirable. While the legal agreements found here are typical of what you might require, it is still comforting to consult an attorney to make sure all of *your* bases are covered and your state's requisites are filled. Having these forms on hand, however, will save you considerable time and money in dealing with your attorney.

ARTICLES OF INCORPORATION

OF

_____

FIRST: I, THE UNDERSIGNED, _____ , whose post office address is _____ being at least twenty-one years of age, do hereby, under and by virtue of the General Laws of the State of Maryland authorizing the formation of corporations, act as the incorporator with the intention of forming the below-named corporation, pursuant to the provisions of the Annotated Code of Maryland, "Corporations and Associations," Title 4, et seq.

SECOND: The name of the corporation is:

_____

THIRD: The purposes for which the Corporation is formed and the business and objects to be carried on by it are as follows:

To engage in, conduct, operate, own and manage a _____ .

To engage in and carry on any other business which may conveniently be conducted in conjunction with any of the business of the Corporation.

To carry out all of or any part of the aforesaid object and purposes, and to conduct its business in all or any of its branches, in any and all states, territories, districts and possessions of the United States of America and in foreign countries.

To borrow or raise moneys for any purposes of the Corporation, and to establish checking accounts, savings accounts and other such money fund accounts as deemed necessary, issue bonds, debentures, notes or other obligations of the Corporation, and at the option of the Corporation, to secure the same by mortgage, pledge, deed of trust or otherwise.

The foregoing objects and purposes shall, except when otherwise expressed, be in no way limited or restricted by reference to or inference from the terms of any other clause of this or any other article of these Articles of Incorporation or any Amendment thereto, and shall each be regarded as independent, and construed as powers as well as objects and purposes.

The Corporation shall be authorized to exercise and enjoy all of the powers, rights and privileges granted to, or conferred upon, corporations of a similar character by the General Laws of the State of Maryland now or hereafter in force, and the enumeration of the foregoing powers shall not be deemed to exclude any powers, rights or privileges so granted or conferred.

FOURTH: The post office address of the principal office of the Corporation in this State is _____ . The name of the Resident Agent of the Corporation in this State is _____ , a citizen of this State who actually resides therein and whose post office address is _____ .

FIFTH: The total number of shares of stock which the Corporation shall have the authority to issue is ONE THOUSAND (1,000) shares, without nominal or par value. Such shares of stock of said Corporation are to be held by each stockholder upon the condition that he or she will not sell, assign, or transfer all or any of such shares without first offering the same for sale to the Corporation, which shall thereupon have the exclusive right to purchase the said stock for a period of thirty (30) days from the date of the original offer to sell, unless the party so offering said stock for sale shall within (30) days withdraw such offer prior to actual acceptance in writing. In the event that the Corporation shall desire not to purchase the said stock so offered for sale, within the thirty (30) days specified then the stock shall be offered to the other shareholders in proportion to the respective stock ownership who shall then have thirty (30) days to accept such offer. If any other stockholder then desires not to purchase said stock so offered for sale, within the thirty (30) days specified then the stock shall be considered to have been offered to the other stockholders in proportion to the respective stock ownership. The price to be paid for the stock so offered shall be the appraised value of such stock as it is determined by an agreed upon appraisal at the time of the offer of sale or if the seller has a bona fide offer from another party the price shall be equal to that offer without regard to anyother appraisal that this section may provide for. In case of a dispute as to the amount to be paid for such stock, such amount shall be ascertained by three (3) appraisers; one to be appointed by the stockholder offering the stock for sale; one by the stockholder offering to purchase the same, or by the Corporation, if it is offering to purchase; and one by the two so appointed. The decision of two of said appraisers shall be final and binding. Compliance with the above condition in regard to the sale, transfer and assignment of the shares of stock of the said Corporation shall be a condition precedent to the transfer of such shares of stock on the books of the Corporation. In the event that neither bona fide shareholder nor the Corporation shall desire to purchase the said stock so offered for sale, within the thirty (30) days specified above for the Corporation and the thirty (30) days for the stockholder, then and only in that event may the said stock offered for sale be sold and transferred on the books of the Corporation to the purchaser thereof.

SIXTH: The corporation shall have one or more directors, limited to seven (7), and shall never have less than one. The names of the directors who shall act until the first annual meeting or until their successors are duly chosen and qualify are:

                _____
                _____
                _____
                _____

SEVENTH: The following provisions are hereby adopted for the purpose of defining, limiting and regulating the powers of the corporation and of the directors and stockholders:

(a) Notwithstanding any provision of law requiring a greater proportion than a majority of the votes of all current stockholders of the corporation entitled to be cast, the corporation may take or authorize such action upon the concurrence of a majority of the aggregate number of the votes entitled to be cast thereon.

(b) The corporation reserves the right from time to time to make any amendment of its articles of incorporation, now or herafter authorized by law, including any amendment which alters the contract rights, as expressly set forth in its articles of incorporation, of any outstanding stock.

(c) The authority to make, alter, and repeal the By-Laws of the corporation shall be vested in the Board of Directors, but the Board of Directors may delegate such authority in whole or in part to the stockholders entitled to vote.

(d) By Agreement of all current stockholders of the corporation, each holder of any of the shares of the capital stock of the corporation shall be entitled to purchase or subscribe for any unissued stock or any additional shares of stock to be issued by reason of any increase of the authorized capital stock of the corporation for a period of thirty days, and after expiration of said thirty days, any such unissued stock or such additional authorized issue of any stock may be issued and disposed of pursuant to such Agreement among the current stockholders to such person, firms, corporations or associations and upon such terms as may be deemed advisable by the Board of Directors or the current stockholders in the exercise of its or their discretion.

(e) The corporation may indemnify any person who is serving or has served as a director or officer of the corporation or, at its request, as a director or officer of any other corporation in which it owns shares of capital stock or of which it is a creditor, against expenses actually and necessarily incurred by him or her, in connection with the defense of any action, suit or proceeding in which he or she is made a party by reason of being or having been a director or officer of the corporation or of such other corporation, except in relation to matters as to which such person is adjudged in such action, suit or proceeding to be liable for negligence or misconduct in the performance of duty; provided there is a determination that such person acted in good faith and in a manner he reasonably believed to be in or not opposed to the best interest of the corporation. Such indemnification shall not be deemed exclusive of any other rights to which any person may be entitled, under By-Law, agreement, vote, of stockholders or otherwise.

EIGHTH: The duration of the Corporation shall be perpetual.

IN WITNESS WHEREOF, I have signed these Articles of Incorporation the _____ day of _____.

_____

STATE OF MARYLAND
COUNTY OF MONTGOMERY, to wit:

I HEREBY CERTIFY that on this _____ day of _____, before me, the subscriber, a Notary Public of the State and County aforesaid, personally appeared _____, who acknowledge the aforegoing Articles of Incorporation to be his act.

WITNESS my hand and notarial seal the day and year last above written.

_____

# VERSION 2

## ARTICLES OF INCORPORATION

### OF

_____

ARTICLE ONE—NAME—The name of this corporation is _____

ARTICLE TWO—PURPOSES—The purpose for which this corporation is formed is _____.

ARTICLE THREE—REGISTERED OFFICE: REGISTERED AGENT—The address of the initial registered office of the corporation is:

_____
(Address)

_____
(City)

_____
(County)

_____
(State)

and the name of its initial registered agent at such address is _____.

_____

ARTICLE FOUR—DURATION—The period of this corporation's duration is _____.
       (limited period/perpetual duration)

ARTICLE FIVE -DIRECTORS-(a) The number of directors constituting the initial board of directors is _____, and the names and addresses of the persons who are to serve as directors until the first annual meeting of the shareholders or until their successors are elected and qualified are:

| | |
|---|---|
| _____ | _____ |
| (Name) | (Name) |
| _____ | _____ |
| (Address) | (Address) |
| _____ | _____ |
| (City) | (City) |
| _____ | _____ |
| (County) | (County) |
| _____ | _____ |
| (State) | (State) |
| | |
| _____ | _____ |
| (Name) | (Name) |
| _____ | _____ |
| (Address) | (Address) |
| _____ | _____ |
| (City) | (City) |
| _____ | _____ |
| (County) | (County) |
| _____ | _____ |
| (State) | (State) |

(b) The number of directors of the corporation set forth in Clause (a) of this Article shall constitute the authorized number of directors until changed by an amendment of these articles of incorporation or by a bylaw duly adopted by the vote or written consent of the holders of a majority of the then outstanding shares of stock in the corporation.

ARTICLE SIX—INCORPORATORS—The names and addresses of the incorporators are:

| | |
|---|---|
| _____ | _____ |
| (Name of incorporator A) | (Name of incorporator B) |
| _____ | _____ |
| (Address) | (Address) |
| _____ | _____ |
| (City) | (City) |
| _____ | _____ |
| (County) | (County) |
| _____ | _____ |
| (State) | (State) |
| | |
| _____ | _____ |
| (Name of incorporator C) | (Name of incorporator D) |
| _____ | _____ |
| (Address) | (Address) |
| _____ | _____ |
| (City) | (City) |
| _____ | _____ |
| (County) | (County) |
| _____ | _____ |
| (State) | (State) |

ARTICLE SEVEN—CAPITALIZATION—The total number of shares of all classes of stock which the corporation shall have authority to issue is _____, divided into _____ shares of common stock at _____ Dollars ($ _____ ) par value each and _____ shares of preferred stock, at _____ Dollars ($ _____ ) par value each. The designations and powers, preferences, and rights, and the qualifications, limitations, or restrictions of the classes of stock are as follows: _____
_____
_____
_____

This corporation will not commence business until it has received for the issuance of its share consideration of the value of _____ Dollars ($ _____ ), consisting of money, labor done, or property actually received, which sum is not less than _____ Dollars ($ _____ ).

This Article can be amended only by the vote or written consent of the holders of _____ percent (____%) of the outstanding shares.

In witness whereof, for the purpose of forming a corporation under the laws of the State of _____, we, the undersigned, have personally executed these articles of incorporation on this _____ day of _____, 19 ____.

_____        _____
(Signature of incorporator A)     (Signature of incorporator B)

_____        _____
(Signature of incorporator C)     (Signature of incorporator D)

STATE OF _____

COUNTY OF _____

The foregoing instrument was acknowledged before me this _____ day of _____, 19 _____, by _____. In witness whereof I have hereunto set my hand and seal.

My commission expires _____.

_____
(Notary Public)

# HOW AND WHERE TO FILE INCORPORATION PAPERS

| State | What to File | Where to File It | Filing Fee (Domestic Corp.) | Filing Fee (Foreign Corp.) | Franchise Tax (Domestic) | Franchise Tax (Foreign) |
|---|---|---|---|---|---|---|
| AL | AI | County Probate Judge of county where business is located | $45 | $45 | $25+(1) | same |
| AK | AI | Department of Commerce and Economic Development Pouch D Juneau 99811 | $35+ | $35+ | $100 (every 2 yrs.) | $200 (every 2 yrs.) |
| AZ | AI | Corporation Commission 2222 West Encanto Blvd. Phoenix 85009 SS | $50 | $50 | NONE | NONE |
| AR | AI | Corporate Department State Capitol Bldg. Little Rock 72201 SS | $15+ | $50+ | $11+(1) | same |
| CA | AI | 111 Capitol Mall Sacramento 95814 SS | $65 | $550 | $200+(2) | same |
| CO | AI | 1575 Sherman Ave. Denver 80203 | $22.50 | $100 | NONE | NONE |

AI=Articles of Incorporation; CI=Certificate of Incorporation
SS=Secretary of State

| State | What to File | Where to File It | Filing Fee (Domestic Corp.) | Filing Fee (Foreign Corp.) | Franchise Tax (Domestic) | Franchise Tax (Foreign) |
|---|---|---|---|---|---|---|
| CT | CI | SS 30 Trinity St. PO Box 846 Hartford 06115 | $50+ | $150+ | 10% of net income | same |
| DE | CI | SS Dover 19901 SS | $10+ | $10+ | $20+(1) | $30 |
| FL | AI | Charter Section Tallahassee 32304 SS | $35+ | $45+ | $10 | same |
| GA | AI | 225 Peachtree St. NE Atlanta 30303 | $15 | $100 | $10+(2) | same |
| HI | AI | Department of Regulatory Agencies 1010 Richards St. Honolulu 96813 SS | $50+ | $50+ | NONE | NONE |

| | | | | | | |
|---|---|---|---|---|---|---|
| ID | AI | State House<br>Boise 83720<br>SS | $60 | $60 | $20+(2) | same |
| IL | AI | Corporation Division<br>Springfield 62706<br><br>SS | $\frac{1}{10}$ of 1% of stated capital | $\frac{1}{10}$ of 1% of stated capital | $25+(3) | same |
| IN | AI | State House # 155<br>Indianapolis 46204<br>SS | $30+ | $30+ | NONE | NONE |
| NV | AI | Corporation Division<br>Capitol Bldg.,<br>   Capitol Complex<br>Carson City 89710 | $50+ | $50+ | NONE | NONE |
| NH | Record of Organi-zation | SS<br>Concord 03301<br><br>SS | $60+ | $100 | $60+(1) | $150 |
| NJ | CI | State House<br>Trenton 08625<br>State Corporation<br>Commission | $25+ | $165 | $25+(4) | $50+(4) |
| NM | AI | Corporation and Franchise<br>   Tax Departments<br>PO Drawer 1269<br>Santa Fe 87501<br>SS | $50+ | $100+ | $10+(4) | same |
| NY | CI | Division of Corporations<br>162 Washington Ave.<br>Albany 12231<br>SS | $10+ | $10+ | 10% net NY income | same |
| NC | AI | Corporations Division<br>116 West Jones St.<br>Raleigh 27603<br>SS | $40+ | $40+ | $10+(1) | same |
| ND | AI | Division of Corporations<br>Bismarck 58505<br>SS | $25+ | $75+ | NONE | NONE |
| OH | AI | Division of Corporations<br>30 East Broad St.<br>Columbus 43215<br>SS | $50+ | $50+ | $50+(3) | same |
| OK | AI | State Capitol Bldg., Rm. 101<br>Oklahoma City 73105 | $3+ | $18+ | $10+(3) | same |
| OR | AI (Form 11-B) AI and | Corporation Commission<br>Commerce Bldg.<br>Salem 97310<br>Secretary of the<br>Commonwealth | $10 | $50 | $10+(2) | $200 |

| | | | | | | |
|----|----|----|----|----|----|----|
| PA | Registry Statement | of Pennsylvania Corporation Bureau Harrisburg 17120 | $75 | $150 | 1¢/$10 stock | same |
| RI | AI | SS Providence 02903 SS | $80+ | $15+ | $100+(1) $10+ | same |
| SC | AI | Box 11350 Columbia 29201 SS | $45+ | $45+ | (based on dividends) | same |
| SD | AI | State Capitol Pierre 57501 SS | $40+ | $50+ | NONE | NONE |
| TN | Charter | Corporation Division Nashville 37219 SS | $10+ | $300 | $10+(1) | $25+ (based on gross receipts in TN) |
| TX | AI | Corporation Division Sam Houston State Office Bldg. Austin 78711 SS | $100 | $500 | $55+(3) | same |
| UT | AI | State Capitol Bldg., Rm. 203 Salt Lake City 84114 SS | $25+ | $25+ | $25+(2) | same |
| VT | Articles of Association | Montpelier 05602 State Corporation Commission | $20+ | $60 | NONE | NONE |
| VA | AI | Box 1197 Richmond 23209 SS | $20+ | $60+ | $20+(1) | same |
| WA | AI | Corporation Division Legislative Bldg. Olympia 98504 SS | $50+ | $50+ | $30+(1) | same |
| WV | AI | Corporation Division Charleston 25305 SS | $30+ | $260+ | $20+(1) | $35+( 1) |
| WI | AI (Form 2) | Corporation Division State Capitol Bldg. Madison 53702 SS | $55+ | $55+ | 2.3% or more of income | same |
| WY | AI | Division of Corporations Cheyenne 82002 | $50+ | $50+ | $10+(4) | same |

# BANK GUARANTY

WHEREAS _____

(hereinafter described as "Debtor") is now or may hereafter become indebted or obligated to _____ (hereinafter called the "Bank") for debts or obligations as hereinafter defined (hereinafter referred to as "liabilities" or "liability") and said Debtor now desires or hereafter may desire to enter into transactions whereby said Debtor may become liable to, indebted or obligated to, said Bank for such liabilities, and the undersigned (hereinafter called "Guarantor", whether one or more than one) has agreed to guarantee any existing liabilities of said Debtor to Bank as well as any liability of said Debtor to said Bank hereafter arising, and has requested said Bank to engage in, or to continue to engage in, transactions with said Debtor to the extent that the Bank may agree thereto, but the Bank by the acceptance hereof does not obligate itself to engage in any such transaction or transactions.

NOW, THEREFORE, in consideration of the premises and the sum of One Dollar ($1.00) to the Guarantor in hand paid by the Bank, receipt of which is hereby acknowledged, and of the existing liabilities of Debtor to Bank, and to induce the Bank to continue in effect the existing liabilities, and to induce the Bank, at its option, at any time or from time to time, to extend future financial accommodations to Debtor, and to permit Debtor to incur or become subject to future liabilities to Bank, the undersigned Guarantor hereby unconditionally and directly (and jointly and severally if more than one), gurantees to the Bank the due performance, including, but not being limited to, the prompt payment when due, of Debtor's liabilities to Bank, the Guarantor (jointly and severally as aforesaid) hereby promising to pay to the Bank, its successors and assigns upon demand, any and all liabilities of said Debtor to Bank. The words "liabilities" or "liability" are used herein with respect to Debtor in the most comprehensive sense and include any and all advances, debts, obligations and liabilities of Debtor (individually or jointly and severally with others) to Bank heretofore, now, or hereafter made, incurred or created, whether formal or informal, however arising, whether due or not due, absolute or contingent, determined or undetermined, and whether Debtor may be liable individually or jointly with others, and whether Debtor's liability shall be as maker, drawer, endorser, acceptor, assignor, guarantor, surety or otherwise, or whether the recovery thereupon may be or hereafter become barred by any statute of limitations, or whether such liabilities may be or hereafter become unenforceable by reason of death, present or future lack of capacity of Debtor or otherwise. Guarantor agrees to pay to Bank, upon demand, Debtor's liabilities as aforesaid, together with all interest thereon and attorneys' fees, costs and expenses of collection incurred by the Bank in enforcing such liabilities.

Guarantor waives any right to require Bank to proceed against Debtor or to proceed against or exhaust any security or collateral held by Bank. Guarantor authorizes Bank, without notice or demand and without affecting Guarantor's liability hereunder, from time to time, to renew, extend, accelerate, modify, and/or compromise Debtor's liability for any indebtedness, and Guarantor shall continue to be liable for same as so renewed, extended, accelerated, modified, and/or compromised, further that Bank shall have a right of setoff against all moneys, securities and other property of Guarantor now or hereafter in the possession of or on deposit with Bank, with the right to apply same to any indebtedness of Debtor or Guarantor hereunder, without previous notice or demand. Any indebtedness of Debtor to Guarantor is hereby subordinated to the liability of Debtor to Bank, and upon request of Bank shall be collected, enforced and received by Guarantor as trustee for Bank and paid over to Bank on account of the liability of Debtor to Bank but without releasing Guarantor with respect to any balance due Bank as provided for herein. The liability of Guarantor hereunder shall not in any manner be affected, released or discharged by any change, exchange or alteration of any collateral or other security held by Bank for payment of or as security for any liability of Debtor or the loss, surrender or release of any such collateral or security, or the failure by Bank to safeguard same or to realize thereon or to perfect a lien thereon or otherwise to take any action with respect thereto, nor shall the Bank be required to notify Guarantor of any violation by Debtor of any of its agreements or arrangements with Bank whether pertaining to any collateral or security or otherwise.

This Guaranty shall be a continuing one and shall bind the Guarantor (and his, her, its, or their respective personal representatives, executor, administrators, and successors) for all liabilities of Debtor to Bank, until notice in writing (sent by registered or certified mail to Bank at its home office) of desire to terminate this Guaranty has been received by the Bank, each such Guarantor so giving notice to remain liable for all liabilities of the Debtor contracted before the receipt by Bank of such notice; nor shall any such notice from any one or more of the undersigned in any manner affect, modify or lessen the obligation hereunder of the other undersigned, if any, who have failed to give such notice.

Guarantor hereby waives all notices whatsoever with respect to this Guaranty and the Debtor's Liabilities to Bank, including but not being limited to, notice: of the Bank's acceptance hereof and intention to act in reliance hereon, of its reliance hereon, of the present existence or future incurring of any of the Debtor's Liabilities to Bank, of the amount, terms and conditions thereof, any acceleration of the maturity thereof, and of any defaults thereon. Guarantor hereby consents to the taking of, or failure to take, from time to time without notice to Guarantor, any action of any nature whatsoever with respect to the Debtor's Liabilities to Bank, with respect to the taking, release, or realization upon collateral, if any, and with respect to any rights against any Person or Persons (including the Debtor and any Guarantor) or in any property, including but not being limited to, any renewals, extensions, modifications, postponements, compromises, indulgences, waivers, surrenders, exchanges and releases, and Guarantor will remain fully liable hereunder notwithstanding any of the forgoing; provided, however, that the granting of a release of the liability hereunder of all of the Guarantors or of less than all of the Guarantors shall be effective with respect to the liability hereunder of the one or more who are specifically so released but shall in no way effect the liability hereunder of any not so released. The death or incapacity of any of the Guarantors shall in no way affect the liability hereunder of any other of the Guarantors. Guarantor hereby waives the benefit of all laws now or hereafter in effect in any way limiting or restricting the liability of Guarantor hereunder.

In addition to all other liability of Guarantor hereunder, Guarantor also agrees to pay to the Bank on demand all costs and expenses which may be incurred in the enforcement of the Debtor's Liabilities to Bank or the liability of Guarantor hereunder. Such expenses shall include all counsel fees incurred by Bank before the filing of any suit to enforce this Guaranty, and in the event of suit shall include an additional 15% of Debtor's Liabilities to Bank then remaining unpaid. If any of the Debtor's Liabilities to Bank is not duly performed, including the prompt payment when due of any amount payable thereon, all the Debtor's Liabilities to Bank shall at the Bank's option be deemed to be forthwith due and payable for the purposes of this Guaranty and the liability of Guarantor hereunder. No delay in making demand on Guarantor for performance or payment of Guarantor's obligations hereunder shall prejudice the right to enforce said performance or payment.

In the event of suit by Bank, Bank at its option may join in one action the Debtor and Guarantor, or may bring successive suits in any order against any one or more of them. The liability of Debtor and each of the Guarantors shall be joint and several.

Each person signing his name as a Guarantor hereto agrees that his liability shall be absolute and not subject to any condition that some other person sign his name as Guarantor hereunder.

POWER OF ATTORNEY TO CONFESS JUDGMENT: Guarantor hereby authorizes and empowers any attorney of any court of record in the United States or elsewhere, without prior notice or demand for payment, to appear for him, her, it or them and to confess judgment against him, her, it or them in favor of _____ or any other party then entitled to enforce the terms of this Guaranty, in any court having jurisdiction, or before any justice of the peace or similar official, for the full amount then due by Guarantor under such Guaranty, including court costs and reasonable attorneys' fee. The provisions of this paragraph pertaining to power to confess judgment shall be fully applicable unless its applicability is waived by a Bank officer by (1) inserting a check mark in the following block ☐ and (2) signing his name on the following line _____
_____.

This Guaranty shall inure to the benefit of the Bank, its successors, assigns, endorsees and any Person or Persons, including any banking institution or institutions, to whom the Bank may grant any interest in the Debtor's Liabilities to Bank or any of them, and shall be binding upon Guarantor and Guarantor's executors, administrators, successors, assigns and other legal representatives.

IN WITNESS WHEREOF, Guarantor, intending to be legally bound and intending this to be a sealed instrument, has duly executed this Guaranty under seal this _____ day of _____ , 19_____.

**(THIS SIDE FOR CORPORATE USE)**          **(THIS SIDE FOR INDIVIDUAL USE)**

_____          _____ (SEAL)

**(Name of Company)**

_____          _____ (SEAL)
                      **President**

**By**_____          _____ (SEAL)
                      **Secretary**

**(Corporate Seal)**                      _____ (SEAL)

# BILL OF SALE (VERSION 1)

The undersigned,

for a valuable consideration, the receipt of which is hereby acknowledged, do _____ hereby grant, bargain, sell, and convey to the personal property described as

The seller _____ do _____ for _____ heirs, executors and administrators covenant and agree to warrant and defend the title to the property, goods, and chattels hereby conveyed, against the just and lawful claims and demands of all persons whomsoever.

Dated _____ 19_____

STATE OF _____ )
                          ) ss.
COUNTY OF _____ )

On _____ 19_____ before me, the undersigned, a Notary Public in and for said County, personally appeared _____ and known to me to be the person(s) whose name(s) _____ subscribed to the within instrument and acknowledged that _____ executed same.
WITNESS my hand and official seal.

Seal _____

Notary Public in and for said State

# BILL OF SALE (VERSION 2)

## OF

_____

STATE OF              )
                     )   ss:

COUNTY               )

KNOW YE ALL MEN BY THESE PRESENTS,

That I, _____, of _____ _____
                                                             (Street Address)     (City)

_____, for and in consideration of payment of the sum of
      (State)   (Zip)

$_____, the receipt of which is hereby acknowledged, do hereby grant,

bargain, sell, and convey to: _____, of _____
                                                                  (Street Address)

_____, and his/her heirs, executors, administra-
   (City)         (State)   (Zip)

tors, successors, and assigns the following property:

     I hereby warrant that I am the lawful owner of said property and that I have full legal right, power, and authority to sell said property. I further warrant said property to be free of all encumbrances and that I will warrant and defend said property hereby sold against any and all persons whomsoever.

     IN WITNESS WHEREOF, I, the Seller, have hereto set my hand and seal this _____ day of _____, 19_____.

                       (Signed) _____

## BUSINESS PLAN

Entire books have been written about the business plan, as if the discovery of business plans were like the invention of the wheel or motherhood. A Business Plan simply is:

The road map a business person needs to find his or her way in the uncharted territory of a new business or an expanded one. It is the blueprint without which, it would be difficult and even hazardous to begin construction of an enterprise.

The purposes of a business plan are to (1) guide the entrepreneur in developing or expanding a business with reasonable assurance of orderly progress and success, and (2) present to the person or institution from whom you might want to borrow money for the financing of your enterprise, whether that party be a banker, finance company, government bureau, or a relative.

While there are numerous ways to go about creating such a business plan—including spending several thousand dollars to an attorney, CPA, or business consultant to prepare one—*you* are still needed to give wings to the ultimate plan. Since you will most likely be responsible for the Plan's execution, performance, and promises to be fullfilled, you might as well prepare it. We have provided the skeleton of such a Plan—a series of worksheets that are suggested by a multitude of experts.

# BUSINESS PLAN I
## STATIONERY

(If the business plan is to be used as a presentation to a potential lender or financial institution, a cover letter, printed on good stationery, should introduce you and the purpose of your presentation. For example:)

Dear (name) or Gentlemen:

We are requesting a loan of $ _____ for the purpose of _____
_____.
Repayment is anticipated over a period of _____.
The source of repayment will be _____.
We are offering as collateral the items listed on the accompanying exhibit, complete with appraised valuation, having an approximate current value of $_____.
Your consideration of this loan request will be appreciated, as it will be vital in the successful execution of our business plan, described in the following pages. Should further information be required, please contact us at _____.

Cordially,


(signature)

Name
Title


encl.: Business Plan for
_____

# BUSINESS PLAN II
## BUSINESS IDENTIFICATION

1.  The name of the business is _____

2.  Business address _____

3.  Actual location _____

4.  Telephone _____

5.  Tax ID or Social Security number _____

6.  Principals involved in business and contact addresses
    _____
    _____
    _____

7.  Accountant of record and address and phone

    _____

8.  Attorney of record and address and phone

    _____

9.  Banker, location, and phone

    _____

10. Insurance agent, address, and phone

    _____

11. Other business consultant or adviser, address, and phone

    _____

# BUSINESS PLAN III
## PURPOSE

1. **The goals of the proposed business are**

   _____
   _____
   _____

2. **If an existing business, state purpose of acquisition or expansion**

   _____
   _____

3. **Your experience to enable you to successfully manage the above-described enterprise**

   _____
   _____

4. **How much money will be needed**
   **From your own investment** _____
   **Other personal lenders** _____
   **Loan requested from this institution** _____

5. **How will you make use of these funds?**

   _____

6. **How will they benefit the proposed business?**

   _____

7. **What is your repayment plan?**

   _____

8. **Please verify your (7) statement**

   _____

9. **Available collateral and market value**

   _____

10. **Is the collateral (9) pledged to or owned by persons or institutions other than you?**

    _____

# BUSINESS PLAN IV
## DESCRIPTION OF BUSINESS

1. The legal description of the proposed business
   _____

2. If it is a corporation, where has it been or will it be incorporated?
   _____

3. Regular or S corporation? _____

4. Classification _____

5. Is this a new business? _____
   Expansion of an existing business? _____
   Purchase of another's business? _____

6. When are you projecting to begin operation?
   _____

7. If an existing business, outline existing history
   _____
   _____

8. Operating schedule of business
   _____

9. Seasonal? _____ Year-round business? _____

10. How will you operate the premises? Stock? Inventory? Personnel?
    _____
    _____

11. List of suppliers and products to be supplied
    _____

12. Terms of supply acquisition or credit available
    _____

13. Quotations for above
    _____

14. Will suppliers render any technical or management assistance?
    _____

15. If you use outside contractors, who are they and what will they be supplying? Their terms?
    _____

16. If you are planning to construct a building, supply all specifics, costs, titles
    _____

17. What R&D or market research have you done?
    _____

18. What is your competition?
    _____

19. Why will this business be successful and profitable?
    _____

# BUSINESS PLAN V
# YOUR MARKET

1. Primary market: ethnic composition, age group(s), neighborhood, economic level, social level, sex, and so forth.

   _____

   _____

2. Size of market: area, population

   _____

   _____

3. What is your expected coverage or market penetration?

   _____

   _____

4. What is anticipated growth potential?

   _____

   _____

5. Will you be able to share in this market growth? How?

   _____

   _____

6. How will you finance this anticipated growth?

   _____

7. How will you price your product/service? At what profit?

   _____

   _____

8. What about your competition? Their pricing? Give examples.

   _____

   _____

9. How will you advertise/promote your product/service? What available media? At what costs?

   _____

   _____

10. Advertising budget and schedule anticipated

    _____

    _____

11. What service do you need to render? What provisions can you make for this demand?

    _____

    _____

12. Will credit be offered? What kind?

    _____

13. How will you handle credit delinquencies?

    _____

14. If you have developed any logos, slogans, ads, promotional aids, attach copies or samples.

    _____

    _____

# BUSINESS PLAN VI
## COMPETITION

1. Names and locations of your nearest competitors

   _____

   _____

2. Do you have any realistic information on their status? Proof?

   _____

   _____

3. How will you be competitive? Better?

   _____

4. How will you be different? Be specific about your advantages and how you can meet and beat competition, if needed?

   _____

   _____

5. Do you have any figure on their market share?

   _____

   _____

6. What plans can you advance on getting some of that market share? Over what time period? At what cost?

   _____

   _____

   _____

# BUSINESS PLAN VII
## LOCATION

1. **Give reason for choosing the location you have**
   _____

2. **What's the neighborhood like?**
   _____

3. **Zoning?** _____

4. **Other area businesses? Any competitive?**
   _____
   _____

5. **Why is this location your first choice?**
   _____

6. **What other locations have you explored?**
   _____
   _____

7. **What is the rental or operating cost? Is this compatible with your budgetary needs?**
   _____
   _____

8. **Is this location permanent? If not, when will it change?**

9. **Is the building you are in or will occupy leased or owned by you?**
   _____

10. **Describe the lease terms, taxes, escalator clause**
    _____

11. **Please enclose a floor plan of the facility**
    _____

12. **If you need to make alterations or renovations, attach revised floor plans and cost estimates.**

# BUSINESS PLAN VIII
## MANAGEMENT

1. Attach detailed resume of each principal in the business.
2. Name each principal and related business experience in reference to the new business.

   _____

3. What are job descriptions of each of the above? Salaries? Fringe benefits?

   _____
   _____
   _____
   _____

4. What external management assistance can you call on, if and when necessary?

   _____
   _____
   _____

# BUSINESS PLAN IX
## PERSONNEL

1. Will you need to hire any people? If so, what are the job titles, functions, and expected salaries?

   _____

2. What training and fringe benefits must you provide?

   _____

3. Can you do with part-time employees?

   _____

4. Are any of the proposed employees family members?

   _____

5. A succession policy, in the event you become incapable of managing the business yourself

   _____

   _____

## BUSINESS PLAN X
## FINANCIAL INFORMATION

1. Balance sheet—for the past three years if an established business; current if a new business
2. Operating statement—same as (1)
3. Projected cash flow—month-by-month if a new business; for three years, quarterly, if an established business
4. Break-even analysis—same as (3)
5. Financial statement for each principal, co-signor, or guarantor of the business
6. Personal or business tax returns for the past year
7. Capital equipment: if you need any, attach list of items, estimated cost or value of each
8. Appraisal form from a bank-approved appraiser showing existence and current value of any real estate, vehicles, equipment, and machinery owned by the business
9. Are there any other assets that you now own or might own in the near future not shown above that are important to disclose?

_____

_____

_____

## BUSINESS PLAN XI
## BUYING A BUSINESS INFORMATION

1.  Who started the business you are buying and when?
    _____

2.  What do you think are the real reasons that this business is for sale?
    _____

3.  Who determined the acquisition price? How much is it?
    _____

4.  How much will you pay for goodwill? _____

5.  Will seller take back any portion of the purchase price as a loan? On what terms?
    _____

6.  If a reason for selling is declining sales, can you reverse the trend? How?
    _____
    _____

7.  What else can you do to make this acquisition successful?
    _____

8.  Attach a list of visible assets—creditors and their terms, value and age of inventory, capital assets, any liabilities for which you will be responsible, appraisers' confirmations, photos of building and/or location.

# BUSINESS PLAN XII
## MISCELLANEOUS CHECKLIST

1. If the business is a franchise, enclose a set of the Franchise Agreement
2. Copy of any pertinent contracts
3. Copy of any business agreements
4. Any management contract
5. Copy of maintenance agreements
6. Roster of major customers, annual purchases, terms
7. List of principal suppliers, annual volume, terms
8. Credit card and credit system you use
9. Any publicity that might have been generated
10. Annual report, if one was prepared
11. Copy of insurance carried
12. Any patents or copyrights owned
13. Any other pertinent legal documents

## BY-LAWS

By-laws are additions to a corporation's charter. They are like codicils, or commentaries on the Bible (Talmud), or Amendments to the Constitution. By-laws are rules that the members of a corporation adopt for the proper running of their company. They cannot be in opposition to laws of the government under which the business is incorporated. By-laws, being self-imposed by members of the organization, help to conduct that business in its special way. They pertain to the rights and duties of the members of a specific organization only.

# BYLAWS: BUSINESS CORPORATION

**ARTICLE ONE—OFFICES**—The principal office of the corporation shall be located at:

_____
(Address)

_____
(City)

_____
(County)

_____
(State)

The board of directors shall have the power and authority to establish and maintain branch or subordinate offices at any other locations.

**ARTICLE TWO—STOCKHOLDERS—**

**SECTION 1. ANNUAL MEETING:** The annual meeting of the stockholders shall be held on the _____ day in the month of _____ in each year, beginning with the year 19_____, at _____ o'clock _____, for the purpose of electing directors and for the transaction of such other business as may come before the meeting. If the day fixed for the annual meeting shall be a legal holiday in the State of _____, such meeting shall be held on the next succeeding business day. If the election of directors is not held on the day designated herein for any annual meeting of the shareholders, or at any adjournment thereof, the board of directors shall cause the election to be held at a special meeting of the stockholders as soon thereafter as is convenient.

**SECTION 2. SPECIAL MEETINGS:** Special meetings of the stockholders, for any purpose or purposes, unless otherwise prescribed by statute, may be called by the president or by the board of directors, and shall be called by the president at the request of the holders of not less than _____ of all the outstanding shares of the corporation entitled to vote at the meeting.

**SECTION 3. PLACE OF MEETING:** The board of directors may designate any place _____ the State of _____, as the place of meeting for any annual meeting or for any special meeting called by the board of directors. A waiver of notice signed by all stockholders entitled to vote at a meeting may designate any place, either within or without the State of _____, as the place for the holding of such meeting. If no designation is made, or if a special meeting is otherwise called, the place of meeting shall be the principal office of the corporation in

_____
(City)

_____
(State)

**SECTION 4. NOTICE OF MEETING:** Written or printed notice stating the place, day, and hour of the meeting and, in case of a special meeting, the purpose or purposes for which the meeting is called, shall be delivered not less than _____ nor more than _____ days before the date of the meeting, either personally or by mail, by or at the direction of the president, or the secretary, or the officer or persons calling the meeting, to each shareholder of record entitled to vote at such meeting. If mailed, such notice shall be deemed to be delivered when deposited in the United States mail, addressed to the shareholder at his or her address as it appears on the stock transfer books of the corporation, with postage thereon prepaid. Notice of each meeting shall also be mailed to holders of stock not entitled to vote, as herein provided, but lack of such notice shall not affect the legality of any meeting otherwise properly called and noticed.

SECTION 5. CLOSING TRANSFER BOOKS OR FIXING RECORD DATE: For the purpose of determining stockholders entitled to notice of, or to vote at, any meeting of stockholders or any adjournment thereof, or stockholders entitled to receive payment of any dividend, or to make a determination of shareholders for any other proper purpose, the board of directors of the corporation may provide that the stock transfer books shall be closed for a stated period, but not to exceed _____ days. If the stock transfer books shall be closed for the purpose of determining stockholders entitled to notice of, or to vote at, a meeting of stockholders, such books shall be closed for at least _____ days immediately preceding such meeting. In lieu of closing the stock transfer books, the board of directors may fix in advance a date as the record date for any such determination of stockholders, such date in any event to be not more than _____ days, and in case of a meeting of stockholders, not less than _____ days prior to the date on which the particular action requiring such determination of stockholders is to be taken.

If the stock transfer books are not closed and no record date is fixed for the determination of stockholders entitled to notice of, or to vote at, a meeting of stockholders, or of stockholders entitled to receive payment of a dividend, the date that notice of the meeting is mailed or the date on which the resolution of the board of directors declaring such dividend is adopted, as the case may be, shall be the record date for such determination of stockholders. When a determination of stockholders entitled to vote at any meeting of stockholders has been made as provided in this section, such determination shall apply to any adjournment thereof except where the determination has been made through the closing of the stock transfer books and the stated period of closing has expired.

SECTION 6. QUORUM: A majority of the outstanding shares of the corporation entitled to vote, represented in person or by proxy, shall constitute a quorum at a meeting of stockholders. If less than a majority of such outstanding shares are represented at a meeting, a majority of the shares so represented may adjourn the meeting from time to time without further notice. At such adjourned meeting at which a quorum is present or represented, any business may be transacted that might have been transacted at the meeting as originally notified. The stockholders present at a duly organized meeting may continue to transact business until adjournment, notwithstanding the withdrawal of enough stockholders to leave less than a quorum.

SECTION 7. PROXIES: At all meetings of stockholders, a stockholder may vote by proxy executed in writing by the stockholder or by his or her duly authorized attorney-in-fact. Such proxy shall be filed with the secretary of the corporation before or at the time of the meeting. No proxy shall be valid after _____months (number)

from the date of its execution unless otherwise provided in the proxy.

SECTION 8. VOTING OF SHARES: Subject to the provisions of any applicable law or any provision of the articles of incorporation or of these bylaws concerning cumulative voting, each outstanding share entitled to vote shall be entitled to one vote on each matter submitted to vote at a meeting of stockholders.

ARTICLE THREE—BOARD OF DIRECTORS—

SECTION 1. GENERAL POWERS: The business and affairs of the corporation shall be managed by its board of directors.

SECTION 2. NUMBER, TENURE, AND QUALIFICATION: The number of directors of the corporation shall be _____. Directors shall be elected at the annual meeting of stockholders, and the term of office of each director shall be until the next annual meeting of stockholders and the election and qualificaiton of his or her successor. Directors need not be residents of the State of _____, and need/need not be stockholders of the corporation.

SECTION 3. REGULAR MEETINGS: A regular meeting of the board of directors shall be held without notice other than this bylaw immediately after and at the same place as the annual meeting of stockholders. The board of directors may provide, by resolution, the time and place for holding additional regular meetings without other notice than such resolution. Additional regular meetings shall be held at the principal office of the corporation in the absence of any designation in the resolution.

SECTION 4. SPECIAL MEETINGS: Special meetings of the board of directors may be called by or at the request of the president or any two directors, and shall be held at the principal office of the corporation or at such other place as the directors may determine.

SECTION 5. NOTICE: Notice of any special meeting shall be given at least _____ before the time fixed for the meeting, by written notice delivered personally or mailed to each director at this business address, or by telegram. If mailed, such notice shall be deemed to be delivered when depostied in the United States mail so addressed, with postage thereon prepaid, not less than _____ days prior to the commencement of the above-stated notice period. If notice is given by telegram, such notice shall be deemed to be delivered when the telegram is delivered to the telegraph company. Any director may waive notice of any meeting. The attendance of a director at a meeting shall constitute a waiver of notice of such meeting, except where a director attends a meeting for the express purpose of objecting to the transaction of any business because the meeting is not lawfully called or convened. Neither the business to be transacted at, nor the prupose of, any regular or special meeting of the board of directors need be specified in the notice or waiver of notice of such meeting.

SECTION 6. QUORUM: A majority of the number of directors fixed by these bylaws shall constitute a quorum for the transaction of business at any meeting of the board of directors, but if less than such majority is present at a meeting, a majority of the directors present may adjourn the meeting from time to time without further notice.

SECTION 7. BOARD DECISIONS: The act of the majority of the directors present at a meeting at which a quorum is present shall be the act of the board of directors except that vote of not less than _____ percent (_____%) of all the members of the board shall be required for the amendment of or addition to these bylaws.

SECTION 8. VACANCIES: Any vacancy occuring in the board of directors may be filled by the affirmative vote of a majority of the remaining directors though less than a quorum of the board of directors. A director elected to fill a vacancy shall be elected for the unexpired term of his or her predecessor in office. Any directorship to be filled by reason of an increase in the number of directors shall be filled by election at an annual meeting or at a special meeting of stockholders called for that purpose.

SECTION 9. COMPENSATION: By resolution of the board of directors, the directors may be paid their expenses, if any, of attendance at each meeting of the board of directors, and may be paid a fixed sum for attendance at each meeting of the board of directors or a stated salary as director. No such payment shall preclude any director from serving the corporation in any other capactiy and receiving compensation therefor.

SECTION 10. PRESUMPTION OF ASSENT: A director of the corporation who is present at a meeting of the board of directors at which action on any corporate matter is taken shall be presumed to have assented to the action taken unless his or her dissent shall be entered in the minutes of the meeting or unless he or she shall file a written dissent to such action with the person acting as the secretary of the meeting before the adjournment thereof or shall forward such dissent by registered mail to the secretary of the corporation immediately after the adjournment of the meeting. Such right to dissent shall not apply to a director who voted in favor of such action.

ARTICLE FOUR—OFFICERS—

SECTION 1. NUMBER: The officers of the corporation shall be a president, one or more vice-presidents (the number thereof to be determiend by the board of directors), a secretary, and a treasurer, each of who shall be elected by the board of directors. Such other officers and assistant officers as may be deemed necessary may be elected or appointed by the board of directors. Any two or more offices may be held by the same person, except the offices of _____
_____.

SECTION 2. ELECTION AND TERM OF OFFICE: The officers of the corporation to be elected by the board of directos shall be elected annually at the first meeting of the board of directors held after each annual meeting of the stockholders. If the election of officers is not held at such meeting, such election shall be held as soon thereafter as is convenient. Each officer shall hold office until his or her successor has been duly elected and qualilfied or until his or her death or until he or she resigns or is removed in the manner hereinafter provided.

SECTION 3. REMOVAL: Any officer or agent elected or appointed by the board of directors may be removed by the board of directors whenever in its judgment the best interests of the corporation would be served thereby, but such removal shall be without prejudice to the contract rights, if any, of the person so removed.

SECTION 4. VACANCIES: A vacancy in any office because of death, resignation, removal, disqualification or otherwise, may be filled by the board of directors for the unexpired portion of the term.

SECTION 5. POWERS AND DUTIES: The powers and duties of the several officers shall be as provided from time to time by resolution or other directive of the board of directors. In the absence of such provisions, the respective officers shall have the powers and shall discharge the duties customarily and usually held and performed by like officers of corporations similar in organization and business purposes to this corporation.

SECTION 6. SALARIES: The salaries of the officers shall be fixed from time to time by the board of directors, and no officer shall be prevented from receiving such salary by reason of the fact that he or she is also a director of the corporation.

ARTICLE FIVE—CONTRACTS, LOANS, CHECKS, AND DEPOSITS—

SECTION 1. CONTRACTS: The board of directors may authorize any officer or officers, agent or agents, to enter into any contract or execute and deliver any instrument in the name of and on behalf of the corporation, and such authority may be general or confined to specific instances.

SECTION 2. LOANS: No loans shall be contracted on behalf of the corporation and no evidences of indebtedness shall be issued in its name unless authorized by a resolution of the board of directors. Such authority may be general or confined to specific instances.

SECTION 3. CHECKS, DRAFTS, OR ORDERS: All checks, drafts, or other orders for the payment of money, notes, or other evidences of indebtedness issued in the name of the corporation shall be signed by such officer or officers, agent or agents of the corporation and in such manner as shall from time to time be determined by resolution of the board of directors.

SECTION 4. DEPOSITS: All funds of the corporation not otherwise employed shall be deposited from time to time to the credit of the corporation in such banks, trust companies, or other depositories as the board of directors may select.

ARTICLE SIX—CERTIFICATES FOR SHARES: TRANSFERS—

SECTION 1. CERTIFICATES FOR SHARES: Certificates representing shares of the corporation shall be in such form as shall be determined by the board of directors. Such certificates shall be signed by the president or a vice-president and by the secretary or an assistant secretary. All certificates for shares shall be consecutively numbered or otherwise identified. The name and address of the person to whom the shares represented thereby are issued, with the number of shares and date of issue, shall be entered on the stock transfer books of the corporation. All certificates surrendered to the corporation for transfer shall be canceled and no new certificate shall be issued until the former certificate for a like number of shares shall have been surrendered and canceled, except that in case of a lost, destroyed, or mutilated certificate a new one may be issued therefor on such terms and indemnity to the corporation as the board of directors may prescribe.

SECTION 2. TRANSFER OF SHARES: Transfer of shares of the corporation shall be made in the manner specified in the Uniform Commercial Code. The corporation shall maintain stock transfer books, and any transfer be registered thereon only on request and surrender of the stock certificate representing the transferred shares, duly endorsed. The corporation shall have the absolute right to recognize as the owner of any shares of stock issued by it, the person or persons in whose name the certificate representing such shares stands according to the books of the corporation for all proper corporate purposes, including the voting of the shares represented by the certificate at a regular or special meeting of stockholders, and the issuance and payment of dividends on such shares.

ARTICLE SEVEN—FISCAL YEAR—Cross out either Paragraph A or Paragraph B:
a) The fiscal year of the corporation shall be the calendar year or begin on the _____ day of _____ of each year and end at midnight on the _____ day of _____ of the following year.

OR

b) The fiscal year of the corporation shall be as follows:
_____
_____
_____

ARTICLE EIGHT—DIVIDENDS—The board of directors may from time to time declare, and the corporation may pay, dividends on its outstanding shares in the manner and on the terms and conditions provided by law and its articles of incorporation.

ARTICLE NINE—SEAL—The board of directors shall provide a corporate seal, which shall be circular in form and shall have inscribed thereon the name of the corporation and the state of incorporation and the words "Corporate Seal." The seal shall be stamped or affixed to such documents as may be prescribed by law or custom or by the board of directors.

ARTICLE TEN—WAIVER OF NOTICE—Whenever any notice is required to be given to any stockholder or director of the corporation under the provisions of these bylaws or under the provisions of the articles of incorporation or under the provisions of law, a waiver thereof in writing, signed by the person or persons entitled to such notice, whether before or after the time stated therein, shall be deemed equivalent to the giving of such notice.

ARTICLE ELEVEN—AMENDMENTS—These bylaws may be altered, amended, or repealed and new bylaws may be adopted by the board of directors at any regular or special meeting of the board; provided, however, that the number of directors shall not be increased or decreased nor shall the provisions of ARTICLE TWO, concerning the stockholders, be substantially altered without the prior approval of the stockholders at a regular or special meeting of the stockholders, or by written consent. Changes in and additions to the bylaws by the board of directors shall be reported to the stockholders at their next regular meeting and shall be subject to the approval or disapproval of the stockholders at such meeting. If no action is then taken by the stockholders on a change in or addition to the bylaws, such change or addition shall be deemed to be fully approved and ratified by the stockholders.

# BYLAWS: NONPROFIT CORPORATION

**ARTICLE ONE—OFFICES—**The principal office of the corporation shall be located at:

_____
(Address)

_____
(City)

_____
(County)

_____
(State)

The corporation may have other such offices, either within or without the State of _____, as the board of directors may determine from time to time.

**ARTICLE TWO—MEMBERS—**

**SECTION 1. CLASSES OF MEMBERS:** The members of the corporation shall be divided into _____ classes as follows: _____

_____
_____
_____

The qualifications for membership in each class shall be: _____

_____
_____
_____
_____

**SECTION 2. ELECTION OF MEMBERS:** Any person interested in becoming a member of the corporation shall submit a written and signed application, on a form approved by the board of directors, to the secretary of the corporation. Such application shall be accompanied by the written sponsorship of _____ members in good standing or _____ directors. During the formative period of the corporation, each application shall be considered by the board of directors at its regular _____ meeting, or at any special meeting of the board, and approved or disapproved. Applicants whose applications are so approved shall become members of the corporation on payment of the required initiation fee and dues.

As soon as the membership committee shall have been formed, as provided hereinafter, all applications for membership shall be submitted to the membership committee, duly considered by the committee, and approved or disapproved by a majority vote of the committee. On approval of his or her application by the membership committee and payment of the required initiation fee and dues, the application shall become a member of the corporation.

Any applicant who has been disapproved by the membership committee, or any sponsor of such applicant, shall have the privilege of review by the membership at large, according to such procedure as may be fixed by the board of directors.

SECTION 3. VOTING RIGHTS: Each member in good standing shall be entitled to one vote on each matter submitted to a vote of the members.

SECTION 4. TERMINATION OF MEMBERSHIP: The board of directors, by affirmative vote of _____ of all the members of the board, may suspend or expel a member for cause after an appropriate hearing, and, by a majority vote of those present at any regularly constituted meeting, may terminate the membership of any member who becomes ineligible for membership, or suspend or expel any member who shall be in default in the payment of dues for the period fixed hereinafter.

SECTION 5. RESIGNATION: Any member may resign by filing a written resignation with the secretary, but any such resignation shall not relieve the member so resigning of the obligation to pay any dues, assessment, or other charges theretofore accrued and unpaid.

SECTION 6. REINSTATEMENT: On written request signed by a former member and filed with the secretary, the board of directors, by the affirmative vote of _____ of the members of the board, may reinstate such former member to membership on such terms as the board of directors may deem appropriate.

SECTION 7. TRANSFER OF MEMBERSHIP: Membership in this corporation is not transferable or assignable.

ARTICLE THREE—MEETINGS OF MEMBERS

SECTION 1. ANNUAL MEETING: The annual meeting of the members shall be held at:

_____
(Address)

_____
(City)

_____
(County)

_____
(State)

on the _____ day in the month of _____ in each year, beginning with the year 19 _____, at _____ o'clock _____, for the purpose of electing directors and for the transaction of such other business as may come before the meeting. If the day fixed for the annual meeting shall be a legal holiday in the State of _____, such meeting shall be held on the next succeeding business day. If the election of directors is not held on the day designated herein for any annual meeting of the members, or at any adjournment thereof, the board of directors shall cause the election to be held at a special meeting of the members as soon thereafter as is convenient.

SECTION 2. SPECIAL MEETINGS: Special meetings of the members, for any purpose or purposes, unless otherwise prescribed by statute, may be called by the president or by the board of directors, and shall be called by the president at the request of the holders of not less than _____ of the members having
(majority fraction)

voting rights, at _____
(a place designated by the board of directors or as the case may

be).

If no designation is made, or if a special meeting is otherwise called, the place of meeting shall be the principal office of the corporation in the State of _____, and consent to the holding of such a meeting, such a meeting shall be valid without call or notice, and at such meeting any corporate action may be taken.

SECTION 3. NOTICE OF MEETING: Written or printed notice stating the place, day, and hour of the meeting and, in case of a special meeting, the purpose or purposes for which the meeting is called, shall be delivered either personally or by mail, to each member entitled to vote at such a meeting, not less than _____ nor more than _____ days before the date of the meeting, either personally or by mail, by or at the direction of the president, or the secretary, or the officer or persons calling the meeting. If mailed, such notice shall be deemed to be delivered when deposited in the United States Mail, addressed to the member at his or her address as it appears on the records of the corporation, with postage thereon prepaid.

SECTION 4. INFORMAL ACTION BY MEMBERS: Any action required by law to be taken at a meeting of the members, or any action that may be taken at a meeting of members, may be taken without a meeting if a consent in writing, setting forth the action so taken, is signed by all the members entitled to vote with respect to the subject matter thereof.

SECTION 5. QUORUM: Members holding _____ percent (_____%) of the votes that may be cast at any meeting shall constitute a quorum at such meeting. If a quorum is not present at any meeting of members, a majority of the members present may adjourn the meeting from time to time without further notice.

SECTION 6. PROXIES: At any meetings of members, a member entitled to vote may vote by proxy executed in writing by the member or by his or her duly authorized attorney-in-fact. No proxy shall be valid after _____ months from the date of its execution unless otherwise provided in the proxy.

SECTION 7. VOTING BY MAIL: Where directors or officers are to be elected by members or any class or classes of members, such election may be conducted by mail in such manner as the board of directors shall determine.

ARTICLE FOUR—BOARD OF DIRECTORS—

SECTION 1. GENERAL POWERS: The business and affairs of the corporation shall be managed by its board of directors. Directors need not be residents of the State of _____ and need/need not be members of the corporation.

SECTION 2. NUMBER, TENURE, AND QUALIFICATIONS: The number of directors of the corporation shall be _____. Directors shall be elected at the annual meeting of members, and the term of office of each director shall be until the next annual meeting of members and the election and qualification of his or her successor.

SECTION 3. REGULAR MEETINGS: A regular meeting of the board of directors shall be held without notice other than this bylaw immediately after and at the same place as the annual meeting of members. The board of directors may provide, by resolution, the time and place for holding additional regular meetings without other notice than such resolution. Additional regular meetings shall be held at the principal office of the corporation in the absence of any designation in the resolution.

SECTION 4. SPECIAL MEETINGS: Special meetings of the board of directors may be called by or at the request of the president or any two directors, and shall be held at the principal office of the corporation or at such other place as the directors may determine.

SECTION 5. NOTICE: Notice of any special meeting shall be given at least _____ hours before the time fixed for the meeting, by written notice delivered personally or sent by mail or telegram to each director at his or her address as shown by the records of the corporation. If mailed, such notice shall be deemed to be delivered when deposited in the United States mail so addressed, with postage thereon prepaid. If notice is given by telegram, such notice shall be deemed to be delivered when the telegram is delivered to the telegraph company. Any director may waive notice of any meeting. The attendance of a director at a meeting shall constitute a waiver of notice of such meeting, except where a director attends a meeting for the express purpose of objecting to the transaction of any business because the meeting is not lawfully called or convened. Neither the business to be transacted at, nor the purpose of, any regular or special meeting of the board of directors need by specified in the notice or waiver of notice of such meeting, unless specifically required by law or by these bylaws.

SECTION 6. QUORUM: A majority of the board of directors shall constitute a quorum for the transaction of business at any meeting of the board of directors, but if less than such majority is present at a meeting, a majority of the directors present may adjourn the meeting from time to time without further notice.

SECTION 7. BOARD DECISIONS: The act of the majority of the directors present at a meeting at which a quorum is present shall be the act of the board of directors, unless the act of a greater number is required by law or by these bylaws.

SECTION 8. VACANCIES: Any vacancy occurring in the board of directors and any directorship to be filled by reason of an increase in the number of directors, shall be filled by the board of directors. A director elected to fill a vacancy shall be elected for the unexpired term of his or her predecessor in office. Each such appointment by the board *shall/shall not* be subject to the approval or disapproval of the members at the next *regular/special* meeting of the members.

SECTION 9. COMPENSATION: Directors as such shall not receive any stated salaries for their services, but by resolution of the board of directors, a fixed sum and expenses of attendance, if any, may be allowed for attendance at any regular or special meetings of the board. Nothing herein contained shall be construed to preclude any director from serving the corporation in any other capacity and receiving compensation therfor.

## ARTICLE FIVE—OFFICERS—

SECTION 1. NUMBER: The officers of the corporation shall be a president, one or more vice-presidents (the number thereof to be determiend by the board of directors), a secretary, and a treasurer, and such other officers as may be elected in accordance with the provisions of this article. The board of directors may elect or appoint such other officers, including one or more assistant secretaries and one or more assistant treasurers, as it shall deem desirable, such officers to have the authority and perform the duties prescribed, from time to time, by the board of directors. Any two or more offices may be held by the same person, except the offices of _____.

SECTION 2. ELECTION AND TERM OF OFFICE: The officers of the corporation shall be elected annually by the board of directors at the annual meeting of the board of directors. If the election of officers is not held at such meeting, such election shall be held as soon thereafter as is convenient. New offices may be created and filled at any meeting of the board of directors. Each officer shall hold office until his or her successor has been duly elected and qualified.

SECTION 3. REMOVAL: Any officer or agent elected or appointed by the board of directors may be removed by the board of directors whenever in its judgment the best interests of the corporation would be served thereby, but such removal shall be without prejudice to the contract rights, if any, of the person so removed.

SECTION 4. VACANCIES: A vacancy in any office because of death, resignation, removal, disqualification or otherwise, may be filled by the board of directors for the unexpired portion of the term.

SECTION 5. POWERS AND DUTIES: The powers and duties of the several officers shall be as specified from time to time by resolution or other directive of the board of directors. In the absence of such specifications, each officer shall have the powers and shall discharge the duties customarily and usually held and performed by like officers of corporations having the same or similar general purposes and objectives as this corporation.

## ARTICLE SIX—COMMITTEES—

SECTION 1. COMMITTEES OF DIRECTORS: The board of directors, by resolution adopted by a majority of the directors in office, may designate one or more committees, each of which shall consist of two or more directors, which committees, to the extent provided in such resoution, shall have and exercise the authority of the board of directors in the managment of the corporation; but the designation of such committees and the delegation thereto of authority shall not operate to relieve the board of directors, or any individual director, of any responsibility imposed on it or him or her by law.

SECTION 2. MEMBERSHIP COMMITTEE: At the first annual meeting of the members, or such special meeting of the members as may be called for the purpose, the members shall take from their number no fewer than _____ nor more than _____ persons, who shall constitute the membership committee. Of the committee members first elected _____ shall serve for one year, _____ for two years, and _____ for three years or _____. At annual meetings of the members thereafter, the members shall be elected to the committee for one-year terms to fill the terms as they expire. Any vacancy occuring in the committee by death, resignation, withdrawal from membership, or otherwise, shall be filled by majority vote of all the remaining members of the committee. Any person so elected shall serve for the remainder of the term of his or her predecessor.

The committee, when formed, shall organize itself, shall elect from its members a chairman and a secretary, and shall perform the functions and discharge the duties, concerning the consideration, approval, and election of new members, as are given to the committee elsewhere in these bylaws, or by resolution of the board of directors, or by resolution of the members.

SECTION 3. OTHER COMMITTEES: Other committees not having and exercising the authority of the board of directors in the management of the corporation may be designated by a resolution adopted by a majority of the directors present at a meeting at which a quorum is present. Except as otherwise provided in such resolution, members of each such committee shall be members of the corporation, and the president of the corporation shall appoint the members thereof. Any member thereof may be removed by the person or persons authorized to appoint such member whenever in their judgment the best interests of the corporation shall be served by such removal.

ARTICLE SEVEN—CONTRACTS, DEPOSITS, AND GIFTS—
SECTION 1. CONTRACTS: The board of directors may authorize any officer or officers, agent or agents, to enter into any contract or execute and deliver any instrument in the name of and on behalf of the corporation, and such authority may be general or confined to specific instances.

SECTION 2. CHECKS, DRAFTS, OR ORDERS:: All checks, drafts, or other orders for the payment of money, notes, or other evidences of indebtedness issued in the name of the corporation shall be signed by such officer or officers, agent or agents of the corporation and in such manner as shall from time to time be determined by resolution of the board of directors. In the absence of such determination by the board of directors, such instruments shall be signed by the treasurer or an assistant treasurer and countersigned by the president or a vice president of the corporation.

SECTION 3. DEPOSITS: All funds of the corporation not otherwise employed shall be deposited from time to time to the credit of the corporation in such banks, trust companies, or other depositaries as the board of directors may select.

SECTION 4. GIFTS: The board of directors may accept on behalf of the corporation any contribution, gift, bequest, or devise for any purpose of the corporation.

**ARTICLE EIGHT—CERTIFICATES OF MEMBERSHIP—**

**SECTION 1. CERTIFICATES OF MEMBERSHIP:** The board of directors shall provide for the issuance of certificates evidencing membership in the corporation, which certificates shall be in such form as may be determined by the board. Such certificates shall be signed by the president or a vice president and by the secretary or an assistant secretary and shall be sealed with the seal of the corporation. All certificates evidencing membership of any class shall be consecutively numbered. The name and address of each member and the date of issuance of the certificate shall be entered on the records of the corporation. If any certificate is lost, mutilated, or destroyed, a new certificate may be issued therefor on such terms and conditions as the board of directros may determine.

**SECTION 2. ISSUANCE OF CERTIFICATES:** When a member has been elected to membership and has paid any initiation fee and dues that may then be required, a certificate of membership shall be issued in his or her name and delivered to him or her by the secretary.

**ARTICLE NINE—BOOKS AND RECORDS—**The corporation shall keep correct and complete books and records of account and shall also keep minutes of the proceedings of its members, board of directors, committees having and exercising any of the authority of the board of directors, and the membership committee, and shall keep at the principal office a record giving the names and addresses of the members entitled to vote. All books and records of the corporation may be inspected by any member, or his or her agent or attorney, for any proper purpose at any reasonable time.

**ARTICLE TEN—FISCAL YEAR—**Cross out either Paragraph A or Paragraph B:

a) The fiscal year of the corporation shall be the calendar year or begin on the _____ day of _____ of each year and end at midnight on the _____ day of _____ of the following year;

OR

b) The fiscal year of the corporation shall be as follows: _____

_____

_____

**ARTICLE ELEVEN—DUES—**

**SECTION 1. ANNUAL DUES:** The board of directors shall determine from time to time the amount of initiation fee, if any, and annual dues payable to the corporation by members of each class, and shall give appropriate notice to the members.

**SECTION 2. PAYMENT OF DUES:** Dues shall be payable in advance on the first day of _____ in each year. Dues of a new member shall be prorated from the first day of the month in which such new member is elected to membership.

**SECTION 3. DEFAULT AND TERMINATION OF MEMBERSHIP:** When any member of any class is in default in the payment of dues for a period of _____ months from the beginning of the period for which such dues became payable, his or her membership may thereupon be terminated by the board of directors as provided hereinabove.

**ARTICLE TWELVE—SEAL**—The board of directors shall provide a corporate seal, which shall be (Describe seal and inscription thereon) _____

_____

_____

_____

**ARTICLE THIRTEEN—WAIVER OF NOTICE**—Whenever any notice is required to be given under the provisions of (cite State nonprofit corporation statute) _____ or under the provisions of the articles of incorporation or the bylaws of the corporation, a waiver thereof in writing, signed by the person or persons entitled to such notice, whether before or after the time stated therein, shall be deemed equivalent to the giving of such notice.

**ARTICLE FOURTEEN—AMENDMENTS OF BYLAWS**—These bylaws may be altered, amended, or repealed and new bylaws may be adopted by (choose one):

a) a majority of the directors present at any regular or special meeting, if at least _____ day's written notice is given of intention to alter, amend, repeal, or adopt new bylaws at such meeting.

OR

b) vote of the members at any regular or special meeting.

OR

c) _____

_____

_____

## CODICIL TO WILL

Last Wills and Testaments are not irrevocable, monolithic documents. During most lifetimes, individuals who make out their wills have changes of mind or wish to add some provision to the existing will. The existing will will not have to be changed—that is the purpose of the codicil. The latter, then, is a supplement to the will whose purpose is to add, subtract from, modify, qualify, or revoke the original document. It, too, needs to be properly prepared and witnessed, then attached to all existing copies of the will.

# CODICIL TO WILL

This is my (first) (second) (third) CODICIL to the will dated _____ of _____ of the following address, _____ in the city of _____ State of _____.

    1. I revoke clause _____ of my will and substitute the following new clause for it:

    2. In all other respects I confirm my will.

In witness to which CODICIL, I have signed my name to it below on _____ 19_____

Signed by me _____

in our presence and by us in (his) (her) presence

and in the presence of each other:

Witness 1: _____

(printed name) _____

Address _____

Occupation _____

Witness 2: _____

(printed name) _____

Address _____

Occupation _____

                                 _____
                                   (your signature)

## COMMERCIAL LEASE

A *commercial* lease is usually intended for a property that is to be used for business purposes, as contrasted with residential, industrial or agricultural functions. Commercial leases are usually of 5, 10, 15 years or longer duration. This contract, which transfers use or occupancy of land, space, structures or even equipment for a stated period of time, obligates the party that leases the property (the lessee) for an enormous amount of money. Take a modest-size store of 2,000 square feet that rents the first year for $10 a square foot, the following four years for $12 a square foot, and the final five years of a ten-year lease for $15 a square foot. The total obligation under these terms amounts to $266,000 over the 15-year period. Clauses in the commercial lease can add substantial additional sums—such as for insurance, maintainence, taxes, improvements, water and sewerage, utilities, and even dues to merchants associations or commercial parks. A careful reading of the sample lease here, and a double-check with a competent attorney, are recommended prior to signing such a document.

# SAMPLE COMMERCIAL LEASE

This lease for a business property made between:
(1) _____ (the "Landlord")
            (landlord name)
and
(2) _____ (the "Tenant")
            (tenant name)
The Landlord and the Tenant hereby agree as follows:
1. The Landlord hereby grants the Tenant a lease of the premises described on the floor plan attached located at:

_____
                    (address and floor, if any)
_____ (the "Premises")
The parties agree that the Premises have a rented area of _____ square feet, excluding the exterior walls.
2. The term of this lease commences on _____ and ends on _____. If the Tenant continues in occupation of the Premises with the consent of the Landlord after expiration of the term of this lease, the Tenant shall be deemed to be leasing the premises on a month-to-month basis and on the same terms described in this lease.
3. The Tenant may use the Premises for _____. and for no other pur-
                                        (business purpose)
pose, unless agreed to in writing by Landlord.
4. (a) The Tenant shall pay the Landlord a "base rent" of _____ dollars ($_____) per year in equal monthly installments of _____ dollars ($_____) in advance on or before the first of each month commencing on _____ with the base rent for any broken portion of a calendar month in which this lease terminates being prorated.

   (b) The following services and expenses are the responsibility of the Landlord:


   (c) The following services and expenses are the responsibility of the Tenant:


   (d) The Landlord shall invoice the Tenant monthly for additional services rendered by the Landlord. Each invoice payable in full 30 days after delivery of such itemized service. The Tenant is deemed to have agreed to the accuracy of the amount charged in any invoice for additional rent which he or she has not challenged in writing within the same 30 days.

   (e) The Tenant shall also pay the Landlord as "additional rent" all of the total costs reasonably incurred by the Landlord, including but not limited to legal fees, of curing any default of the Tenant under this lease, including but not limited to en-

230

forcing payment of rent and regaining lawful possession of the Premises, due on demand.

5. The Landlord shall be solely responsible for repairs or improvements to the structure and to the exterior of the building.

6. Any services and expenses pertaining to the use by the Tenant of the Premises, not mentioned in this lease, are the responsibility and expense of the Tenant.

7. The Landlord agrees that so long as the Tenant complies with the terms of this lease, the Tenant may occupy and enjoy the Premises without any interruption from the Landlord.

8. The Landlord is not liable for any damage to the Tenant's property or for any injury to any person in or coming to or from the Premises, however caused, and the Tenant agrees to indemnify the Landlord against the financial consequences of any such liability. Tenant shall purchase and maintain public liability insurance in the amount of no less than _____ dollars ($_____) and shall provide a copy of such policy of this insurance to the Landlord immediately upon occupancy.

9. The Landlord may terminate this lease for any one of the following or any other cause permitted by law:

    (a)   15 days' arrears of rent or additional rent;

    (b)   the bankruptcy or insolvency of the tenant;

    (c)   an unauthorized change in the use of the Premises by the Tenant, and any change which affects the Landlord's building insurance or which constitutes a nuisance.

    (d)   substantial damage to or destruction of the Premises;

    (e)   any sale or material change in use of the building in which the Premises are located by the Landlord;

    (f)   any unauthorized assignment or subletting of this lease by the Tenant;

    (g)   any significant willful or negligent damage to the Premises caused by the Tenant or by persons permitted on the Premises by Tenant.

10. The Tenant may not assign or sublet the premises, in whole or in part, or allow the Premises to be used by any other person without the written consent of the Landlord, which consent will not be unreasonably withheld.

11. The Tenant shall keep the Premises in a sound state of repair and cleanliness and shall not make improvements or alterations to the Premises without the written consent of the Landlord, which consent shall not be unreasonably withheld.

12. At the end of the lease, the Tenant shall deliver vacant possession to the Landlord of the Premises in the same condition as at the commencement of the lease, reasonable wear and tear excepted. The Landlord may, in the Landlord's sole discretion, elect to keep any of the Tenant's improvements, alterations, or fixtures.

13. Any written notice required or permitted to be given by this lease is sufficiently given if sent by ordinary or electronic mail to the last known address of the party for whom the notice is intended. Any written notice sent in accordance with this paragraph is deemed, for the purposes of this lease, received by the addressee on the seventh day after mailing unless actually received before.

**14.** This lease binds and benefits the parties and their respective heirs, successors, and permitted assigns.

**15.** If not in default under this lease, the Tenant has the right to renew this lease for a further term of _____ years by giving written notice of renewal to the Landlord in the six-month period immediately before the expiration of the original fixed term of this lease. The renewed lease is granted on the same terms as set out in this lease except as to base rent and without any further right of renewal. The base rent payable by the Tenant in the renewed term may be agreed between the Landlord and Tenant but, failing such agreement before commencement of the renewed term of the lease, the amount of the base rent shall be settled by arbitration in accordance with the rules of the American Arbitration Association in force at that time and judgment on the arbitration award may be entered in any court of competent jurisdiction.

Executed under seal on _____, 19 _____.
(date)

Signed, sealed, and

delivered in the presence of:

_____     _____
(signature of witness)               (signature of landlord)
for the Landlord                     The Landlord

_____     _____
(signature of witness)               (signature of tenant)
for the Tenant                       The Tenant

## COMPANY POLICY HANDBOOK

This could be a "book" of many pages or a single sheet setting forth the company's policies. As soon as even one employee is hired, some form of company policy handbook is desirable. Situations and relations between employer and employees rarely remain status quo. A handbook tries to account not only for present conditions, but also anticipate future needs. In this litigious age it is wise to spell out all facets of a business's operation—hours, vacations, other off-time, duties, dress code, behavior, credit, purchases from the company, responsibilities, and expectations. The proposed handbook herewith has tried to present all possible employer-employee problems and serve as a basic instrument upon which you can build an employer policy suited to your own needs.

If your business employs or plans to employ more than your brother-in-law, it is probably a sound idea to prepare a written statement setting forth how you want to run your business. This could be a single page or a multipage booklet. Like a business plan that gives you and your banker a blueprint of your management direction, a company or EMPLOYEE HANDBOOK can prevent future problems with employees. Since it will not be written in stone, it can always be changed as circumstances dictate. Such a written policy statement should include:

Reminder of what benefits employees may regard as their due and that such benefits represent a substantial and voluntary contribution by the company.

A statement that policies attempt to establish consistency of company policies from department to department, smooth over possible resentment of employees who might not realize that restrictions or regulations apply equitably to all.

An invitation to enlist employee's interest and participation in the achievement of company objectives.

In addition to general policy matters, there are 12 sections that are recommended for inclusion or at least consideration:

1. Equal employment opportunity
2. Quality of products or services
3. Health, safety and environmental protection
4. Compliance with Anti-Trust Law
5. Government security requirements
6. Practices regarding payments and contributions
7. Standards of conduct in government transactions
8. Relationships with external suppliers
9. International relationships and practices
10. Customer service and satisfaction
11. Reimbursement of business expenses
12. Employee's outside business interests

Discounted purchases from the company should also be made a matter of oral or written company policy.

# COMPANY
# POLICY
# HANDBOOK

**For:** _____

**No.** _____

**This Company Policy Handbook Is the Property of (Company)**

# I.

# COMPANY POLICY HANDBOOK:
# Equal Employment Opportunity

This company believes that employee happiness and satisfaction, as well as company efficiency and profitability, can best be enhanced and maintained by recruiting, hiring, training, compensating, and advancing employees on a basis of merit.

This policy will be promoted without regard to an employee's race, color, religion, national origin, sex, age, veteran status, or handicap.

Owners and managers of the company are each responsible to apply this policy, implement, and monitor it. The employee is always invited to submit in writing, or present orally, any suggestions or complaints that might either enhance this policy of Equal Employment Opportunity or cause corrections to be made.

# II.

# COMPANY POLICY HANDBOOK:
# Quality of Product and Services

Quality is the principal ingredient of our product and/or service. Quality produces employee satisfaction and pride. Quality not only makes customers happy, but keeps them happy. Quality is not only an advance commitment, but an insurance policy that will bring customers back and assure employees' and company survival. As a business advisor put it, "If you cannot do it right the first time, will you have time to do it over again?" Will you, indeed, be given the opportunity to do it over again?

It is the company's job, and that of its managers, to keep all employees informed, to train them properly, and to motivate them to perform their best. Employees are encouraged to contribute suggestions that will enhance the quality of this company's output and to seek information, training, and assistance that will assure quality products and services.

For quality control and performance to be effective, the cooperation of management, employees, and suppliers is necessary, both inside the company and without. The company will provide appropriate rewards to all within its company, as well as those without, who make positive contributions to the implementation of this policy.

# III.

# COMPANY POLICY HANDBOOK: Health, Safety and Environmental Protection

This company and its management are pledged to operate its business in a manner that will not jeopardize the health and safety of its employees and customers, nor expose them to unreasonable risks.

This policy will be rigidly enforced and monitored to comply with known federal, state, and local laws, regulations, industry practices, and humanitarian concerns. Health, Safety, and Environmental Protections are concerns that need to be observed both inside the company and outside, such as by drivers and agents of the company. Observance of sound standards is important to everyone's well-being, to help reduce absenteeism and improve efficiency, promote good public relations for the company and its products and services, and protect our fragile environment. The company will endeavor to post pertinent information in locations accessible to employees, or to disseminate such information personally, to hold training sessions if desirable, and to coordinate such activities with insurance, health, and governmental agencies. Employees' observance and suggestions are always welcome.

# IV.

# COMPANY POLICY HANDBOOK: Compliance with Anti-Trust Laws

The principal federal statutes with which company employees must be familiar are included in what is called the Sherman Anti-Trust Act. The company and each of its employees, but in particular those employees who are in management positions or represent the company at outside functions and activities, must be familiar with the general principles embodied in this Act—involving fair trade, pricing, terms of sale, distribution methods, market share, quotations, and more. If there is any doubt about an employee's actions in these areas, the employee is urged to discuss this matter with management.

The Act, and this company's policy, therefore, hereby specifically prohibits all employees from entering into any agreement, or understanding, explicit or implied, in writing or oral, with a competitor or a third party acting for the competitor, which will limit competition or unfairly restrict his opportunity to do business.

The Act holds companies as well as employees in management positions personally accountable. Anti-trust laws apply to the United States as well as to activities with other countries.

# V.

# COMPANY POLICY HANDBOOK: Government Security Requirements

This paragraph is added only when the company is engaged in selling products or services to the U.S. Government and appropriate employee security is mandated. The company will provide functional guidance in all phases of security applicable to the protection of personnel, products, facilities, services, and classified information, in compliance with Federal regulations that require such protection.

# VI.

# COMPANY POLICY HANDBOOK: Payments and Contributions

While in many foreign countries payments to government and private-sector officials are often common practice, such "unofficial" remunerations are frowned upon in this country. Contributions, however, are made in many instances, primarily to non-profit and charitable endeavors, and sometimes, as a company policy, to political candidates during election time.

Payments and contributions to outsiders contacted in the course of business are heavily based on the employee's sound judgment. They should never be considered bribes or kickbacks, but be limited to dues, payment for luncheons and meetings, or small token gifts that could aid a business transaction or foster good relations.

Employees are urged to check with management prior to any contemplated payment or contribution, to have such transactions charged to the company and paid through normal company channels, or to rely on an established budget that may be established for such purposes.

# VII.

# COMPANY POLICY HANDBOOK: Government Transactions

If and when this company engages in business with the Federal or state governments, or any foreign government, proper legal conduct is mandatory. Wherever and whenever possible, such conduct will be discussed and determined by the company in advance, but if guidelines are not clear, any company employee having such contact should consult with company management prior to any action.

It is the objective of the company to be a trusted, reliable, and even-handed supplier of goods and services to any branch of a government. Scrupulously honest allocations of costs, nondisclosure of any information to outside contacts, adherence to contracts and specifications, avoidance of improper payments and gratuities, and observance of existing government policies, conflicts of interest and anti-trust provisions must be maintained at all times.

While dealings with governmental entities are desirable and of considerable benefit to the company and its employees, the rules of doing so are stricter. Employees of this company are advised to discuss these rules if they are not completely clear.

# VIII.

# COMPANY POLICY HANDBOOK: Relationships with External Suppliers

Employees working on behalf of the company to secure materials and services from suppliers must provide equal opportunities for small and large suppliers to earn a share of this company's purchases. In accordance with government protocol, equal opportunities should be given to small suppliers, businesses operated by women and minorities, and disadvantaged suppliers. It is to be borne in mind that ethical standards and legal requirements, as well as the practical considerations of the marketplace, have to be our criteria.

In evaluating dealings with suppliers of any size or type, the common criteria that make for intelligent buying decisions must be observed. These include: quality, reliability, price, technical excellence, service, and the safeguarding of confidential and proprietary information.

It is usually desirable to make comparative inquiries as to the above qualities, perhaps on an annual basis, with other suppliers in the field.

# IX.

# COMPANY POLICY HANDBOOK: International Relationships

Whether the company is at the present time engaged in international trade or plans to do so in the future this phase of the company's business requires special procedures , skills, and observances.

The federal and state governments encourage trade with overseas business partners. Laws and regulations govern these transactions that are often different from those employed in domestic trade. Cultures, languages, and sensitivities in foreign countries often vary starkly from those in the United States. Product quality, packaging, and paperwork for overseas-destined shipments must be even more stringently checked than comparable sales to domestic consumers.

It is the task of every employee of the company to be knowledgeable of the special requirements of international trade and to assist in the successful promotion of this phase of the company's operation.

# X.

# COMPANY POLICY HANDBOOK: Customer Service and Satisfaction

This company is in business to satisfy its customers. The company's customers are the reason that you are employed and paid. Without our satisfied customers, there would be no company and no jobs. It is therefore the task of every employee to understand each customer's needs, to deliver and provide services and goods that will give each customer satisfaction and to constantly observe the following credo:

Listen to every customer and identify his needs correctly;

Understand what the customer expects of the company and of you and try to accommodate him to the best of your ability;

Always try your best to respond to the customer's needs and expectations, within the bounds of good business practices;

Make only promises that you know you and the company can fulfill;

If you are aware of changes, shortages, delays, improvements, and so forth that specifically affect the customer, communicate these to the customer quickly and honestly;

Understand the relationships faced by fellow-employees, such as sales representatives and managers, in regard to customers and support their efforts toward the company's goal of total customer satisfaction;

Do not try to shoulder unmanageable problems by yourself, but discuss them with supervisors and management. Customers are not always perfect, but they are our customers.

# XI.

# COMPANY POLICY HANDBOOK: Reimbursement of Business Expenses

Authorized business travel, hotel and food costs, entertaining customers and prospects, costs of memberships in business and professional associations, admission to pertinent trade shows, and small purchases of materials and supplies for company use are some of the expenditures that employees might make and that will be reimbursed by the company.

Reimbursement of expenses for or on behalf of the company should be verified by either a properly issued purchase order and/or a dated receipt from the entity creating a business expense. Proper dating and itemization of reimbursable items is important for the records of the company.

In the event of planned business travel, advance purchases of tickets for travel accommodations or reservations made by the company are preferred. It is advisable when entertaining any major purchases or commitments, that these are made within planned budgets, or that advance checks or cash be drawn if such expenditures can be accurately determined.

# XII.

# COMPANY POLICY HANDBOOK: Outside Business Interests

Any situation or transaction engaged in by an employee outside of the company is generally that employee's responsibility and right, unless such activity poses a conflict, potential or actual, with the company.

The company recognizes and respects the right of its employees to engage in outside financial, business and social activities, providing that such activities (1) are legal, (2) do not impair the employee's ability to fulfill his/her functions in the conduct of his employment, (3) do not involve the misuse of company time, funds, products or property, and (4) do not discredit the good name of the company.

Should there be any doubt as to the employee's activities outside of the company, the employee is invited to discuss such activities without recrimination with a member of management. A written copy of such outside activities may be requested by the company.

(optional)

# XIII.

# COMPANY POLICY HANDBOOK: Purchases from the Company

Employees who have been continuously employed for at least _____ months and who work a minimum of _____ hours a week, are entitled to purchase products from the company at _____ percent (%) discount from list price.

Payments for such items must be made in cash at the time of purchase, unless arrangement is made to deduct such sum from current earnings or other arrangements are made by the company before the purchased item(s) leaves the company premises.

It is understood that such items are for the personal use of the employee and/or family, and are not for resale.

# CONTRACTOR AGREEMENT

THIS AGREEMENT is hereby entered into this _____ day of
_____, 19_____, between _____, of _____
                                                            (Street
_____, hereinafter called Owner,
Address)      City)      (State)    (Zip)
and _____, of _____
                           (Street      Address)              City)
_____, hereinafter called the Contractor.
(State)  (Zip)

The said parties, for the considerations hereinafter mentioned, hereby agree to

the following:

## DESCRIPTION OF THE WORK

1. The Contractor shall provide all materials and labor required to perform
all of the work for:


as shown on the drawing(s), and set forth in the specifications and/or descrip-
tion(s) prepared by _____, which drawing(s) and specifi-
cations and/or description(s) are identified by the signatures of the parties to this
agreement, and which form a part of this agreement and are incorporated by reference herein for all purposes.

## PAYMENT

2. Under the terms of this agreement, the Owner agrees to pay the Contractor, for materials to be furnished and work to be done, the sum of
_____ ($ _____), subject to any additions or de-
ductions as hereinafter provided for in this agreement, and to make the following
payments:


and that the final payments shall be made subject to the hereinafter stated conditions of this agreement. It is agreed that no payment made under this agreement
shall be considered conclusive evidence of full performance of this contract, either wholly or in part by the Contractor, and that acceptance of payment shall not
be considered by the Contractor to be acceptance by the Owner of any defective
materials or workmanship.

## LIENS

3. Final payment shall not be due until such time as the Contractor has provided the Owner with a release of any liens arising from this agreement; or receipts for payment in full for all materials and labor for which a lien could be filed; or a bond satisfactory to the Owner indemnifying the Owner against any lien.

## TIMELY COMPLETION OF THE WORK

4. The Contractor agrees that the various portions of the work shall be completed on or before the following dates:

and the entire work shall be completed on or before the _____ day of _____, 19_____.

In the event the work is not completed by the aforementioned date, the Owner shall be entitled to receive as damages from the Contractor, the sum of _____ ($ _____) per _____, it being agreed that the aforementioned sum is reasonable, taking into account the difficulty in determining the exact amount of damages the Owner would sustain in the event of said delay, and that the agreed sum shall be considered as liquidated damages.

If the Contractor is delayed in the completion of the work, by acts of God, fire, flood, or any other unavoidable casualties; or by labor strikes, late delivery of materials; or by neglect of the Owner, his agents or representatives; or by any subcontractor employed by the Contractor; the time for completion of the work shall be extended for the same period as the delay occasioned by any of the aforementioned causes.

## SURVEYS AND EASEMENTS

5. The Owner shall provide and pay for all surveys. All easements for access across the property of another, and for permanent changes, and for the construction or erection of structures shall also be obtained and paid for by the Owner.

## LICENSES, PERMITS AND BUILDING CODES

6. The Contractor shall obtain and pay for all permits and licenses required for the prosecution and timely completion of the work. The Contractor shall comply with all appropriate regulations relating to the conduct of the work and shall advise the Owner of any specifications or drawings which are at variance therewith.

## MATERIALS AND EQUIPMENT

7. The Contractor shall provide and pay for all materials, tools and equipment required for the prosecution and timely completion of the work. Unless otherwise specified in writing, all materials shall be new and of good quality.

## SAMPLES

8. Whenever the Owner may require, the Contractor will furnish for approval all samples as directed, and the work shall be in accordance with approved samples.

## LABOR AND SUPERVISION

9. In the prosecution of the work the Contractor shall at all times keep a competent foreman and a sufficient number of workers skilled in their trades to suitably perform the work.

The foreman shall represent the Contractor and, in the absence of the Contractor, all instructions given by the Owner to the foreman shall be binding upon the Contractor as though given to the Contractor. Upon request of the foreman, instructions shall be in writing.

## ALTERATIONS AND CHANGES

10. All changes and deviations in the work ordered by the Owner must be in writing, the contract sum being increased or decreased accordingly by the Contractor. Any claims for increases in the cost of the work must be presented by the Contractor to the Owner in writing, and written approval of the Owner shall be obtained by the Contractor before proceeding with the ordered change or revision.

In the event that additional work, not shown on the drawings and/or not described in the specifications, is required to comply with laws, regulations, or building codes, such additional work shall be considered as done under the terms of this agreement.

## CORRECTIONS OF DEFICIENCIES

11. The Contractor agrees to reexecute any work which does not conform to the drawings and specifications, warrants the work performed, and further agrees that he shall remedy any defects resulting from faulty materials or workmanship which shall become evident during a period of one year after completion of the work. This provision shall apply with equal force to all work performed by subcontractors as to work that is performed by direct employees of the Contractor.

## PROTECTION OF THE WORK

12. It shall be the responsibility of the Contractor to reasonably protect the work, the property of the Owner, and adjacent property and the public, and the Contractor shall be responsible for any damage, injury or death resulting from his negligence or from any intentional act of the Contractor or the Contractor's employees, agents, or subcontractors.

## CLEANING UP

13. The Contractor shall keep the premises free from the accumulation of waste and, upon completion of the work, shall remove all waste, equipment, and other materials and leave the premises in clean condition.

## CONTRACTOR'S LIABILITY INSURANCE

14. The Contractor shall obtain insurance to protect himself against claims for property damage arising out of his or any subcontractor's performance of this contract; and to protect himself against claims under provisions of Workman's Compensation and any similar employee benefit acts, and from claims for bodily injury, including death, due to performance of this contract by the Contractor or any subcontractor employed for the performance of this contract.

## OWNER'S LIABILITY INSURANCE

15. It shall be the responsibility of the Owner, at the Owner's option, to obtain insurance to protect himself from the contingent liability of claims for property damage and bodily injury, including death, that may arise from the performance of this contract.

## FIRE INSURANCE WITH EXTENDED COVERAGE

16. The Owner shall obtain fire insurance with extended coverage at 100 percent of the value of the entire structure, including materials and labor related to the work described in this agreement. Certificates of insurance shall be filed with the Contractor if he so requests. The aforesaid fire insurance need not include tools, equipment, scaffolding, or forms owned or rented by the contractor, and subcontractor, or their respective employees.

## OWNER'S RIGHT TO TERMINATE THE AGREEMENT

17. In the event the Contractor shall fail to meet the provisions of this agreement, the Owner shall, after seven (7) days' written notice to the Contractor and his surety, have the right to take possession of the premises in order to complete the work as specified in the agreement. The Owner may deduct the cost thereof from any payment then and thereafter due to the Contractor or may, at his option, terminate the agreement, take possession of any materials, and complete the work as he deems appropriate. If the unpaid balance of the contracted sum exceeds the Owner's expenses of completing the work, such excess shall be paid to the Contractor. If such expense shall exceed the unpaid balance, the Contractor shall pay the difference to the Owner.

## CONTRACTOR'S RIGHT TO TERMINATE THE AGREEMENT

18. In the event the Owner shall fail to pay the Contractor within seven (7) days after the date upon which payment shall become due, the Contractor shall have the right, after seven (7) days' written notice to the Owner, to stop work and may, at his option, terminate the agreement and recover from the Owner payment for all work executed, plus any loss sustained, plus a reasonable profit, plus damages.

In the event the work is stopped by any court or other public authority for a period of thirty (30) days through no fault of the Contractor, the Contractor shall have the right to stop work and may, at his option, terminate the agreement and recover from the Owner payment for all work executed, plus any loss sustained, plus a reasonable profit, plus damages.

## ASSIGNMENT OF RIGHTS

19. Neither the Owner nor the Contractor shall have the right to assign any rights or interest occurring under this agreement without the written consent of the other, nor shall the Contractor assign any sums due, or to become due, to him under the provisions of this agreement.

## ACCESS AND INSPECTION

20. The Owner, Owner's representative, and public authorities shall at all times have access to the work.

An appropriately licensed representative of the Owner, whose authority shall be set forth in writing by the Owner, shall have the authority to direct removal of any materials and the taking down of any portions of the work failing to meet drawings, specifications, laws, regulations, or building codes; the reexecution of said work deemed as being done under the provisions of Article 11 of this agreement.

Any other removal of materials or taking down of portions of the work as directed by the Owner's representatives shall be in writing and at the sole expense of the Owner.

## ATTORNEY FEES

21. Attorney fees and court costs shall be paid by the defendant in the event that judgment must be obtained, and is, to enforce this agreement or any breach thereof.

IN WITNESS WHEREOF, the parties hereto set their hands and seals the day and year written above.

_____          _____
Witness as to Owner                      Owner

_____          _____
Witness as to Contractor                 Contractor

## CORPORATE MINUTES OF SHAREHOLDERS

These are transcriptions or other written records of meetings that corporations hold periodically, usually at least annually, with those individuals who own shares, or at least major shares, in the company. Minutes are normally retained by the corporation indefinitely. Frequently they are disseminated to shareholders, whether they were present or not. This eliminates any future objections or charges of secrecy and corporate actions considered detrimental to the shareholder's interests.

# CORPORATE MINUTES OF SHAREHOLDERS MEETING

A meeting of shareholders of _____

was duly called and held on _____ 19_____at _____

_____

commencing at _____ (AM) (PM).

With the approval of the shareholders present, _____

acted as chairperson of the meeting and _____

acted as secretary and recorded the minutes. The chairperson acknowledged that the required quorum was present to conduct business and that the meeting was properly constituted. On motions duly made and seconded, it was voted that

1.   The minutes of the last meeting of shareholders be taken as read.

2.   The following resolutions were voted on:

There being no further business to transact at this time, it was voted to adjourn the meeting.

Dated _____ 19_____

Secretary _____          Chairperson _____

(typed) _____          (typed) _____

# CREDIT ACTION (ADVERSE)
## (TO FIND OUT REASON FOR REQUEST)

Date _____

**Dear**

On _____, I was notified that my application for credit dated _____ was denied based upon information received by you from a source other than a consumer credit reporting agency.

Pursuant to my right under the Fair Credit Reporting Act, Title 15 USC, Sec. 1681m(b), I hereby request that the nature of the information received by you be disclosed to me.

Please forward such information to me at the above address.

Thank you for your prompt attention to this matter.

Sincerely,

# CREDIT INFORMATION SHEET

HUSBAND ............................................................ ADDRESS ........................................................................................

AGE ...................... OWN OR RENT ................................ NO. YEARS PRESENT ADDRESS ....................................

HOME PHONE ........................ PLACE OF EMPLOYMENT ............................................................................

BUSINESS PHONE ........................ POSITION HELD ........................................................ NO. YEARS ..................

BASE SALARY PER YEAR $........................................ OVERTIME PER YEAR AVG. $..................................

BONUSES $................................... OTHER INCOME $............................................ SOURCE $..............................

WIFE ........................................................................ AGE ..................................................

PLACE OF EMPLOYMENT ........................................ BUSINESS PHONE ............................................

POSITION HELD ........................................................ NO. YEARS ........................................

BASE SALARY PER YEAR $.................................... OVERTIME OR BONUSES $..................................

OTHER INCOME $.............................................. SOURCE ........................................

NUMBER CHILDREN ........................ AGES ........................ OTHER DEPENDENTS ....................................

PRESENT RENT $............................ PRESENT MORTGAGE PAYMENT $........................ IPTI ................ EQUITY $......................

| INSTALLMENT PAYMENTS: | BALANCE UNPAID | MONTHLY PAYMENT |
|---|---|---|
| AUTO: .......................................... | $........................................ | $........................................ |
| ........................................................ | $........................................ | $........................................ |
| ........................................................ | $........................................ | $........................................ |

ALIMONY ........................ CHILD SUPPORTS ........................ OTHER ........................................

ARE THERE ANY JUDGMENTS OR LAWSUITS CURRENT $........................ TYPE ..................................

........................................................................................................................................................

REFERENCES:

NAME ........................................ ADDRESS ........................................ PHONE ......................

NAME ........................................ ADDRESS ........................................ PHONE ......................

ASSETS:

CASH ON HAND      $........................................

CHECKING      $........................ BANK ........................................

SAVINGS      $........................ BANK ........................................

GOVERNMENT BONDS $........................ CASH VALUE ........................ INSURANCE CASH VALUE ......................

REMARKS (Insert Unusual Circumstances) ..........................................................................................

........................................................................................................................................................

I (we) certify the above information to be true and accurate to the best of our knowledge.

HUSBAND ........................................................................

DATE ........................................      WIFE ........................................................................

251

# DISCLOSURE AGREEMENT: CONFIDENTIAL INFORMATION

Agreement made this _____, 19_____, between:

_____ and _____
(Name of Owner)                          (Name of Company)
herein referred to as Owner              herein referred to as the Company,
of                                       of

_____                _____
(Address)                                (Address)

_____                _____
(City)                                   (City)

_____                _____
(County)                                 (County)

_____                _____
(State)                                  (State)

Owner hereby submits to and grants the company permission to disclose to the members of the company certain confidential information hereinafter defined, under the following terms and conditions:

SECTION ONE—The owner has developed and maintains confidential information including but not limited to the following: information concerning secret processes, formulas, machines, components, inventions, creations, systems, designs, materials, software, assembly techniques, pending patent applications, compositions, improvements, ideas, specifications, or arts relating to products and services, as well as financial projections, financing plans, and other business information related to present or prospective business activities of the company. All information, and all documents, records, notebooks, drawings, photographs, and any repositories or representations of such information are hereinafter referred to as confidential information.

SECTION TWO—The owner desires to make available certain of the confidential information for the sole purpose of evaluating said information in reference to potential commercial use of the company or to selling an interest in a business venture which relates to such confidential information.

In consideration of the disclosure of any such confidential information to the company, the company agrees to hold such confidential information in confidence and not to divulge it, in whole or in part, to any third party, except in confidence to those of its employees (if any) who require knowledge of the same for purposes for which it has been disclosed to the undersigned. Each of the said employees shall first have agreed in writing to abide by this agreement to maintain confidentiality of such information. The company further agrees not to use any of the confidential informaiton in any way for its own benefit, except for the purpose specified above, without the prior written permission of the owner.

SECTION THREE—The obligation of the company under this agreement shall not apply to information which, at the time of disclosure to the company, is within the public domain or which thereafter becomes part of the public domain through no act or failure to act of the company.

SECTION FOUR—The company agrees to promptly return to the owner all documentary or written information acquired from the owner pursuant to or in connection with this agreement, and all copies thereof. The company may, at its option, give written agreement to the owner to retain for its records one copy of each document or writing if owner agrees, and if each copy thus retained is clearly marked to indicate the confidential nature of the information contained therein and the limitation of the use thereof by the company as set forth hereinabove.

In witness whereof, the parties have executed this agreement on this _____ day of _____, 19_____.

_____    _____
(Signature of Owner)                (Signature of company agent)

                                    _____
                                    (Title of company agent)

# DISPUTED ACCOUNT—SETTLEMENT OFFER

**Date**

**To:**

**Dear**

**re:**     <u>**Disputed Account**</u>

        **Ref.:** _____

        **Amount $** _____

**We dispute the balance indicated above as owing by us for the following reason(s):**

**Without admitting liability and solely for the purpose of a rapid and equitable resolution of this disputed matter, we are prepared to offer and immediate payment of $ _____ in full settlement of this disputed account.**
**If this proposal is acceptable to you, please advise us in writing. We will send the acceptable payment by return mail.**

**Very truly yours,**


**(Title/Company)**

## DISTRIBUTORSHIP AGREEMENT

A distributor is an individual or a firm that acts as an intermediary between a manufacturer and a retailer. The distributor usually maintains a warehouse or other storage facility in which he keeps the manufacturers' merchandise, as well as vehicles with which to deliver such merchandise to ultimate retail customers. Retailers buy merchandise from the distributor instead of dealing directly with a manufacturer, thus being able to obtain goods more quickly, in smaller quantities and from a variety of sources, both domestic and imported. The price of merchandise is obviously just a little higher, but the advantages outweigh the small cost increase. A manufacturer then executes an agreement with the distributor to fulfill the latter's function, usually within a specifically assigned territory and under conditions that are mutually beneficial. The agreement herewith covers a great many circumstances, though you might have others that apply to your situation. Agreements made with distributors in other states and even other countries should be made with the advice of a local lawyer, as laws in interstate or foreign distribution and relationships could vary.

# DISTRIBUTORSHIP AGREEMENT

Agreement made this _____, 19____, between:
                    (month and day)      (yr.)

_____   and   _____
(Name of Seller)                          (Name of Distributor)
herein referred to as Seller, of          herein referred to as distributor of

_____         _____
(Address)                                 (Address)

_____         _____
(City)                                    (City)

_____         _____
(County)                                  (County)

_____         _____
(State)                                   (State)

## RECITALS

The purpose of this agreement is to establish the distributor as an authorized, wholesale distributor for the sale and service of products of seller and to set forth the respective duties, obligations, and responsibilities of seller and of distributor in the sale of these products by seller to the distributor and the sale and servicing of these products by the distributor.

Distributor has elected to enter into this agreement with seller with confidence in seller's integrity and expressed intention to deal fairly with its distributors, and with knowledge of the customer acceptance of products of seller.

Seller has elected to enter into this agreement with distributor with recognition that seller's success depends upon financially sound, responsible, efficient, vigorous, and successful independent wholesale distributors whose business conduct is free of false, deceptive or misleading advertising, merchandising, pricing, and service practices, and with confidence in distributor's integrity and ability, and in the distributor's expressed intention to deal fairly with seller and its customers, and to perform and carry out distributor's duties, obligations, and responsibilities as set forth in this agreement.

It is the expectation of each of the parties that by entering into this agreement, and by the full and faithful observance and performance of its duties, obligations and responsibilities, a mutually satisfactory relationship between them will be established and maintained.

In consideration of the mutual agreements and acknowledgments herein made, the parties hereto agree as follows:

SECTION ONE—RIGHTS GRANTED—Seller hereby grants to distributor a non-exclusive right upon the terms and conditions hereinafter contained, to purchase, inventory, promote, and resell seller's products.

**SECTION TWO—PRODUCT COVERAGE—**As used herein, the term *seller's prod-ucts* shall mean and be limited to the service parts and accessories manufacture and/or sold by seller in the following categories: _____

(specify categories)

_____

_____

_____

**SECTION THREE—TERMS OF SALE—**All sales of seller's products to distributor shall be made under and subject to the provisions of this agreement at such prices and on such terms as seller shall establish from time to time. Resale prices shall be fixed by distributor except that seller reserves the right to enter into fair-trade agreements to the extent permitted by federal and state laws.

**SECTION FOUR—MARKETING POLICIES—**Distributor will at all times maintain adequate inventories of seller's products and will promote vigorously and effec-tively the sale of seller's products through all channels of distribution prevailing in distributor's primary marketing area in conformity with seller's established mar-keting policies and programs. Distributor will use its best efforts to sell seller's products to aggressive, reputable, and financially responsible dealers providing satisfactory consumer service throughout distributor's primary marketing area. Distributor is authorized to enter into written agreements with its dealers relating to the purchase, resale, and service of seller's products on forms approved by seller for this purpose.

**SECTION FIVE—MERCHANDISING POLICIES—**Seller will provide distributor with continuous and comprehensive merchandising assistance in the form of _____

(list

_____

types of assistance, such as national advertising programs, product and sales

_____

training, sales promotions)

and distributor agrees to make full use of such assistance in carrying out seller's merchandising and sales promotion policies.

**SECTION SIX—SALES POLICIES—**Sales quotas, giving reasonable regard to past performance and market potential of seller's products, may be established by seller from time to time. Distributor agrees to provide sales training and sales promotions, and distributor agrees to make full use of such assistance in carrying out seller's merchandising and sales promotion policies.

**SECTION SEVEN—ADVERTISING POLICIES—**Seller will cooperate with distribu-tor and its dealers in providing for continuous and effective advertising and pro-motion of seller's products throughout distributor's principal marketing area and distributor agrees to participate in, actively promote and faithfully comply with the terms and conditions of such cooperative advertising and merchandising pro-grams as seller may establish and offer to distributor from time to time.

SECTION EIGHT—PRODUCT WARRANTY POLICIES—(a) Seller's products are sold to distributor at prices which contemplate that such products are free from defect in manufacture and workmanship at the time of sale. In the event that any product is proved to seller's satisfaction to have been defective at time of sale, seller will make an appropriate adjustment in the original sales price of said product.

(b) Seller agrees to protect distributor and hold it harmless from any loss or claim arising out of inherent defects in any of seller's product existing at the time such product is sold by seller to distributor, provided that distributor gives seller immediate notice of any such loss or claim and cooperates fully with seller in the handling thereof. Distributor agrees to protect seller and hold it harmless from any loss or claim arising out of the negligence of distributor, distributor's agents, employees, or representatives in the installation, use sale or servicing of seller's products.

(c) In the event that any dealer shall, with respect to any of seller's products purchased from distributor, fail to discharge his or her obligations to the original consumer pursuant to the terms and conditions of seller's product warranty and consumer service policies, distributor agrees to discharge promptly said unfulfilled obligations.

SECTION NINE—ORDER PROCESSING AND SHIPMENT POLICES—Seller will employ all best efforts to fill distributor's orders promptly upon acceptance but reserves the right to allot available inventories as it deems best. Seller shall not be liable for failure to ship seller's products specified in any accepted order because of strikes, differences with workmen, inability to secure transportaion facilities, or other circumstances beyond its control. Distributor shall not be liable for failure to accept shipments of products ordered from seller when such failure is due to strikes or any other cause beyond distributor's control, provided seller receives notice in writing to suspend such shipments prior to delivery to carrier.

SECTION TEN—FINANCIAL POLICIES—It is the intent and understanding of the parties, and the essence of this agreement that distributor shall:

(a) Maintain and employ in connection with distributor's business and operations under this agreement such net working capital and net worth as may be required to enable distributor properly and fully to carry out and perform all of distributor's duties, obligations and responsibilities under this agreement.

(b) Pay promptly all amounts due seller in accordance with terms of sale extended by seller from time to time.

(c) Furnish seller with financial statements in such form as seller may reasonably require from time to time for credit purposes.

(d) Furnish, at seller's request, a detailed reconcilement of seller's statements of account with distributor's records, listing all differences, and showing net amount distributor acknowledges to be due seller.

Shipments may be suspended at seller's discretion in the event that distributor fails to promptly and faithfully discharge each and every provision of this paragraph.

SECTION ELEVEN—USE OF SELLER'S NAME—Distributor will not use, authorize or permit the use of, the name " _____ " or any other trademark
(seller's name)
owned by seller as part of its firm, corporate or business name or in any way, except to designate products purchased from seller under the terms of this agreement. Distributor shall not contest the right of seller to exclusive use of any trademark or trade name used or claimed by seller.

SECTION TWELVE—RELATIONSHIP OF PARTIES—During the term hereof the relation between seller and distributor is that of merchandiser and vendor. Distributor, its agents, and employees shall, under no circumstances, be deemed agents or representatives of seller. Distributor will not modify any of seller's products without written permission from seller. Distributor will not modify any of seller's products without written permission from seller. Neither distributor nor seller shall have any right to enter into any contract or commitment in the name of, or on behalf of the other, or to bind the other in any respect whatsoever.

SECTION THIRTEEN—TERM OF AGREEMENT—This agreement shall continue in full force and effect from and after the date as of which this agreement has been executed until terminated by either party under the provisions of Paragraph 14 hereof.

SECTION FOURTEEN—TERMINATION—The following provisions shall govern the termination of the agreement:

(a) Either party may terminate without cause by written notice given to the other not less than _____ days prior to the effective date of such notice.
(number)

(b) Seller may terminate at any time by written notice given to distributor not less than _____ days prior to the effective day of such notice in the event
(number)
seller decides to terminate all outstanding parts-and-accessories distributor agreements and to offer a new or amended form of distributor agreement.

(c) Seller may terminate by notice given to distributor, effective immediately, in any of the following events: (a) failure to distributor to fulfill or perform any one or more of the duties, obligations, or responsibilities undertaken by him or her pursuant to SECTIONS TEN, ELEVEN, and TWELVE, (b) any assignment or attempted assignment by distributor of any interest in this agreement with seller's written consent; (c) any sale, transfer, or relinquishment, voluntary or involuntary, by operation of law or otherwise of any material interest in the direct or indirect ownership or any change in the management of the distributor; (d) failure of distributor for any reason to function in the ordinary course of business; (e) a disagreement between or among managers, principals, partners, officers or stockholders of distributor which in the opinion of seller may affect adversely the ownership, operation, management, business or interest of distributor or seller; (f) conviction in a court of competent jurisdiction of distributor, or a manager, partner, principal officer or major stockholder thereof for any violation of law tending, in seller's opinion, to affect adversely the operation or business of distributor or the good name, goodwill, or reputation of seller, products of seller, or distributor;

or (g) submission by distributor to seller of false or fraudulent reports or statements, including without limitation, claims for any refund, credit, rebate, incentive, allowance, discount, reimbursement or other payment by seller.

(d) In the event either party has any business relations with the other party after termination of this agreement, such relations shall not be construed as a renewal of this agreement or as a waiver of such termination, but all such transactions shall be governed by terms identical with the provisions of this agreement relating thereto unless the parties hereto execute a new agreement superceding this agreement.

SECTION FIFTEEN—OBLIGATIONS UPON TERMINATION—Upon termination of this agreement distributor shall cease to be an authorized distributor of seller and:

(a) All amounts owing by distributor to seller shall, notwithstanding prior terms of sale, become immediately due and payable.

(b) All unshipped orders shall be canceled without liability of either party to the other.

(c) Distributor will resell and deliver to seller upon demand, free and clear of all liens and encumberances, such of seller's products and materials bearing seller's name as seller shall elect to repurchase, at a mutually agreed price but not in excess of seller's current distributor price for said products and materials.

(d) Neither party shall be liable to the other because of such termination for compensation, reimbursement or damages on account of the loss of prospective profits or anticipated sales, or on account of expenditures, investments, leases, or commitments in connection with the business or good will of seller or the distributor or for any other reason whatsoever growing out of such termination.

SECTION SIXTEEN—USE OF NAME PROHIBITED AFTER TERMINATION—Upon termination of this agreement, distributor will remove and not thereafter use any sign containing the name and trademark "_____", or any
(seller's name)

other trademark owned by seller and immediately destroy all stationery, advertising matter and other printed matter in its possession or under its control containing the word "_____", or such other trademarks.
(seller's name)

Distributor will not at any time after such termination use or permit any such trademark to be used in any manner in connection with any business conducted by it or in which it may have an interest, or otherwise whatsoever as descriptive of or referring to anything other than merchandise or products of seller. Regardless of the cause of termination, distributor will immediately take all appropriate steps to remove and cancel its listings in telephone books, and other directories, and public records, or elsewhere which contain the name "_____"
(seller's name)

or other such trademarks. If distributor fails to obtain such removals or cancellations promptly, seller may make application for such removals or cancellations on behalf of distributor and in distributor's name and in such event distributor will render every assistance.

SECTION SEVENTEEN—ACKNOWLEDGEMENTS—Each party acknowledges that no representation or statement, and no understanding or agreement, has been made, or exists, and that in entering into this agreement, he or she has not relied upon anything done or said or upon any presumption in fact or in law, (a) with respect to this agreement, or to the duration, termination, or renewal of this agreement, or with respect to the relationship between the parties, other than as expressly set forth in this agreement; or (b) that in any way tends to change or modify the terms, or any of them, of this agreement or to prevent this agreement becoming effective; or (c) that in any way affects or relates to the subject matter hereof. Distributor also acknowledges that the terms and conditions of this agreement, and each of them, are reasonable and fair and equitable.

SECTION EIGHTEEN—TERMINATION OF PRIOR AGREEMENTS—This agreement terminates and supersedes all prior seller-distributor agreements, if any, between the parties hereto.

SECTION NINETEEN—ASSIGNMENTS—Neither this agreement or any right hereunder nor interest herein may be assigned by distributor.

SECTION TWENTY—NO IMPLIED WAIVERS—Except as expressly provided in this agreement, waiver by either party, or failure by either party to claim a breach, of any provision of this agreement shall not be, or held to be a waiver of any breach or subsequent breach, or as affecting in any way the effectiveness of such provision.

SECTION TWENTY-ONE—EFFECT OF DETERMINATION BY SELLER—Any determination to be made, opinion to be formed, or discretion to be exercised by seller in connection with any provision of this agreement shall be made, formed or exercised by seller alone and shall be final, conclusive and binding upon the parties hereto.

SECTION TWENTY-TWO—NOTICES—Any notices required or permitted by this agreement, or given in connection herewith, shall be in writing and may be by personal delivery or by first-class registered mail, postage prepaid. Notices to seller shall be delivered to or addressed to the office of the secretary or seller at:

_____
(Address)

_____
(City)

_____
(County)

_____
(State)

Notices to distributor shall be delivered to or addressed to distributor at distributor's principal place of business set forth herein.

SECTION TWENTY-THREE—AMENDMENT—Notwithstanding anything in this agreement to the contrary, seller shall have the right to amend, modify, or change this agreement in case of legislation, government regulation, or changes in circumstance beyond the control of seller that might affect materially the relationship between seller and distributor.

**SECTION TWENTY-FOUR—EXECUTION ON BEHALF OF SELLER**—This agreement shall bind seller when it bears the signature of _____
(appropriate officer of
_____ of seller and is delivered to distributor. Distributor acknowledges
seller)
notice that no one except _____ of seller is author-
(appropriate officer of seller)
ized to make or execute any other agreement relating to the subject matter hereof on behalf of seller, or in any manner to enlarge, vary or modify the terms of this agreement, and to terminate this agreement on behalf of seller, and then only by an instrument in writing.

**SECTION TWENTY-FIVE—GOVERNING LAW**—This agreement has been signed by distributor and sent to seller for final approval and execution, and has been signed and delivered on behalf of seller. The parties hereto intend this agreement to be executed as an agreement of the State of _____
and to be construed in accordance with the laws of the State of
_____.

In witness whereof, the parties have executed this agreement in the City of _____ , State of _____ on
_____, 19_____.
(month)          (day)                    (yr.)


_____          _____
(Signature of Distributor)          (Signature of Seller)

# EXCLUSIVE DISTRIBUTORSHIP CONTRACT

Agreement made this _____, 19_____, between (month and day)

_____ and _____
(Name of company)                    (Name of distributor)
herein referred to as company, of    herein referred to as distributor, of

_____              _____
(Address)                            (Address)

_____              _____
(City)                               (City)

_____              _____
(County)                             (County)

_____              _____
(State)                              (State)

SECTION ONE—EXCLUSIVE APPOINTMENT—Distributor is hereby appointed on an exclusive basis for the sale of the company's _____ and (principal product)

other products in the territory composed of _____ (specify territory)

for the period commencing _____, 19_____, and terminating (month)        (year)

_____, 19_____. The company assumes no responsibility, (month)      (year)

however, with regard to any of its products that may be shipped into distributor's territory by others. The company furthermore reserves the right to sell in the territory of distributor any of its products or parts thereof to the United States, any state government, any department or bureau thereof, and any contractor or subcontractor thereof.

SECTION TWO—RESTRICTIONS ON DISTRIBUTORSHIP—Distributor agrees not to solicit or accept orders for, or sell, or deliver, outside of such territory, any merchandise manufactured or sold by the company. Distributor will not sell, distribute, or promote the sale of any line of products competitive to those supplies by the company either in such territory or elsewhere.

SECTION THREE—DUTIES OF DISTRIBUTOR—Distributor agrees to promote the sale of the company's products in such territory, to maintain a sales organization of sufficient size to cover the territory and to serve the trade in the territory promptly and adequately, to furnish to the company such reports, information, and data as the company may from time to time require, and to conform to all merchandising policies of the company as may be from time to time announced.

SECTION FOUR—COMPLIANCE WITH AGREEMENT—Distributor hereby accepts such appointment and agrees to make all sales of the company's merchandise only in accordance with this agreement.

In witness whereof, the parties have executed this agreement in the City of _____, State of _____, the day and year first above written.

_____              _____
(Signature of company)               (Signature of distributor)

## APPLICATION FOR EMPLOYER IDENTIFICATION NUMBER

Every business that starts operation needs to apply to the Department of the Treasury, Internal Revenue Service (IRS) for a Form SS-4. After processing the completed form, the IRS will then assign an identification number to the business which must be used on all tax returns and other official papers and correspondence.

Form **SS-4**

(Rev. August 1988)
Department of the Treasury
Internal Revenue Service

# Application for Employer Identification Number

(For use by employers and others. Please read the attached instructions before completing this form.) **Please type or print clearly.**

1  Name of applicant (True legal name. See instructions.)

2  Trade name of business if different from item 1

3  Executor, trustee, "care of name"

4  Mailing address (street address) (room, apt., or suite no.)

5  Address of business, if different from item 4. (See instructions.)

4a  City, state, and ZIP code

5a  City, state, and ZIP code

6  County and State where principal business is located

7  Name of principal officer, grantor, or general partner. (See instructions.) ▶

8  Type of entity (Check only one.) (See instructions.)

☐ Individual SSN _____
☐ REMIC
☐ State/local government    ☐ National guard
☐ Other nonprofit organization (specify)_____
☐ Farmers' cooperative
☐ Estate    ☐ Trust
☐ Other (specify) ▶

☐ Plan administrator SSN _____
☐ Personal service corp.
☐ Other corporation (specify) _____
☐ Federal government/military

☐ Partnership

☐ Church or church controlled organization

If nonprofit organization enter GEN (if applicable)_____

8a  If a corporation, give name of foreign country (if applicable) or state in the U.S. where incorporated ▶

Foreign country

State

9  Reason for applying (check only one)

☐ Started new business
☐ Hired employees
☐ Created a pension plan (specify type) ▶_____
☐ Banking purpose (specify) ▶

☐ Changed type of organization (specify) ▶_____
☐ Purchased going business
☐ Created a trust (specify) ▶_____
☐ Other (specify) ▶

10  Business start date or acquisition date (Mo., day, year) (See instructions.)

11  Enter closing month of accounting year (See instructions.)

12  First date wages or annuities were paid or will be paid (Mo., day, year). **Note:** *If applicant is a withholding agent, enter date income will first be paid to nonresident alien. (Mo., day, year).*   .   .   .   .   .   .   .   .   .   .   .   .   .   .   .   .   .   .   ▶

13  Enter highest number of employees expected in the next 12 months. **Note:** *If the applicant does not expect to have any employees during the period, enter "0."*   .   .   .   .   .   .   .   .   .   .   ▶

| Nonagricultural | Agricultural | Household |
|---|---|---|
| | | |

14  Does the applicant operate more than one place of business?   .   .   .   .   .   .   .   .   .   .   .   .   ☐ Yes   ☐ No
    If "Yes," enter name of business. ▶

15  Principal activity or service (See instructions.) ▶

16  Is the principal business activity manufacturing?.   .   .   .   .   .   .   .   .   .   .   .   .   .   .   ☐ Yes   ☐ No
    If "Yes," principal product and raw material used. ▶

17  To whom are most of the products or services sold?  Please check the appropriate box.          ☐ Business (wholesale)
    ☐ Public (retail)          ☐ Other (specify) ▶          ☐ N/A

18  Has the applicant ever applied for an identification number for this or any other business?.   .   .   .   .   .   .   .   ☐ Yes   ☐ No
    **Note:** *If "Yes," please answer items 18a and 18b.*

18a  If the answer to item 18 is "Yes," give applicant's true name and trade name, if different when applicant applied.

    True name ▶                                        Trade name ▶

18b  Enter approximate date, city, and state where the application was filed and the previous employer identification number if known.

| Approximate date when filed (Mo., day, year) | City, and state where filed | Previous EIN |
|---|---|---|
| | | |

Under penalties of perjury, I declare that I have examined this application, and to the best of my knowledge and belief, it is true, correct, and complete.

Telephone number (include area code)

Name and title (please type or print clearly) ▶

Signature ▶                                        Date ▶

**Note:** *Do not write below this line.    For official use only.*

| Please leave blank ▶ | Geo. | Ind. | Class | Reason for applying |
|---|---|---|---|---|
| | | | | |

**For Paperwork Reduction Act Notice, see instructions.**          ✶U.S. Government Printing Office: 1988-523-133/00332          Form **SS-4** (Rev. 8-88)

## EQUIPMENT LEASING AGREEMENT

This agreement is unusually long, but it covers a lot of ground. For most small business people it is largely unexplored ground. Leasing rather than buying equipment can be an advantage for most business people, especially if they are undercapitalized. Leasing, even if it costs a little more than buying equipment outright, can conserve much needed capital. If the lease costs 10 percent more than comparable equipment purchased outright, then that cost might be equivalent to the 10 percent interest paid on a loan—provided such borrowed capital is available. Another advantage to leased equipment is that expected obsolescence is avoided. At the end of a lease period, the equipment can be turned in for a new model—or dropped altogether, if it was found that the leased equipment was not cost-effective. Still, leasing equipment can be quite complicated. The agreement here spells out the many possible pitfalls and problems. Even if some or most of them are not applicable, it flags the entrepreneur on the possible pitfalls before they have a chance to happen.

# EQUIPMENT LEASING AGREEMENT

This rental agreement, made the _____ day of _____, 19_____, by and between _____ (hereinafter called Lessor) located at _____, and _____, (hereinafter called Lessee) located at _____.

WITNESSETH

1. EQUIPMENT—The Lessee hereby leases from the Lessor, and the Lessor leases to the Lessee, the following personal property (hereinafter called "Equipment"), on the terms and conditions set forth below:

2. WARRANT INDEMNITY AND DAMAGES—Lessor will purchase at its cost a 100 percent service contract from the equipment installer to provide service for all Equipment listed above, for the term of this Lease. The Lessor is hereby released from any and all liability by the Lessee for any and all damages that might be caused either directly or indirectly by failure of said Equipment.

3. TERM—This rental agreement shall continue in force for a term of _____ beginning on the _____ day of _____, 19_____ and ending on the _____, 19_____.

4. INSTALLATION COST—Lessee agrees to pay on presentation of a billing all installation cost for the Equipment being installed.

5. RENT AND OTHER CHARGES—During and for the term hereof, commencing on the commencement date, Lessee covenants and agrees to pay Lessor for the listed Equipment, without previous notice or demand therefor, and without deduction, set-off or abatement a monthly rental of _____ for each and every month for the term of the agreement. Said monthly payment is due in advance on the _____ day of each month beginning _____. Lessee covenants and agrees to pay, as additional rent, a late fee equal to 10 percent (10%) of any rent due, if said payments are not paid within fifteen (15) days of their due date. All payments due under the terms of the Lease shall be made to the office of _____. Rent checks are to be made payable to _____.

6. LOCATION—The Equipment shall be installed at above location of the Lessee and thereafter kept at that location and shall not be removed therefrom without Lessor's prior written consent.

7. ASSIGNMENT—Without Lessor's prior written consent, Lessee shall not (a) assign, transfer, pledge, hypothecate or otherwise dispose of this Lease or any interest therein, or (b) sublet or lend the Equipment or permit it to be used by anyone other than Lessee or Lessee's employees.

Lessee shall keep the Equipment free and clear of all levies, liens and encumbrances. Lessor may assign this Lease and/or mortgage in Equipment, in whole or in part, without notice to Lessee; and its assignee or mortgagee may reassign this Lease and/or such mortgage, without notice to Lessee. Each such assignee and /or mortgagee shall have all of the rights but none of the obligations of Lessor under this Lease. Lessee shall recognize each such assignment and/or mortgage and shall not assert against the assignee and/or mortgagee any defense, counterclaim, or set-off that Lessee may have against Lessor. Subject to the foregoing, this Lease insures to the benefit of and is binding upon heirs, legatees, personal representatives, survivors and assigns of the parties hereto.

8. USE—Lessee shall use the Equipment in a careful manner and shall comply with all laws relating to its possession, use or maintenance.

9. INSPECTION—At all reasonable times during business hours, Lessor shall have the right to inspect the Equipment and to observe its use.

10. ALTERATIONS—Lessee shall not make any alterations, additions or improvements to the Equipment without Lessor's prior written consent. All additions and improvements made to the Equipment shall belong to and become the property of Lessor.

11. INSURANCE: LOSS AND DAMAGE TO EQUIPMENT: INDEMNITIES—

   (a) Lessee shall and hereby agrees to maintain in force, during the Initial Lease Term hereof and renewal thereof, adequate public liability insurance covering the Equipment and insuring both Lessee and Lessor against any loss, damage, claim, suit, action, or liability arising out of the ownership, possession, maintenance, operation or use of the Equipment.

   Without relieving Lessee from its contractual obligation to maintain such insurance or from its liability for failure to do so, it is agreed that in the event of such failure, or if such insurance proves to be inadequate to pay in full any loss, damage, claim, suit, action or liability of or against Lessor and relating to the Equipment or arising out of its ownership, possession, maintenance, operation or use, then Lessee, in any such event, hereby indemnifies and agrees to save Lessor harmless against and from any such loss, damage, claim, suit, action, or liability whatsoever.

   (b) Lessee will provide at its own expense "All-Risk" Physical Damage Insurance covering the Equipment naming Lessor as "named insured" and will provide Lessor the original of said insurance policy. The limits of said policy will be an amount not less than $_____, and will conform with any co-insurance requirements of any such insurance contract. If, however, the Equipment shall consist in whole or in part of licensed motor vehicles, then as to such vehicles, in lieu of the insurance coverage described in the foregoing provisions, Lessee will provide, at its own expense, comprehensive insurance (actual cash value) and One Hundred Dollars ($100.00) deductible collision insurance covering Lessor as the owner of such vehicles. Should any Equipment listed in (1) above be of a further specialized nature, Lessee will provide, at Lessee's expense, the form of insurance policy suitable to such specialized equipment. Lessee hereby appoints Lessor its attorney-in-fact to make claim for, receive payment of and execute or endorse all documents, checks or drafts for loss or damage or return premium under any insurance policy issued as to the Equipment.

Lessee shall promptly, on acquiring knowledge thereof, notify Lessor of any loss, damage, injury, or accident involving the Equipment, and shall make available to Lessor all information and documents pertinent thereto.

(c) Lessee hereby assumes and shall bear the entire risk of loss and damage to the Equipment from any and every cause whatsoever to the extent not covered by the foregoing provisions relating to insurance. No loss or damage to the Equipment or any part thereof shall relieve Lessee from any obligations to pay the rent provided in this Lease, except and only to the extent that Lessor shall be satisfied and made whole from the insurance coverage above described. In the event of loss or damage of any kind whatsoever to any item of Equipment which is not so covered by such insurance coverage, it shall: (i) replace the same in good repair, condition and working order; or (ii) replace the same with like equipment in good repair condition and working order, and execute the necessary instruments to subject such replacement equipment to the terms of this Lease.

Lessee agrees to indemnify Lessor against and hold it harmless from any and all claims, actions, suits, proceedings, costs, expenses, fines, damages, and liabilities, including counsel fees, arising out of, connected with, or resulting from the Equipment, including, without limitation, its manufacture, selection, delivery, possession, and use of operation.

12. SURRENDER—Upon the expiration or earlier termination of this Lease, Lessee shall return the Equipment in good repair (at its expense), ordinary wear and tear resulting from proper use thereof, excepted.

13. TAXES—During the Initial Lease Term and any renewal thereof, Lessee shall keep the Equipment free and clear of all liens and encumbrances and shall pay all license fees, personal property taxes, sales taxes, registration and recording fees, assessments, charges and taxes, (municipal, state and federal), if any, which may now or hereafter be imposed upon the ownership, leasing, sale, possession or use of the Equipment

other than income taxes. If Lessee fails to pay any said fees, assessments, charges or taxes, Lessor shall have the right, but shall not be obligated, to pay the same, in which event, the cost thereof shall be repayable to Lessor with the regular payment of rent. Lessee's obligations hereunder shall continue after the expiration of the Initial Lease Term and any renewal thereof as to those expenses incurred or accrued during such terms.

14. DEFAULT—If Lessee fails to pay any rent or other amount herein provided within fifteen (15) days after the same is due and payable, or if Lessee fails to perform any other provision hereof within ten (10) days after the Lessor shall have demanded in writing performance thereof, or if any proceeding in bankruptcy, receivership or insolvency shall be commenced by or against Lessee or its property, or if Lessee makes any assignment for the benefit of its creditors, Lessor shall have the right but shall not be obligated to exercise any one or more of the following remedies: (a) to sue for and recover all rents and other amounts then due or thereafter accruing under this lease; (b) to take possession of any and all of the Equipment, wherever it may be located, without demand or notice, without any court order or other process of law, and without incurring any liability to Lessee for any damages occasioned by such taking of possession; (c) to sell any or all of the Equipment at public or private sale for cash or on credit and to recover from Lessee all costs of taking possession, storing, repairing and selling the Equipment, an amount equal to 10 percent (10%) Of the actual cost to Lessor of the Equipment sold, and the unpaid balance of the total rent for the initial term of this Lease attributable to the Equipment sold, less the net proceeds of such sale; (d) to terminate this Lease as to any or all items of Equipment; (e) in the event Lessor elects to terminate this lease as to any or all items of Equipment, to recover from Lessee as to each item subject to said termination the worth at the time of such termination, of the excess, if any, of the amount of rent reserved herein for said item for the balance of the term hereof over the then reasonable rental value of said item for the same period of time; (f) to pursue any other remedy now or hereafter existing at law or in equity. Notwithstanding any such action that Lessor may take, including taking possession of any or all of the Equipment, Lessee shall remain liable for the full performance of all its obligations hereunder, provided, however, that if Lessor in writing terminates this Lease, as to any item of Equipment, Lessee shall not be liable for rent in respect of such item accruing after the date of such termination. In addition to the foregoing, Lessee shall pay Lessor all costs and expenses, including reasonable attorney's fees incurred by Lessor in exercising any of its rights or remedies hereunder.

15. NOTICES—Any written notice or demand under this agreement may be given to a party by mailing it to the party at its address set forth above, or at such address as the party may provide in writing from time to time. Notice or demand so mailed shall be effective when deposited in the United States mail, duly addressed and with postage prepaid.

16. CHOICE OF LAW—This Lease shall be governed by and construed in accordance with the laws of the State of _____.

17. OWNERSHIP—The Equipment is, and shall at all times remain, the property of the Lessor; and Lessee shall have no right, title or interest herein thereto except as expressly set forth in this Lease. Lessor may attach identifying labels on Equipment.

18. ENTIRE AGREEMENT: WAIVER—This instrument constitutes the entire agreement between Lessor and Lessee. No agent or employee of the supplier is authorized to bind Lessor, to waive or alter any term or condition printed herein or add any provision hereto. Except as provided in paragraph 5 hereof, a provision may be added hereto or a provision hereof may be altered or varied only by a writing signed and made a part hereof by an authorized officer of Lessor. Waiver by Lessor of any provision hereof in one instance shall not constitute a waiver as to any other instance.

In witness whereof, the parties hereto set their hands and seals:

**Witness or Attest By:**     Date:     For:   Lessor

_____   _____   _____

                                      By

**Witness or Attest By:**     Date:     For:   Lessee

_____   _____   _____

                                      By

**FREEDOM OF INFORMATION REQUEST**

A national law called the Freedom of Information Act was passed by Congress in 1966 and amended in 1974 and 1976. Under its provisions an individual or a business can petition any government agency for information within its files—except in matters of national security. This act established the principle that the public has the right to know what the federal agencies do on the taxpayer's behalf. It makes federal government decisions and records more accessible to any citizen. The enclosed form can be used to make your request to any federal agency.

# FREEDOM OF INFORMATION ACT/ PRIVACY ACT REQUEST

**Attn:**

This is a request under provisions of Title 5 USC, Sec. 552, the Freedom of Information Act, and Title 5 USC, Sec. 552a, the Privacy Act.

Please furnish me with copies of all records on me retrievable by the use of an individual identifier and by the use of any combination of identifiers (e.g., name + date of birth + Social Security number, and so on) that are contained in the following systems of records:

In order to identify myself and to facilitate your search of records systems, I provide the following information:

| Last Name | First | Middle | |
|---|---|---|---|

| Street | City | State | Zip |
|---|---|---|---|

| Date of Birth | Place of Birth | Sex | Social Security No. |
|---|---|---|---|

## GENERAL PARTNERSHIP AGREEMENT

Entering into a partnership to conduct a business together, even among relatives, is one of the most sensitive and potentially destructive business acts possible. An agreement executed prior to the start of the business together is most vital. It is like a marriage contract and if every exigency is not anticipated ahead of time and spelled out clearly in this document, disagreements that can crop up in later years can lead to circumstances worse than a divorce. It must be emphasized that such an agreement is very important. No partnership should be started without the clear understanding of all common and mutual problems, made at a time when heads are clear and relationships unencumbered with possible business and financial problems. If no unanimity exists on these or additional terms you might wish to add, an ombudsman should be employed to iron out all points in dispute. This could be an attorney, an accountant, a banker, or a friend known to and trusted by both sides, but preferably not a relative.

# GENERAL PARTNERSHIP AGREEMENT

THIS GENERAL PARTNERSHIP AGREEMENT is made and entered as of the _____ day of _____, 19    , by and among the undersigned parties.

<u>WITNESSETH:</u>

WHEREAS, the parties hereto desire to join together in a partnership pursuant to the Uniform Partnership Act of the State of                    for the purposes of (i) purchasing property located in the State of                 , and being more particularly described on Schedule B (attached hereto): (ii) holding the property as an investment and for the production of income; and (iii) carrying on any and all activities related thereto; and

WHEREAS, the parties hereto desire to set forth in full and in writing the terms and provisions of their agreements and understandings in this General Partnership Agreement (hereinafter "Agreement").

NOW, THEREFORE, in consideration of the foregoing, of the mutual promises of the parties hereto, and of other good and valuable consideration, the receipt and sufficiency of which is hereby acknowledged, it is hereby agreed as follows:

1. <u>Formation of Partnership.</u> The undersigned parties do hereby form a general partnership (hereinafter "Partnership"), pursuant to the Uniform Partnership Act of the State of Maryland.

2. <u>Principal Office of Partnership.</u> The principal office and place of business of the Partnership shall be
                , and may have such other or additional offices as the partners shall deem advisable.

3. <u>Business of the Partnership.</u> The business of the Partnership shall consist of (i) acquiring and owning in the Partnership Property; (ii) leasing, selling, maintaining, or operating the Partnership Property as an investment and for the production of income; and (iii) carrying on any and all activities related thereto.

4. <u>Partners; Percentages of Partnership Interest.</u> Unless otherwise indicated, (i) the terms "partner" and "partners" shall mean those persons designated as in Schedule A, and (ii) the percentage shown after the name of each partner in Schedule A shall represent the "partnership interest" or "partnership interests" of such partner for all purposes of this Agreement.

5. <u>Capital Contributions; Capital Accounts.</u>

A.  The partners shall contribute cash or property in the proportion shown opposite their respective names on Schedule A, and such amount shall constitute the Partners' respective "Capital Accounts."

B.  The The Capital Accounts of the Partners shall be increased to reflect the partners' respective shares of partnership profits or additional contributions, and shall be reduced to reflect the Partners' respective shares of partnership losses, deductions or distributions.

6. <u>Profits and Losses.</u> The profit of the Partnership shall be shared and the losses of the Partnership shall be borne, by the partners, *pro rata,* in proportion to their respective percentages of partnership interest.

7. **Term of Partnership.** The term of the Partnership shall commence as of the date of execution of this Agreement, and it shall continue until _____, and thereafter from year to year, unless previously terminated in accordance with provisions hereinafter stated.

8. **Legal Title to Partnership Property.**

A. The "Partnership Property" shall consist of and mean the property described on Schedule B (attached hereto), and any additions to the property of the Partnership to the extent representing Capital Contributions or purchased with Partnership funds or with funds procured by the Partnership or any of the partners on behalf of the Partnership.

Legal title to the Partnership Property shall be held in the name of the Partnership, or in whatever other manner the partners determine to be in the best interests of the Partnership. The partners may arrange to have title taken and held in the name of trustees, nominees or straw parties including the partners, for the Partnership.

B. It is expressly understood and agreed that the manner of holding title to the Partnership Property (or any part thereof) is solely for the convenience of the Partnership; accordingly, the spouse, heirs, executors or administrators, beneficiaries, distributees, successors, or assigns of any partner shall have no right, title or interest in or to any Partnership Property by reason of the manner in which title is held, but all such property shall be treated as Partnership Property subject to the terms of this Agreement.

9. **Management of Business.** Acting with the express approval of all partners, any partner may contract with any person, firm or corporation, including itself or any partner, as an entity and any firm or corporation in which it (or any of the partners) may have an interest, at reasonable and competitive rates of compensation, commission or remuneration, for (i) the development, construction, management and maintenance of the Partnership Property, (ii) the placement of refinancing or mortgages on the Partnership Property, (iii) the lease, sale, assignment, or transfer of the Partnership's interest in the Partnership Property (or any part thereof), as well as any other services which may at any time be necessary, proper, convenient or advisable to conduct the business of the Partnership.

10. **Distribution of Net Cash Flow, Sale and Refinancing Proceeds.**

A. So far as practicable, any net cash flow of the Partnership shall be distributed semi-annually among the partners, but such distribution may be made more or less frequently if the partners shall deem it advisable to do so.

B. For all purposes of this Agreement, the term "net cash flow" shall mean any funds available for distribution.

C. The net cash flow of the Partnership available for distribution shall be distributed among all of the partners in proportion to their respective Capital Accounts to the extent of such Capital Accounts, and thereafter in proportion to their respective shares of Partnership interest.

D. Notwithstanding any other provisions of this Agreement in the event of the refinancing (which term "refinancing" is hereby defined for all purposes of this Agreement to include the recasting, modifying, increasing or extending) of any mortgage on any of the Partnership Property, and if the Partnership is not dissolved or the Partnership Property sold, any proceeds that are not used to finance capital improvements or replacements (hereinafter in this Agreement sometimes referred to as "excess refinancing proceeds"), shall, after payment of or provision for (to the extent the partners deem appropriate) all liabilities to creditors of the Partnership (including the repayment of any loans made to the Partnership), be distributed as net cash flow pursuant to Paragraph 10C.

11. Assignability of Partnership Interests.

A. The partners shall not transfer, assign, pledge, encumber, sell or otherwise dispose of their interests as partners in the Partnership or enter into any agreement as a result of which any person, firm or corporation shall have a partnership interest, either alone or with it, in the Partnership, without the consent of all of the other partners.

B. Unless named in this Agreement, no person shall be considered a partner hereof. The Partnership, each partner and any other person having business with the Partnership need deal only with partners so named; they shall not be required to deal with any person by reason of an assignment by a partner or by reason of the dissolution or liquidation of a partner.

12. Dissolution of Partnership.

A. The Partnership shall be dissolved upon the occurrence of any of the following events:

The adjudication of insanity, incompetency, the dissolution, liquidation or bankruptcy (or death) of any partner, the withdrawal of any partner, or the occurrence of any other event causing the dissolution of a partnership under the laws of the State of Maryland.

B. Upon dissolution of the Partnership, the remaining partner (that is, the partner other than the insane, incompetent, bankrupt, liquidated, deceased, withdrawn, or insolvent partner), or in the case of dissolution, all other partners shall continue to operate the Partnership business in the ordinary course pending commencement of any winding up of the Partnership affairs.

C. In the event of the dissolution of the Partnership by reason of the events specified in Paragraph A, then the remaining partner (if there is one) shall elect whether or not to continue ownership of the Partnership property. If the remaining partner shall elect to continue, he shall provide a written appraisal of the Partnership property to the outgoing partner within thirty (30) days of the event of dissolution and the appraised value provided shall govern as the selling price, unless the outgoing partner objects to it, and provides a second written appraisal of the property to the remaining partner within sixty (60) days of the event of dissolution. If the partners cannot then agree upon a purchase price, the appraisers named by the respective partners shall appoint a third appraiser who shall provide a written appraisal within ninety (90) days of the event of dissolution, and the appraisal of the third appraiser shall govern. The remaining partner shall pay to the outgoing partner a sum equal to (i) the Percentage of Interest of the outgoing partner times the agreed value of the Partnership property reduced by (ii) the amount of any negative Capital Account balance, within ninety (90) days of the third appraiser's report (or, if sooner, the date upon which the parties agree as to the value of such property). The cost of any appraisal shall be borne by the appointing partner, except that the fee of the third appraiser shall be borne by all partners in proportion to their respective Percentages of Interest. In the event the Partnership is to be dissolved, the provisions of Paragraph D shall apply.

D. In the event the remaining partner decides not to continue, then all of the partners shall proceed with dispatch and without any unnecessary delay to sell or otherwise liquidate the assets and property of the Partnership, and after paying or duly providing for all liabilities to creditors of the Partnership, to distribute the net proceeds and any other liquid assets of the Partnership among the partners in the manner set forth in Paragraph 10C hereof.

E. Any net proceeds from the sale or other disposition of all or substantially all of the property of the Partnership and any other liquid assets of the Partnership shall (to the extent thereof), after payment of or provision for all liabilities (loans made to the Partnership), be distributed among all the partners hereof as net cash flow pursuant to Paragraph 10C of this Agreement.

13. <u>Miscellaneous Provisions.</u>

A. The use of any gender herein shall be deemed to be or include the other genders and the use of the singular herein shall be deemed to be or include the plural (and *vice versa*), wherever appropriate.

B. This Agreement sets forth all (and is intended by all parties hereto to be an integration of all) of the promises, agreements, conditions, understandings, warranties, and representations among the parties hereto with respect to the Partnership, the Partnership business and the Partnership Property, and there are not understandings, warranties or representations, oral or written, express or implied, among them other than as set forth herein.

C. All exhibits hereto are hereby incorporated herein by reference.

14. <u>Governing Law.</u> It is the intention of the parties hereto that all questions with respect to the construction of this Agreement and the rights and liabilities of the parties hereto shall be determined in accordance with the laws of the State of Maryland.

15. <u>Burden and Benefit.</u> This Agreement is binding upon, and inures to the benefit of, the parties hereto and their respective spouses, heirs, executors, administrators, personal and legal representatives, successors, and assigns.

IN WITNESS WHEREOF, the undersigned partners have affixed their signatures and seals as of the day and year first above written.

WITNESS:                                          PARTNERS:

_____        _____

_____        _____

Attach Schedule A
with names of Partners, Addresses,
Percentage of Interest of each,
and Capital Contributions of each

## GUARANTEE FOR PAYMENT

This document is a very tricky one. It concerns a third party who will guarantee or co-sign a debt to another party. For example, a business associate or relative, or in many cases an adult child, makes a loan or buys a house or a car, but does not have sufficient credit or collateral to swing the deal. The guarantor then is asked and does co-sign a note guaranteeing to the lender (property owner, banker, auto dealer, et al.) that the debt will be paid—if not by the recipient then by the guarantor or guarantors. This obligation continues in force until liquidated, no matter what the circumstances. The danger here exists that (1) the guarantor often is under emotional or moral pressure to guarantee the debt, and (2) the beneficiary of the loan or property is usually an adult child, relative or close associate and it is very difficult if not impossible to deny such a request. Sometimes such a guarantee comes up at a future date when the guarantor has all but forgotten that he has co-signed on a deal in which he has absolutely no benefit. Guarantees for Payment require careful consideration, possibly devoid of any emotional impact, as other more direct forms of giving could be considered preferable.

# GUARANTEE FOR PAYMENT

In consideration of the Creditor _____
accepting the payment promise of the Debtor _____
the undersigned Guarantor _____
hereby unconditionally guarantees the Creditor prompt and full payment of all amounts which are now or may become owing by the Debtor to the Creditor.
The obligation of the Guarantor under this guarantee is limited to a maximum amount of _____ dollars ($ _____ ).
This guarantee is intended to operate notwithstanding any renewals, extensions, or indulgences of any kind granted the Debtor by the Creditor, or the release or change of any security given by the Debtor to the Creditor to secure the Debtor's payment promise ("Security"), or any failure or neglect on the part of the Creditor to enforce payment by the Debtor or to protect any Security, and the Creditor may call upon the guarantee as a first, principal obligation without previously demanding payment from the Debtor or any co-guarantor or realizing any Security.
This guarantee is also intended to operate as a continuing, absolute obligation and remains in force until revoked by notice in writing from the Guarantor to the Creditor, which revocation shall not affect the guarantee of prompt and full payment of any amount owed by the Debtor to the Creditor as of the date of actual receipt of notice of revocation by the Creditor.
If more than one person executes this guarantee, their obligation under this guarantee is joint and several.
Given under Seal on_____19_____.

Signed, sealed and delivered in        )
the presence of:                        )
                                        )
_____         )        _____ s
(signature of witness)                  )
for _____             )
                                        )
_____         )        _____ s
(signature of witness)                  )
for _____             )

## INDEPENDENT CONTRACTOR AGREEMENT

An Independent Contractor is an individual who is self-employed and offers his services to a general contractor or subcontractor, or even directly to a business establishment. The Independent Contractor pays a self-employment tax and the contractor or business that hires him need not pay any social security taxes or other fringe benefits on his services. The nature of the Independent Contractor and the possibilities of later repercussions and problems, make it highly desirable that the business person have the Independent Contractor execute and sign a statement setting forth his independent status. Cases have arisen in courts in which tax authorities, insurance companies, and even the Independent Contractor himself have sued the business person at a later time for real or contrived payments or reimbursements. A properly executed and signed Agreement, made before any work is started, will help prevent future problems of this sort.

# INDEPENDENT CONTRACTOR AGREEMENT

Date _____

NAME _____

ADDRESS _____

I, _____, hereby represent to _____ that I am acting as an outside independent contractor in regard to the services I am supplying. I understand that I will be issued a Federal Government Tax Information Form No. 1099, reflecting my earnings for the year. I further represent that I am being engaged by _____ on a job by job basis, to perform various services. The financial arrangements under which I work for the company (or individual) are determined by the work performed. I agree to hold harmless and indemnify _____ against any suits which arise as a result of work performed by me as a (sub)contractor. I understand that I am not an employee of _____, and I am responsible for my own personal income taxes.

Signed _____

Social Security # _____

Witness _____

Date _____

In case of emergency, contact:
_____
_____

## RESIDENTIAL LEASE AGREEMENT

Businesses occasionally acquire residential properties which their owners use as investments. Income from such properties and perhaps the prospect of (1) appreciation in value, or (2) future change in zoning that makes the residential property a commercially-zoned one, makes the use of residential leases one of the many tools of entrepreneurship. The sample lease herewith should provide protection and guidelines for the investor, although if a real estate broker or attorney is employed in the transaction, their lease form will be utilized. In any event, the sample here is typical of most residential leases and its study provides excellent preparation for any eventuality.

# LEASE AGREEMENT (RESIDENTIAL)

This Lease, made this _____ day of _____, by and between _____, Tenant, and _____, Landlord and Agent.

Witnesseth, That the Landlord, in consideration of the covenants and agreements hereinafter mentioned, to be kept and performed by the Tenant, doth demise unto the Tenant the premises known as _____, to be occupied as living quarters, and for no other purpose whatsoever, from 12 noon, the _____ day of _____ for a term of _____ from thence ensuing; and to expire at 12 noon, the _____ day of _____.

And the Tenant, in consideration of said demise, does covenant and agree with the Landlord as follows:

1. It is understood and agreed that Tenant is to commence occupancy of the premises on the _____ day of _____. Tenant is to pay the sum of _____ ($_____) as "pro-rata" rent through the _____ day of _____.

Tenant to pay during the said term of this Lease the rent, _____, payable as follows, to wit: _____ per month, the first installment to become due on the _____ day of _____.

If on the date of this Lease another person is occupying the premises and Landlord is unable to deliver possession on or before the commencement of the term of this Lease, Tenant's right of possession hereunder shall be postponed until said premises are vacated by such other person, and the rent due hereunder shall be abated at the rate of one-thirtieth (1/30) of a monthly installment for each day the possession is postponed.

2. Any and all monthly payments are due and payable in advance, and such payments are to be made to the Landlord or his Agent. If payment of rent is delinquent 5 days beyond due date, there will be a 5% penalty added to monthly rent and Tenant herewith agrees to pay same immediately. Tenant agrees to pay said rent in the manner and at the time herein specified, without deduction or demand.

3. Tenant herewith deposits with Landlord $_____ to secure that Tenant shall fully and faithfully perform all the covenants and conditions of this Lease. This sum shall be returned to the Tenant within approximately forty-five (45) days after the end of the Lease term, less any expenses caused by the breach of any condition of this Lease and any sums due from the Tenant. This deposit shall not be used or applied by Tenant as a substitute for the rent due for any month, including the last month of the Lease. In the event that the Tenant shall breach the Lease, the full amount of the security deposit shall be forfeited.

4. At least 60 days' written notice must be given to Landlord or his Agent of the intention to terminate tenancy, with such notice to expire on whatever day of month the tenancy would terminate. If the Tenant holds over after the expiration of

284

the term of this Lease, a month-to-month tenancy shall exist and all the terms, conditions, and covenants of this Lease shall remain in force. Further, such notice must be accompanied by payment of rent covering the term of the Lease up through the date of termination.

5. The premises are rented to the above Tenant to be used only by the Tenant and shall not be subleased or assigned. The premises will be used solely for residential purposes and be occupied by no more than _____ persons, including children.

6. The premises are rented unfurnished and are equipped with STOVE/OVEN, REFRIGERATOR, DISHWASHER, DISPOSAL, EXHAUST-FAN, WASHING MACHINE, DRYER, CENTRAL AIR CONDITIONING/HEATING SYSTEM, WALL-TO-WALL CARPETING, STORM WINDOWS/SCREENS, LIGHT FIXTURES, ALL OF EXISTING DECORATOR WINDOW TREATMENT, BACK YARD FENCE, AND ANY OTHER ITEMS COMING WITH PREMISES, and are to be returned to the Landlord or Agent at the expiration of occupancy, in as good condition as received (reasonable wear and tear excepted). The occupants are to keep premises neat and clean and free from objectionable features, nuisances and hazards. No alterations, additions, modifications or changes of any nature or description shall be made to the leased premises without the written consent of the Landlord or his Agent. The Tenant will preserve and attend to the reasonable care of any lawn, trees, vines, and shrubbery on said property at the Tenant's expense. Tenant will not permit vehicles to be parked on any portion of lawn that has not been expressly paved or graveled for parking purposes. Tenant agrees that no representations or warranties as to the condition of the premises have been made; and that no other agreement has been made to redecorate, repair or improve the premises unless hereinafter set forth specifically in writing.

7. The Tenant shall promptly pay all bills for utilities charged to the premises, including sewerage charges. If dishwasher, disposal, washing machine, dryer, air conditioners, or other appliances are provided with the leased premises, then the Tenant will be responsible for the cost of repairs and maintenance of the appliances, except when such repairs and maintenance are necessitated by ordinary wear and tear.

8. The Landlord or Agent shall give the Tenant quiet enjoyment for the term of the Lease. The Tenant is responsible for loss or damage from freezing of water pipes or plumbing fixtures in cold weather, or from the stoppage of water closet, which shall be repaired at the expense of the Tenant.

9. Time is the essence of this agreement in all respects, and if the occupants shall fail to make foregoing payments or any of them on time, or use the premises for any other purpose than herein stated, or fail to maintain the premises in the condition herein specified, or shall vacate the premises, each or any of the foregoing acts (among others) shall constitute a violation of this agreement; in which case the Landlord or Agent hereby reserves the right and is hereby expressly given the right to enter the premises and remove any and all belongings and property of the said occupants, and thereby repossess the premises without let or hindrance or any right of damage against them or either of them by said oc-

cupant or anyone occupying said premises with him or her or by his or her consent for so doing.

10. In the event Tenant shall default in the obligation to pay rent and it becomes necessary to retain a lawyer to collect arrearages in rent, Tenant shall be responsible for payment of such legal fees in the amount of twenty-five percent (25%) of the arrearages, with a minimum legal fee of $200.00.

11. If Tenant shall default in the observance of performance of any term or covenant of the Lease and if the Landlord or Agent makes any expenditures or incurs any obligations for the payment of money in connection therewith, including but not limited to attorney's fees, such sums paid or obligations incurred, with interest and costs, shall be deemed additional rent hereunder and shall be paid by Tenant to Landlord or Agent within five (5) days of rendition of any bill or statement to Tenant.

12. It is also understood and agreed that in case of the violation of this agreement in any way by said occupant or occupants, the Landlord or Agent hereby serves and hereby is expressly given the right to take any other action than that specified which is allowable by law for the enforcement of this agreement or otherwise.

13. The Tenant agrees to allow the Landlord or his representatives at any reasonable hour, to enter the said premises for the purpose of inspecting the same, for making any repairs that they may deem necessary or desirable, and two months preceding the expiration of said term will allow the usual notice "for rent" or "for sale" to be placed in front of said premises and remain thereon and property may be shown without hindrance or molestation.

14. The Tenant has no authority to incur any debt or make any charge against the Landlord, his Agent or assigns or create any lien upon the said leased property for any work or material furnished the same.

15. It is further agreed that no waiver or any breach of any covenant, condition or agreement herein shall operate as a waiver of the covenant, condition or agreement itself.

16. If Tenant is in the military service and is transferred out of the Washington Metropolitan area during the term of the Lease, Tenant may terminate this Lease by providing Landlord a copy of the transfer orders AND giving Landlord at least thirty (30) days' written notice of the intention to terminate, with such notice to expire on whatever day of the month the tenancy would terminate, if it were a month-to-month tenancy. (If the Lease would end on the 25th of a certain month, then any notice to terminate under this clause would have to be given 30 days before the 25th of any month.) Further, such notice must be accompanied by payment of rent covering the term of the Lease up through the date of termination.

17. All of the terms, covenants, agreements, and provisions herein contained shall bind and inure to benefit the Landlord, Tenant and Agent, their heirs, executors, administrators, personal representatives, successors, trustees, receivers, and assigns, as applicable, except as otherwise provided herein.

18. If the Landlord or Tenant, husband or wife, should die during the term of this Lease, the surviving spouse of the deceased may terminate this Lease by

giving thirty (30) days' written notice, from rent day to rent day, to the other parties involved in the Lease. This right of termination of Lease must be exercised within ninety (90) days of death of party concerned.

19. Tenant will do nothing and permit nothing to be done or about the premises which will contravene any fire insurance policy covering the same. If Tenant's use or occupancy of the premises increases the premium on any fire insurance policy, Tenant shall pay such increase. It shall be the responsibility of the Tenant to obtain an insurance policy which provides public liability coverage and also provides for the protection of Tenant's personal property.

20. Tenant is not to acquire any pets without Landlord's written consent (birds and fish excepted). _____

_____
Landlord's signature

21. If the property is subject to a condominium regime, a planned unit development, or a homeowners' association, Tenant agrees to abide by all rules and regulations now or hereafter promulgated. Tenant acknowledges that he has been afforded the opportunity to review the present by-laws, rules and regulations. Tenant is not authorized to vote for the Owner at any meeting of the Council of Unit Owners or the Homeowners' Association.

22. Tenant is to be responsible for first $50 for any and all repairs.

23. Tenant is to take good care of the property and the care includes the following ordinary care: Replacing light bulbs, changing furnace filters at least four times a year, recaulking the bath and kitchen areas, refilling freon for air conditioning unit, cutting grass, good lawn and yard care, and so forth.

24. This Lease contains the entire agreement between all parties hereto and shall not be changed or modified in any manner except by an instrument in writing executed by parties hereto.

WITNESS the following signatures this _____ day of _____, 19_____.

Tenant _____ (SEAL)   Landlord _____ (SEAL)

Tenant _____ (SEAL)   Witness _____ (SEAL)

# LEASE RENEWAL OPTION

Date _____

To:

Dear

re: <u>Lease Renewal</u>

This is to notify you that we are exercising the option to renew our lease of _____ for a further term of _____ years, contained in section _____ of the lease.

Please advise us of the rent you propose to charge in the renewed term so that we can decide whether or not to accept the renewal or to submit the matter to arbitration in accordance with the provisions of section _____ of the lease.

Very truly yours,

Signature _____

Company _____

## EXCLUSIVE RIGHT-TO-SELL LISTING AGREEMENT

This is an agreement between the owner of a property—land, building, or business—and a broker, giving the latter complete and total rights to sell your property and collect a commission on the transaction. If another party sells the property, or if the owner sells the property directly, the broker or agent who has the Exclusive Right-to-Sell Listing Agreement is still entitled to his agreed commission, unless he also agrees to share it with a second party. Such agreements have the advantage of having the broker apply greater effort to accomplish the sale and to negotiate the best possible price within the shortest possible time. The latter facet of the agreement is important. The owner or seller can and usually does attach a time limit to the agreement—let's say three or six months. The opposite of an exclusive listing is an open listing. The latter allows any broker to try and sell the property and collect full commission and only when one broker (or the owner) sells the property is the open listing canceled.

# LISTING AGREEMENT: EXCLUSIVE RIGHT-TO-SELL

Between the Client:
and (Broker/Consultant):

Client employs Consultant as an independent contractor and exclusive agent, to assist in identifying, presenting, or negotiating a transfer of ownership of Client's business to a suitable buyer.

If Client, through an authorized representative, reaches an agreement to sell its business, and/or assets related to this business, to a buyer introduced to Client through efforts of the Consultant, and if such negotiations result in a change of ownership and/or funding, then Client guarantees that Consultant, irrespective of any previous contract or negotiations, will be compensated as follows:

The amount used in determining Consultant's compensation will be the sum of all amounts used by the parties in the determination of the net settlement. This may include, but is not limited to, such consideration as payment in cash, stock, or in kind; options; fees; notes or other evidence of indebtedness; leases; other arrangements negotiated to offset purchase or option price, such as covenants not to compete; and all other assets to be exchanged in connection with the acquisition, lease and/or funding of such business and/or assets related to this business, to be exchanged in connection with the acquisition, lease and/or funding of such business and/or assets related to the business.

A payment of _____, which will be credited against any fee ultimately due to Consultant arising out of this agreement, is payable to Consultant on _____. The balance of the amount due Consultant, as calculated above, is to be paid in full at the time of final settlement, or closing, if earlier, in cash, money order or by cashier's check.

This agreement shall remain in effect until 30 days from the date Consultant receives written notice of termination from Client, but in no instance shall this agreement be terminated prior to _____. It is understood that Client's obligations to Consultant arising out of contacts and/or negotiations initiated during the term of this agreement shall survive this agreement.

By signing this agreement, the signing party represents that he or she has the unconditional authority to enter into this exclusive agreement on behalf of Client.

Accepted and agreed to , this _____ day of _____, 19_____.

BROKER/CONSULTANT                    CLIENT

BY: _____          BY: _____

## LIVING TRUST

A living trust or a revocable *inter vivos* trust is a legal instrument used to hold assets, such as real estate, stocks, bonds, and bank accounts. With the creation of the living trust, assets are transfered to the trust, but you lose no control over these assets. You can manage your assets during your lifetime as usual and provide for their distribution upon your death. The trust enables you to distribute your assets at the time you desire and to the people you choose, in any amount you choose. It can be a superior alternative to a will, because it provides you with substantial benefits before your demise. The single most important advantage of the living trust is that it escapes probate proceedings—a court-supervised process for testing the validity of a will that can take from three months to three years. A living trust makes funds available for distribution to your heirs(s) immediately after your death,without benefit of court procedures. Also, this instrument is not a matter of public record; your financial affairs and those of your ultimate heirs are totally private. The first step you should undertake is to prepare a property inventory list, such as the sample shown below.

### Property Inventory List

| | |
|---|---|
| Your personal residence | Life insurance policies |
| Second residence, if any | Employee benefits, pension rights |
| Other real estate | IRAs, Keoghs, other plans |
| Cash | Automobiles |
| Savings and checking accounts (numbers and locations) | Other vehicles |
| Mutual or money market funds | Precious metals |
| Bonds, descriptions | Jewelry |
| Stocks, descriptions | Valuable collectibles |
| Government securities | Artworks |
| Other business interests | Household furnishings |
| | Recreational equipment |

**LIVING TRUST FORM FOR SINGLE PERSON WITH BENEFICIARY(IES)**

# The _____ Trust
## 𝔇𝔢𝔠𝔩𝔞𝔯𝔞𝔱𝔦𝔬𝔫 𝔒𝔣 𝔗𝔯𝔲𝔰𝔱

1. I, _____ , of
_____ ,
City of _____ , County of _____ , State of _____ ,
referred to hereinafter as Grantor and/or Trustee, hereby declare that I am the Trustee of the property referred to in this Declaration of Trust agreement as the trust estate, which is fully set forth in the Schedule of Trust Estate Assets attached hereto and made a part hereof.

2. I hereby declare that I hold the trust estate created by this Declaration of Trust agreement and all right to, title to and interest in the trust estate in trust for the use and benefit of: _____
_____ of _____ .

3. Upon my death, the Successor Trustee is hereby directed forthwith to transfer the trust estate and all right to, title to and interest in the trust estate to the named contingent beneficiaries in the following manner, subject to amendment:
_____ of _____(address),
City of _____ , County of _____ , State of
_____ , shall receive _____ from the trust estate;
_____ of _____
City of _____ , County of _____ , State of
_____ , shall receive _____ from the trust estate;
_____ of _____
City of _____ , County of _____ , State of
_____ , shall receive _____ from the trust estate;
_____ of _____
City of _____ , County of _____ , State of
_____ , shall receive _____ from the trust estate.

4. In the event that the income to be received by any beneficiary from the trust estate or his or her share thereof, and from other sources known to the trustee, shall be considered at any time by the trustee to be insufficient for the support, maintenance and education of any such beneficiary or of any person being supported by any such beneficiary, the trustee shall pay to such beneficiary from time to time such amounts from the beneficiary's share of the trust estate as the trustee shall deem sufficient for such purposes.

5. The Grantor reserves the right during his life to amend, modify or revoke this Declaration of Trust agreement in whole or in part, without the consent of any beneficiary and without giving notice to any beneficiary hereunder, by a writing or writings signed and acknowledged by the Grantor, to be effective upon delivery to the Trustee.

6. Upon my death, I shall be succeeded as trustee of the trust estate created by this Declaration of Trust agreement by _____ of _____ . The Successor Trustee shall serve all functions of the trustee that are set forth in the provisions of this Declaration of Trust agreement. In the event of the death of any of the foregoing beneficiaries for whom a trust share is being retained, the trustee shall apportion and distribute the principal thereof per stirpes among the then living lineal or legally adopted descendents of that person, and if there be none, then per stirpes among the then living contingent beneficiaries.

292

7. If the Successor Trustee is unable to serve as trustee for any reason, _____
of _____ shall serve as Contingent Successor Trustee.

8.  The Trustee of this Declaration of Trust has all of the discretionary powers necessary and appropriate to administer this Trust, including but not limited to, the power to sell, mortgage, encumber, pledge, hypothecate, lease, rent or improve, invest and reinvest the trust estate property when such action is deemed to be in the best interest and furtherance of the Trust purposes.

The Trustee may pay income or principal to the beneficiaries or for their benefit, and shall have no obligation to confirm the use of such payments for the use and welfare of any beneficiary.

Any person serving as Trustee hereunder shall serve without bond.

9.  No interest of a Beneficiary of this Trust can be alienated.  No Beneficiary can assign, pledge, encumber or otherwise transfer an interest in the Trust estate, nor shall such interest be garnished, attached, or levied upon or otherwise subjected to any proceedings whether at law or in equity.

10.  Each Beneficiary hereunder shall be liable for his/her proportionate share of any estate tax that may be imposed by any state or federal entity upon the share of the Trust estate held for or distributed to a Beneficiary upon the death of the Grantor or the survivor of the Grantor.

11.  This Declaration of Trust agreement shall be administered and interpreted in accordance with the laws of the State of _____.

12.  This trust shall be known as "The _____ Trust."

13.  I hereby declare that this Declaration of Trust agreement fully and accurately  sets forth the manner in which my trust estate shall be held, managed, disposed by the trustee.

_____

Date

_____

Grantor/Trustee


County of _____

City of _____

State of _____


On_____, 19_____, _____
Grantor/Trustee of the trust estate created  by this Declaration of Trust agreement, came before me and acknowledged that it was his/her free act and deed to execute this agreement.


Notary Seal:                                        _____
                                                                    Notary Public

**LIVING TRUST FORM FOR MARRIED PERSON WITH CHILDREN**

# The _____ Trust
# 𝔇𝔢𝔠𝔩𝔞𝔯𝔞𝔱𝔦𝔬𝔫 𝔒𝔣 𝔗𝔯𝔲𝔰𝔱

1. We, _____ Husband, and
_____ Wife, of
_____,
City of _____ County of _____, State of _____,
referred to hereinafter as Grantors and/or Joint Trustees, hereby declare that we are Joint Trustees of the property referred to in this Declaration of Trust agreement as the trust estate, which is more fully set forth in the Schedule of Trust Estate Assets attached hereto and made a part hereof.

2. We hereby declare that we hold the trust estate created by this Declaration of Trust agreement and all our right to, title to and interest in the trust estate in trust for the use and benefit of: _____
_____ of _____.

3. Upon the death of one of the beneficiaries named in paragraph 2 above, all right to, title to and interest in the trust estate created by this Declaration of Trust agreement shall be held in trust for the use and benefit of the survivor of the two beneficiaries named in paragraph 2 above.

4. Upon the death of the surviving beneficiary (as determined in paragraph 3 above), the trust property shall be equally divided among and, except as hereinafter provided, held or distributed to the Grantors' then living lineal or legally adopted descendants, per stirpes. The trustees shall pay the income from any retained share to or for the benefit of the beneficiary thereof during the period that such share is retained, and at the end of such period the principal thereof shall be distributed to such beneficiary.

5: For purposes of this trust agreement, _____ shall be deemed to be the last surviving spouse, unless there is conclusive proof to the contrary.

6. The share for any living child of the Grantors shall be retained by the trustees until the child reaches the age of _____ years. The share for any grandchild of the Grantors at any time apportioned shall be retained by the trustees until the grandchild reaches the age of _____ years. But in any event the trust shall terminate 20 years after the death of both Grantors.

7. Upon the death of any lineal descendent for whom a trust share is being retained, the trustees shall apportion and distribute the principal thereof per stirpes among the then living lineal or legally adopted descendents of that person, and if there be none, then per stirpes among the then living lineal descendents of the Grantors.

8. In the event that the income to be received by any beneficiary from the trust estate or his or her share thereof, and from other sources known to the trustees, shall be considered at any time by the trustees to be insufficient for the support, maintenance and education of any such beneficiary or of any person being supported by any such beneficiary, the trustees shall pay to such beneficiary from time to time such amounts from the beneficiary's share of the trust estate as the trustees shall deem sufficient for such purposes.

9. The Grantors reserve the right during their joint lives and during the life of the survivor of them to amend, modify or revoke this Declaration of Trust agreement in whole or in part, without the consent of any beneficiary and without giving notice to any beneficiary hereunder, by a writing or writings signed and acknowledged by the Grantors or the survivor, to be effective upon delivery to either Trustee.

10. Upon the death of both Co-Trustees, _____ of _____
_____ shall serve as Successor Trustee.
If the Successor Trustee is unable to serve as the trustee for any reason, _____
of _____ shall serve as Contingent Successor Trustee.

Any Successor Trustee shall have all of the powers and authorities granted to the Trustees or the surviving Trustee as set forth in the provisions of this Declaration of Trust.

11. The Trustees of this Declaration of Trust have all of the discretionary powers necessary and appropriate to administer this Trust, including but not limited to, the power to sell, mortgage, encumber, pledge, hypothecate, lease, rent or improve, invest and reinvest the trust estate property when such action is deemed to be in the best interest and furtherance of the Trust purposes.

The Trustees may pay income or principal to the beneficiaries or for their benefit, and shall have no obligation to confirm the use of such payments for the use and welfare of any beneficiary.

In the event this Declaration of Trust provides for more than one Trustee, the exercise of any and all powers, authorities, discretions and rights granted to said Trustees shall not be construed to require the Trustees to act in unison in order to exercise any Trust power, but each Trustee may individually exercise any of the Trust powers.

In the event of a physical or mental incapacity or death of one of the Co-Trustees, the survivor shall continue as the Sole Trustee with full power and authority to exercise all of the powers granted to the Trustees under this Declaration of Trust.

Any person serving as Trustee hereunder shall serve without bond.

12. No interest of a Beneficiary of this Trust can be alienated. No Beneficiary can assign, pledge, encumber or otherwise transfer an interest in the Trust estate, nor shall such interest be garnished, attached, or levied upon or otherwise subjected to any proceedings whether at law or in equity.

13. Each Beneficiary hereunder shall be liable for his(her) proportionate share of any estate tax that may be imposed by any state or federal entity upon the share of the Trust estate held for or distributed to a Beneficiary upon the death of the Grantors or the survivor of the Grantors.

14. This Declaration of Trust shall be administered and interpreted in accordance with the laws of the State of _____.

15. This trust shall be known as "The _____ Trust."

16. We hereby declare that this Declaration of Trust fully and accurately sets forth the manner in which our trust estate shall be held, managed, disposed by the Trustees.

_____
Date

_____        _____
Grantor/Trustee                                 Grantor/Trustee

County of _____

City of _____

State of _____

On _____, 19_____, _____
and _____ Grantors and Joint Trustees of the trust estate created by this Declaration of Trust agreement, came before me and acknowledged that it was their free act and deed to execute this agreement.

Notary Seal:

_____
Notary Public

# LIVING TRUST FORM FOR MARRIED PERSON WITHOUT CHILDREN

## The _____ Trust

# 𝔇eclaration 𝔒f 𝔗rust

1. We, _____ Husband, and
_____ Wife, of
_____,
City of _____ County of _____, State of _____,
referred to hereinafter as Grantors, hereby declare that we have appointed _____
Trustee of the property referred to in this Declaration of Trust agreement as the trust estate, which is more fully
set forth in the Schedule of Trust Estate Assets attached hereto and made a part hereof.

2. _____ holds the trust estate created by this Declaration of Trust
agreement and all our right to, title to and interest in the trust estate in trust for the use and benefit of:
_____ of _____.

3. Upon the death of one of the beneficiaries named in paragraph 2 above, all right to, title to and interest
in the trust estate created by this Declaration of Trust agreement shall be held in trust for the use and benefit
of the survivor of the two beneficiaries named in paragraph 2 above.

4. Upon the death of the surviving beneficiary (as determined by paragraph 3 above) the trust property shall be
equally divided among and, except as hereinafter provided, held or distributed to the Grantors' then living lineal
or legally adopted descendants, per stirpes. The trustee shall pay the income from any retained share to or for
the benefit of the beneficiary thereof during the period that such share is retained, and at the end of such period
the principal thereof shall be distributed to such beneficiary.

5. For purposes of this trust agreement, _____ shall be deemed to
be the last surviving spouse, unless there is conclusive proof to the contrary.

6. The share for any living child of the Grantors shall be retained by the trustee until the child reaches the age of
_____ years. The share for any grandchild of the Grantors at any time apportioned shall be retained by
the trustee until the grandchild reaches the age of _____ years. But in any event the trust shall
terminate 20 years after the death of both Grantors.

7. Upon the death of any lineal descendent for whom a trust share is being retained, the trustee shall apportion
and distribute the principal thereof per stirpes among the then living lineal or legally adopted descendents of that
person, and if there be none, then per stirpes among the then living lineal descendents of the Grantors.

8. In the event that the income to be received by any beneficiary from the trust estate or his or her share thereof,
and from other sources known to the trustee, shall be considered at any time by the trustee to be insufficient for
the support, maintenance and education of any such beneficiary or of any person being supported by any such
beneficiary, the trustee shall pay to such beneficiary from time to time such amounts from the beneficiary's share
of the trust estate as the trustee shall deem sufficient for such purposes.

9. The Grantors reserve the right during their joint lives and during the life of the survivor of them to amend, modify
or revoke this Declaration of Trust agreement in whole or in part, without the consent of any beneficiary and without
giving notice to any beneficiary hereunder, by a writing or writings signed and acknowledged by the Grantors or
the survivor, to be effective upon delivery to either Trustee.

10. Upon the death of the Trustee, _____ of _____
_____ shall serve as Successor Trustee.

If the Successor Trustee is unable to serve as the trustee for any reason, _____ of _____ shall serve as Contingent Successor Trustee. Any Successor Trustee shall have all of the powers and authorities granted to the Trustees or the surviving Trustee as set forth in the provisions of this Declaration of Trust.

11. The Trustee of this Declaration of Trust has all of the discretionary powers necessary and appropriate to administer this Trust, including but not limited to, the power to sell, mortgage, encumber, pledge, hypothecate, lease, rent or improve, invest and reinvest the Trust estate property when such action is deemed to be in the best interest and furtherance of the trust purposes.

The Trustee may pay income or principal to the beneficiaries or for their benefit, and shall have no obligation to confirm the use of such payments for the use and welfare of any beneficiary.

Any person serving as Trustee hereunder shall serve without bond.

12. No interest of a Beneficiary of this Trust can be alienated. No Beneficiary can assign, pledge, encumber or otherwise transfer an interest in the Trust estate, nor shall such interest be garnished, attached, or levied upon or otherwise subjected to any proceedings whether at law or in equity.

13. Each Beneficiary hereunder shall be liable for his(her) proportionate share of any estate tax that may be imposed by any state or federal entity upon the share of the Trust estate held for or distributed to a Beneficiary upon the death of the Grantors or the survivor of the Grantors.

14. This Declaration of Trust shall be administered and interpreted in accordance with the laws of the State of _____.

15. This trust shall be known as "The _____ Trust."

16. We hereby declare that this Declaration of Trust fully and accurately sets forth the manner in which our trust estate shall be held, managed, disposed by the Trustees.

_____

Date

_____     _____

Grantor/Trustee                                              Grantor

County of _____

City of _____

State of _____

On _____, 19_____, _____

and _____ Grantors and Trustee of the trust estate created by this Declaration of Trust agreement, came before me and acknowledged that it was their free act and deed to execute this agreement.

Notary Seal:                                              _____

                                                                       Notary Public

# MARKET RESEARCH MARKETING PLAN WORKSHEET

**Information Needed**                                    **Source of Information**       **Who Will Do It**

   I. **Market Characteristics**
- 1. Product/Service
- 2. Segment of Market
- 3. Present Consumer Habits
- 4. Dollar Value of Present Market
- 5. Estimated Actual Market Need
- 6. Current Pricing
- 7. Technological Trend
- 8. Distribution
- 9. Success Factors

  II. **Competition**
- 1. Names, Addresses
- 2. Market Share Each
- 3. Market Size Each
- 4. Trend for Each
- 5. Customer Perceptions
- 6. Product/Price/Feature Comparisons
- 7. Distribution Methods
- 8. Promotion Efforts
- 9. Marketing Strategies
- 10. Strengths/Weaknesses

 III. **Technical Factors**
- 1. Materials/Processes

 IV. **Business Climate**
- 1. Economic Conditions
- 2. Government Relations
  - Federal
  - State
  - Municipal
  - Other Jurisdictions
- 3. Political Factors
- 4. Legal Limitations

  V. **Company Resources (Internal)**
- 1. Physical Facilities
- 2. Traffic/Transportation
- 3. Warehousing
- 4. Offices
- 5. Communications
- 6. Engineering
- 7. Marketing
- 8. Financial Resources

# MECHANIC'S LIEN

The undersigned, _____ claimant,
(name exactly as it appears on contractor's license)
claim a mechanic's lien upon the following described real property; City
of _____ County of _____
_____
_____
(description of property where work or materials were furnished, including street
address and legal description)
The claim due and unpaid is $_____ together with interest thereon at the
rate of _____ from the date the balance became due ,
namely _____ which is due claimant, having deducted all
just credits and offsets, for the following work and materials furnished by
claimant:
_____
_____
_____

Claimant furnished work and materials at the request of, and under contract with
_____
_____

The owners, or reputed owners,of the property are (as described in the building
permit application) _____
_____

Firm Name _____

By: _____
(claimant or authorized agent)

## VERIFICATION

I, the undersigned, say, I am the _____ of the foregoing claim for a
mechanic's lien; I have read said claim of mechanic's lien and know the contents
thereof; the same is true of my own knowledge. I declare under penalty of perjury
that the foregoing is true and correct.

Executed on _____ 19_____, at _____
in the State of _____.

Signature: _____

## NON-DISCLOSURE AND NON-COMPETE AGREEMENTS

The first agreement is one in which the employee or associate promised not to reveal any part of the other party's business, product, or invention to anyone else not specifically authorized. The second agreement applies to employees who might leave the company and go into direct competition with their former employer. When an idea for a potential patent or a new process or product is lent or turned over to another party, the original owner usually requests that second party to sign a Non-Disclosure Agreement—valid at least until the two parties have agreed to a mutually satisfactory working together method or remuneration. A Non-Compete Agreement is often required by companies from employees who are in sales or administrative positions, privy to vital sales records, customer lists, patent or process papers, and any information that could be used against the interests of the owner-company. As an example: leading members of an advertising agency, an accounting or law firm, decide to leave the employ of the parent firm, and set up their own company, possibly taking with them information and records of their employer. Many law suits have taken place in such cases that are costly and frequently destructive to both sides. Clear-cut and binding agreements beforehand can avoid or mitigate such unforeseen later problems.

### Non-Disclosure Statement

Great ideas are the stock-in-trade of many entrepreneurs. Many remain just that because the small businessperson does not want to reveal it or is afraid to let go of it without proprietary protection. The following suggested Agreement will provide some protection.

Another step is to write to the Commissioner of Patents, Washington, DC 20231, stating that you are the originator of the idea, invention or potential patent you describe. Request that your submission, described in great detail, be accepted under the Disclosure Documents Program and preserved for a period of two years. The Patent Office will then assign a Disclosure Document number to you.

This procedure affords you the optimum protection for two years and gives you time to develop the idea. Be sure to keep all notes, memos, correspondence, drawings, sketches, research, dates of contacts and persons contacted on behalf of this project, and of course funds expended.

Briefly, a non-disclosure statement should include:

A statement that you are the originator of the disclosed idea

That the person or company to whom you submit your idea or to your knowledge any other person or company has not made public such an idea

That the person or company to whom you submit the idea will not use it without your permission nor reveal any part of it to anyone else

Request a promise of complete confidentiality until such time that you both have agreed to a plan of production, dissemination or commercialization

# NON-COMPETITION AGREEMENT

BE IT KNOWN, FOR GOOD AND VALUABLE CONSIDERATION, the Undersigned                    , agree not to compete with the business of                    (Company) and its lawful successors, assigns and affiliates in accordance with the terms herein.

The term "not compete" as used herein shall mean that the Undersigned shall not directly or indirectly on his own behalf or on behalf of others engage in a business or other commercial activity described as:


whether as an owner, officer, director, lender, investor, employee, agent, consultant, partner, or stockholder (except      as a minority stockholder in a publicly owned company).

This covenant and agreement shall extend                    for a radius of                    miles from the present location of the Company at                    and shall remain in                    effect for                    years from date hereof at which time this agreement shall expire.

In the event of any violation of this agreement, the Company shall be entitled to full equitable and injunctive relief without need to post bond or surety, which rights shall be cumulative with and not necessarily successive or exclusive of any other legal rights to monetary damages that the company may have.

This agreement shall be binding upon and inure to the benefit of the parties, their successors, assigns and personal representatives.

Signed under seal this                    day of                    , 19      .

Witness

_____        _____

_____        _____

## PATENT APPLICATION AND FORMS

Receiving a United States patent for a product or process is a very complicated and exacting task. The majority of inventors who wish to have a patent issued to them, protecting their innovation for an initial 17 years, usually invest in the several thousand dollars that it can cost to have a licensed U.S. patent attorney prepare the appropriate papers, conduct or supervise the necessary search for possibly conflicting patents, having prepared the correct petition, oath, specification, and drawings. However, a private citizen who has an idea for a patent and wishes to conduct his or her own research, can contact the U.S. Department of Commerce, Patent and Trademark Office, Washington, DC 20231, and request all pertinent application and instruction forms. Protecting your future patent prior to the patent award is also possible by filing a "Disclosure Document" through the above office, which protect the device for a period of two years. To conduct a search of patent files and to ascertain whether a conflicting patent might already be in existence, an inventor can personally visit the Scientific Library of the Patent and Trademark Office at Crystal Plaza, 2021 Jefferson Davis Highway, Alexandria, VA 22301. Much patent information may also be available in any of the several dozen Patent Depositary Libraries located across the United States in major public and university libraries. The SBA also has a pamphlet entitled "Introduction to Patents" (No. 6.005, $0.50) that is a good preliminary guide. A patent may also be assigned to another party in return for certain considerations. Suggested forms for these follow.

The wording of patent applications are approximately as follows, consisting of a petition, a specification, an oath stating that the patent application is that of the petitioner, and a set of black-and-white line drawings showing the patented object from two sides.

# PETITION

To the Commissioner of Patents and Trademarks:

Petitioner _____ a citizen of the United States and a resident of _____ in the State of _____ whose post office address is _____ _____ prays that letters patent be granted to him for the new and original design for _____ set forth in the following specification.

Signed _____
(Inventor's/Applicant's full signature)

# SPECIFICATION

To all whom it may concern:

Be it known that I, _____, have invented a new, original, and ornamental design for _____ of which the following is a specification, reference being made to the accompanying drawing, forming a part hereof.

    Fig. 1 is a plan view of a _____ showing my new design.

    Fig. 2 is a side of the _____ (if there is one).

I claim:

The ornamental design for a _____ as shown and described.

                         Signed _____
                         (Inventor's full signature)

(Present black-and-white drawing of device to be patented, showing at least two sides of same in detail and, if necessary, with marginal explanation.)

# PATENT APPLICATION OATH

## OATH

State of _____ s.s. _____

County of _____

_____ , the above-named petitioner, being sworn or affirmed deposes and says that he is a citizen of the United States and a resident of _____ County of _____ State of _____ Zip Code, _____ that he verily believes himself to be the original and sole inventor of the design for _____ described and claimed in the aforegoing specifications; that he does not know and does not believe that the same was ever known or used before his invention thereof, or patented or described in any printed publication in any country before his invention thereof, or more than one year prior to this application, or in public use or on sale in the United States for more than one year to this application; that said design has not been patented or made the subject of an inventor's certificate in any country foreign to the United States on an application filed by him or his legal representatives or assigns more than six months prior to this application; that he acknowledges his duty to disclose information of which he is aware which is material to the examination of this application, and that no application for patent or inventor's certificate on said design has been filed by him or his representatives or assigns in any country foreign to the United States, except as follows _____

signed
(Inventor's full signature)

Sworn to and subscribed before me this _____ day of _____ 19_____.

(Seal)                    signed
                          (Signature of Notary Public)

# PATENT ASSIGNMENT

WHEREAS, I . . . . . . . . . . . ., of . . . . . . . . . . . ., have invented a certain new and useful improvement in . . . . . . . . . . . . for which an application for United States patent letters was filed on . . . . . . . Serial No. . . . . . . . (if the application has been prepared but not yet filed, then state "for which an application for United States patent letters was executed on . . . . . . . . . . ." instead); and,

WHEREAS, . . . . . . . . . . of . . . . . . . . . . ., whose post office address is . . . . . . . . is desirous of acquiring the entire (or portion thereof) right, title and interest in the same;

NOW, THEREFORE, in consideration of the sum of . . . . . . . . . dollars ($), the receipt whereof is hereby acknowledged, and other good and valuable consideration, I, the said . . ., by these presents do sell, assign and transfer unto said . . . . . . ., the full and exclusive right to said invention in the United States and the entire right, title, and interest in and to any and all patent letters that may be granted, therefore in, the United States.

I hereby authorize and request the commissioner of patents and trademarks to issue said letters patent to said . . . . . . . . as the assignee of the entire right, title, and interest in and to the same, for his sole use and behoof; and for the use and behoof of his legal representatives, to the full end of the term for which said patent letters may be granted, as fully and entirely as the same would have been held by me had this assignment and sale not been made.

Executed this . . . . . . . . day of . . . . . . . . 19 . . . . . . . . at . . . . . . . .

State of . . . . . . . . . . . . . . )

                    ) ss:

County of . . . . . . . . . . . . . )

Before me personally appeared said . . . . . . . . and acknowledged the foregoing instruments to be his free act and deed this . . . . . day of . . . . . 19 . . . . . . . . . . .

(Seal)                                    Signed_____

                                                 Notary Public

## POWERS OF ATTORNEY

These are legal instruments in which one person appoints another as his agent. It confers upon the agent the right to perform certain functions on behalf of the principal—acts that are spelled out specifically. The agent can be an attorney, a trust officer at a bank, or a friend or relative. The purpose of such an instrument is to allow the agent to speak for the principal in fiscal matters, legal situations or to act as proxy in voting. A Durable Power of Attorney is usually more limited in purpose and time. It "shall become effective only during such time periods as the (principal) may be mentally or physically incapacitated and unable to care for (his) (her) needs or make competent decisions . . . "

# POWER OF ATTORNEY (Version 1)

STATE OF                  )

                       )    ss.

COUNTY OF              )

KNOW YE ALL MEN BY THESE PRESENTS,

That I, _____, of _____
                                          Street Address      Apt. No.

_____, do hereby make, constitute,
       City       State             Zip

and appoint _____, of _____
                                              Street Address      Apt.

_____, as my true and lawful
No.      City      State             Zip

Attorney-in-Fact, for me and in my name, place, and stead to:

_____

_____

_____

_____

I further give and grant to my said Attorney-in-Fact full power and authority to do and perform every act necessary and proper to be done in the exercise of any of the foregoing powers as fully as I might or could do if personally present, with full power of substitution and revocation, hereby ratifying and confirming all that my said Attorney-in-fact shall lawfully do, or cause to be done by virtue hereof.

This instrument may not be changed orally.

IN WITNESS WHEREOF, I have hereunto set my hand and seal this _____ day of _____, 19_____.

(Signed) _____

# POWER OF ATTORNEY (Version 2)

This Power of Attorney is given to _____
this _____ day of _____, 19_____. By this
Power of Attorney, I hereby authorize _____ to
undertake all actions necessary to the management of my financial affairs during
the period _____, 19_____ through _____,
19_____, including but not limited to the signing of checks, the making of deposits and withdrawals in any account which I may now have or which I may hereafter
have, the preparation and signing of all documents necessary to the management
of my affairs, and all activities reasonably related thereto.

_____
(My signature)

STATE OF_____)
                                                     )    ss:
COUNTY OF_____)

    Subscribed and sworn to before me this _____ day of _____,
19_____.

_____
Notary Public

_____

# Durable Power of Attorney

KNOW ALL MEN BY THESE PRESENTS that I, _____ , residing at _____ , _____ , do hereby nominate, constitute and appoint _____ residing at _____ , _____ , my true and lawful attorney-in-fact, for me and in my name, place and stead, and for my use and benefit:

To ask, demand, sue for, recover, collect, and receive all sums of money, debts, dues, accounts, legacies, bequests, interest, dividends, annuities, and demands whatsoever as are now or shall hereafter become due, owing, payable, or belonging to me and take all lawful ways and means in my name or otherwise for the recovery thereof, and to compromise and agree to the same and give releases or other sufficient discharges for the same;

For me and in my name, to make, seal, and deliver, bargain, contract, agree for, purchase, receive, and take lands, tenements, hereditaments, and accept the deeds and possession of all lands and to lease, let, demise, bargain, sell, remise, release, convey, mortgage, and hypothecate lands, tenements, and hereditaments upon such terms and conditions and under such covenants as _____ shall think fit;

Also to bargain and agree to, buy, sell, mortgage, hypothecate, and in any and every way and manner deal in and with goods, wares, and merchandise, choses in action, and other property in possession or in action, and to make, do, and transact all and every kind of business of whatsoever nature and kind;

Also as my act and deed, to sign, seal, execute, deliver, and acknowledge such deeds, leases, mortgages, bills of lading, bills, notes, receipts, evidence of debt, releases and satisfaction of mortgage, judgements and other debts, and such other instruments in writing of whatsoever kind and nature as may be necessary or proper in the premises;

Also to endorse checks, notes, drafts and any other commercial paper in my name, and to withdraw money from any of my checking or savings accounts at any commercial bank, savings and loan association or other financial institution, and to sign orders or receipts therefore in my name;

And also to transfer any property held in my name into the Declaration of Trust dated _____ , (The _____ Trust);

GIVING AND GRANTING unto my said attorney-in-fact full power and authority to do and perform every act necessary, requisite, or proper to be done in and about the premises as fully as I might or could do if personally present, with full power of substitution and revocation, hereby ratifying and confirming all that my said attorney-in-fact shall lawfully do or cause to be done by virtue hereof.

All power and authority granted herein shall not be affected by my disability, incapacity, or adjudged incompetency. My agent may exercise the powers and authorities described in this durable power of attorney only in the event that I am unable to manage my own financial affairs due to my disability or incapacity.

IN WITNESS WHEREOF, I have hereunto signed my name this _____ day of _____, 19 ___ .

Signed and Acknowledged
in the Presence of:

_____        _____

_____

STATE OF _____ :
                                        SS:
_____ COUNTY:

Before me, a Notary Public in and for said County and State, personally appeared the above-named _____ who acknowledged that _____ did sign the foregoing instrument and that the same is _____ free and voluntary act and deed.

IN TESTIMONY WHEREOF, I have hereunto set my hand and official seal at_____ _____ , _____ , this _____ day of _____ , 19 ____ .

_____
Notary Public

## PROMISSORY NOTES

Such notes or agreements are used when one party lends money or other valuables to another party. A promissory note is what is termed a negotiable instrument and can be assigned to a third party. In such an instrument the issuer of the promissory note agrees to repay his debt in a certain manner and within a specific time period. Usually some form of collateral is quoted that can be attached in case of any default. In a private promissory note the wording is quite simple, as usually two parties deal directly with each other. A commercial promissory note can be more involved, as the borrower can be a partnership or corporation. In the latter cases the lender might require that all parties of a partnership, or all major stockholders and/or officers of a corporation sign a note, or even pledge personal property as collateral.

# PROMISSORY NOTE (Version 1)

$ _____     Date _____

_____ after the above date I promise to pay to the order
(Number of Days)
of _____, the sum of _____ ($ __),
together with interest at _____ percent per annum, payable at .

    The maker and endorser of this note further agree to waive demand, notice of
nonpayment and protest, and in case of suit shall be brought for the collection
hereof, or the same has to be collected upon demand of an attorney, to pay reasonable attorney's fees for making such collection. Deferred interest payments to
bear interest from maturity at _____ percent per annum, payable
semiannually.

(Signed) _____
                                           Maker

(Signed) _____
                                           Endorser

Due _____

# PROMISSORY NOTE (Version 2)

_____                    _____
**Amount**                                          **Date**

      FOR VALUE RECEIVED, the undersigned promises to pay to the order of _____ the sum of _____, with interest until paid at the rate of _____ percent per annum. Said note payable in _____ _____ installments of _____ beginning _____ with a final payment due _____.

      It is understood and agreed that if default be made in the payment of any one of the aforesaid installments when and as the same shall become due and payable, then and in that event, the unpaid balance of said principal sum shall, at the option of the holder thereof, at once become due and payable. This promissory note may be paid in full together with interest thereon at any time prior to its due date without any prepayment penalties.

      If this note is placed with an attorney for collection because of default, the Maker and Endorsers hereof agree to pay an attorney's fee of fifteen percent (15%) of the balance due on the Note, plus all court costs.

      This promissory note shall be governed and construed in accordance with the laws of the _____.

| _____ | _____ | _____ |
|:---:|:---:|:---:|
| **Witness** | **Date** | **Name** |
| _____ | _____ | _____ |
| **Witness** | **Date** | **Name** |
| | | _____ |
| | | **Address** |
| | | _____ |
| | | **Address** |
| | | _____ |
| | | **Telephone** |

# PROMISSORY NOTE (COMMERCIAL)

$ _____     _____, 19_____

**Promise to Pay.** The undersigned borrower (the "Borrower") (jointly and severally if more than one) unconditionally promise(s) to pay to the order of _____ (the "Bank") at any banking office of the Bank, the sum of _____ Dollars together with interest on the unpaid principal balance thereof at an annual rate of (check one box only):

☐ _____%

☐ _____% plus the Prime Rate, which interest rate will change automatically from time to time, effective as of the effective date of each change in the Prime Rate. As used herein, "Prime Rate" means, as of any date, the announced or published prime rate of

☐ _____

_____

_____

_____

Interest shall be computed on the basis of a 360 day year and charged for actual days elapsed. Any principal or interest not paid when due, whether at stated maturity, by acceleration or otherwise (or if this Note is payable on demand, upon demand for payment by the Bank), shall bear interest, payable on demand, at an annual rate of two percent (2%) in excess of the annual rate stated above until paid.

The Borrower promises to pay the principal and interest owing under this Note (check one box only):

☐ in _____ consecutive _____ Monthly _____ Quarterly _____ Semi-annual _____ principal installments of $ _____ each, with a final installment of $ _____ commencing on _____, 19_____ and thereafter on the like day of each above designated period, together with interest on the unpaid principal balance thereof at the annual rate indicated above, payable with each installment of principal as stated herein.

☐ in _____ consecutive _____ Monthly _____ Quarterly _____ Semi-annual _____ installments of principal and interest of $ _____ each, with a final installment of principal and interest of $ _____ commencing on _____, 19_____ and thereafter on the like day of each above designated period.

☐ on demand. Until demand is made, interest shall be payable _____ _____ commencing _____

☐ in one single installment due _____ after the date hereof.

☐ _____

_____

**Security.** As used herein, "Obligations" means all indebtedness hereunder and any renewals, extensions and modifications hereof, together with any now or hereafter existing indebtedness of the Borrower to the Bank whatsoever. "Obligor" means the Borrower and all endorsers, guarantors and sureties of any Obligation. As security for the full and timely repayment of the Obligations (in addition to any collateral under any note, Business Loan Security Agreement, assignment or other document now existing or hereafter executed by the Borrower and/or any other person with respect to any of the Obligations), the Borrower hereby grants to the Bank a security interest in all monies, bank deposits or credits held by the Bank for or owed by the Bank to the Borrower, and, in the event of default hereunder, such monies, deposits or credits may be set off and applied to the payment of any Obligations.

**Default.** The Borrower shall be in default hereunder on the occurrence of any of the following: (a) Non-payment when due of any portion of any Obligation; (b) Any warranty, representation or statement made or furnished to the Bank by or on behalf of the Borrower proving to have been incorrect when made or furnished; (c) The existence of any event of default under the terms of any note, security agreement, guaranty or other document now existing or hereafter executed by the Borrower (singly or jointly with another person or persons) and (or in favor of) the Bank; (d) The existence of any event of default under the terms of any instrument or writing evidencing a debt of the Borrower to someone other than the Bank; (e) Uninsured loss, theft, substantial damage, destruction, or transfer or encumbrance without fair value in return of any of the Borrower's assets; (f) Any Obligor (i) admitting in writing its insolvency or its inability to pay its debts as they mature, (ii) making a general assignment for the benefit of creditors, (iii) commencing a case under or otherwise seeking to take advantage of any bankruptcy, reorganization, insolvency, readjustment of debt, dissolution or liquidation law, statute or proceeding, (iv) by any act indicating its consent to, approval or acquiescence in any such proceeding or the appointment of any receiver of or trustee for it or a substantial part of its property, or suffering any such receivership, trusteeship or proceeding to continue undismissed for a period of thirty (30) days, or (v) becoming a debtor in any case under any chapter of the United States Bankruptcy Code; (g) Any Obligor defaulting under the terms of the guarantee, security or other agreement executed, or which may hereafter be executed, in connection with the Obligation(s); (h) Judgment against, or attachment of property of any Obligor; (i) The Bank deeming itself insecure; (j) Dissolution, merger, consolidation, liquidation or reorganization of any Obligor; or (k) Death of any Obligor. Upon the occurrence of them pursuant to all of the terms set forth above for any deficiencies hereon after the collection, foreclosure, realization or sale of any collateral securing the Obligations, or any part thereof, together with interest, court costs and attorney's fees as provided above.

This Note will be governed by the internal laws of the State of Maryland and, to the extent Federal laws preempt the laws of Maryland, by the laws of the United States. If any part of this Note is declared invalid or unenforceable, such invalidity or unenforceability shall not affect the remainder of this Note, which shall continue in full force and effect. Any provision that is invalid or unenforceable in any application shall remain in full force and effect as to valid applications. In this Note, the term "person" shall include an individual, corporation, an association, a partnership, a trust, and any other legal entity.

This Note is executed under seal on the date first above written. The Borrower represents that the loan proceeds will be solely for business or commercial (excluding agricultural) purposes.

ATTEST or WITNESS:                    BORROWER(S):

By: _____ (SEAL)

By: _____ (SEAL)

## COMMERCIAL NOTE, SECURED & UNSECURED
## THIRD PARTY GUARANTEE

In order to induce _____ (the "Beneficiary") to make the loan to the borrower (the "Borrower") evidenced by the above commercial promissory note (the "Note"), the undersigned Guarantor (jointly and severally if more than one), as primary obligor and not as surety merely, does hereby absolutely, unconditionally and irrevocably guarantee to the Beneficiary, its successors and assigns, the punctual payment by the Borrower of the payments due and the prompt fulfillment of all obligations and liabilities of the Borrower with respect to the Note, as and when the same shall be due, whether at maturity, by acceleration, demand, or otherwise, together with charges and all reasonably incurred expenses of obtaining or endeavoring to enforce or obtain performance or payment thereof or hereof, including, but not limited to, court costs and reasonable attorney's fees not to exceed 25% of the total amount owing hereunder. The Guarantor hereby expressly waives diligence, presentment, demand, protest, notice of dishonor or other notice of any kind whatsoever, and any requirement that any person exhaust any remedy or take any action against the Borrower or take or pursue any other remedy whatsoever, it being expressly understood that the Beneficiary may proceed against the Guarantor without first proceeding against the Borrower or any of its property or assets. The Guarantor authorizes the Beneficiary (or any holder of this Note) to set off and apply to any payment due under this Guarantee all monies, bank deposits or other credits of the Guarantor in the Beneficiary's (or any holder's) possession, and to confess judgment against the Guarantor as provided in the Note. The Guarantor hereby consents to any extension of time for payment of, and hereby waives any defense of invalidity or unforceability of, the obligations guaranteed, and also waives any other circumstance which might in any manner constitute legal or equitable discharge of a guarantor or surety, it being the intent hereof that the obligations of the Guarantor hereunder shall be absolute and unconditional under any and all circumstances and shall not be discharged except by the full and irrevocable payment of the sums hereunder guaranteed in the manner provided herein. No delay on the part of the Beneficiary in exercising any right or remedy hereunder shall preclude the Beneficiary's exercise thereof.

This Guarantee is executed under seal on the date of the Note. This Guarantee will be construed in accordance with the internal laws of the State of _____

ATTEST or WITNESS:                        GUARANTOR(S):

                                          By: _____ (SEAL)

                                          By: _____ (SEAL)

318

## CONFESSED JUDGMENT PROMISSORY NOTE

This is a more forceful promissory note that gives the lender vast powers to collect unpaid debts or to attach pledged property or other collateral without further ado. With such a note the borrower puts himself at the mercy of the lender, virtually becoming a financial chattel to his benefactor. It smacks of some desperation on the part of the borrower and is used in such circumstances, or when the lender suspects that his loan might be jeopardized, compromised, or collection efforts disputed in court. With such an instrument, the lender has already agreed to have a potential judgment entered in favor of attaching his collateral. It puts substantial pressure on the lender to make good his promise to meet his fiscal obligation.

# CONFESSED JUDGMENT PROMISSORY NOTE

$ _____                    _____, 19_____

      For Value received, the undersigned jointly and severally promise to pay to the order of _____ the principal sum of _____ Dollars ($ _____), payable at _____, together with interest thereon at the rate of _____ percent per annum until maturity, both principal and interest being payable in lawful money of the United States as follows:

      Payments of principle plus interest shall be made monthly in the amount of $ _____ beginning _____, with each payment representing $ _____ of principle and $ _____ of interest.

      If any installment of principle or interest hereunder be not paid when due the entire unpaid amount hereof together with interest shall become due and payable forthwith at the election of the holder hereof. Upon default of any of the obligations set forth herein, each maker and endorser authorizes and empowers any attorney, Justice of the Peace, or Clerk of Court of Record in any of the jurisdictions in which the makers or endorsers reside, work or own property, in the State of _____, or in any other jurisdiction, to enter judgment by confesssion against such makers and endorsers, jointly and severally, in favor of _____ or its assigns, for the full amount due plus all costs of collection, including without limitation court costs and reasonable attorney's fees. Each maker and endorser expressly waives any summons or other process, consents to immediate execution of said judgment, and expressly waives benefit of all exemption laws and presentment, demand, protest, and notice of maturity, non-payment and/or protest, and also waives benefit of any other requirements necessary to hold each of them liable as makers and endorsers.

      If any one or more of the words or terms of this Note shall be held to be indefinite, invalid, illegal or otherwise unenforceable, in whole or in part, for any reason, by any court of competent jurisdiction, the remainder of this Note shall continue in full force and effect and shall be construed as if such indefinite, invalid, illegal or unenforceable words or terms had not been contained herein.

      The terms of this Note shall be governed by the laws of the State of _____.

_____(SEAL)

_____(SEAL)

_____(SEAL)

# RENTAL AGREEMENT (GENERAL)

THIS AGREEMENT is made this _____ day of _____,

19_____, between _____, of

_____ _____ _____ _____, here-
(Street Address)            (City)          (State)      (Zip)

inafter called "Owner", and _____, of_____
                                                        (Street Address)

_____ _____ _____, hereinafter called
            (City)           (State)      (Zip)

"Renter."

## PROPERTY

_____
_____
_____
_____
_____
_____

The Owner warrants that to the Best of his/her knowledge and belief the aforesaid property is free of faults or deficiencies which would affect its safe and dependable operation under normal and prudent usage.

## RENTAL PERIOD

The Owner agrees to rent te above-described property to the Renter for a period of _____ beginning _____, and ending _____.

## USE OF PROPERTY

_____
_____

The Renter further agrees that the rented property (1) shall not be used beyond any rated capacity; (2) shall Not Be used for any illegal purpose; (3) shall not be used in any manner for which it was not designed, built, or designated by the manufacturer; (4) will not be used in a negligent manner: (5) will not be operated by any other person without the written permission of the Owner; and (6) will not be removed from the designated area of use or operation.

## AREA OF USE OR OPERATION

The Renter agrees to operate/use the above-described property only at the following location or within the following described area(s):

_____
_____
_____

321

## INSURANCE

The Renter hereby agrees that he/she shall fully indemnify the Owner for any and all damage to or loss of the rented property and any accessories or related equipment during the term of this Agreement whether caused by fire, theft, flood, vandalism, or any other cause, except that which shall be determined to have been caused by a fault or deficiency of the rented property, accessories, or equipment.

## RENTAL RATE

The Renter hereby agrees to pay the Owner at the rate of $ _____ per _____ for the use of said property and any accessories/ equipment. Any fuel used shall be paid for by the Renter.

## DEPOSIT

The Renter further agrees to make a deposit of $ _____ with the Owner, said deposit to be used, in the event of loss of or damage to the rented property and any accessories/equipment during the term of this Agreement, to defray fully or partially the cost of necessary repairs or replacement. In the absence of any damage or loss, said deposit shall be credited toward payment of the rental fee and any excess shall be returned to the Renter.

## RETURN OF PROPERTY TO OWNER

The Renter hereby agrees to return the rented property and any accessories/ equipment to the Owner at _____ no later than _____.

## TERMINATION OF AGREEMENT

It is mutually agreed that the Renter shall have the right to terminate this Agreement at any time by payment of one full day's rental for each 24-hour period or any part thereof, during which the Renter has retained possession of the property and any accessories/equipment during the term of this Agreement.
IN WITNESS WHEREOF, the parties hereto hereby execute this Agreement.

(Signed) _____
(Renter)

(Signed) _____
(Owner)

# REAL ESTATE SALES CONTRACT

Date ............................... 19 ........

RECEIVED FROM ................................................................................ Purchaser(s)

**DEPOSIT**
a deposit of ........................................................... Dollars [$ ................... ]

by Cash, Check, Note (to be redeemed or cashed by) to be held in trust by Agent and to be applied as part payment of the purchase of

**LEGAL DESCRIPTION ADDRESS**
Lot ..............................................................................................

with improvements thereon known as No. ..........................................................

**EQUIPMENT & CHATTELS**
including ........................................................................................

................................................................................................

.......................................................................... upon the following terms of sale.

**PRICE**
Total price
of property ........................................................................... Dollars
[$ ............................... ]

**DOWN PAYT.**
The purchaser agrees to pay $ ......................... cash or certified check at the date of conveyance, of which sum this deposit shall be a part. Should deposit be in excess of cash payment required, excess shall be applied to the cost of closing and remaining funds, if any, returned to Purchaser.

**FIRST TRUST**
The Purchaser is to: place [   ] assume [   ] or give seller [   ] an FHA _____ VA _____ conventional _____ first deed

of trust secured on said premises of $ ............. due as amortized and bearing interest at the rate of ............ % per annum, or prevailing rate at time of settlement, payable approximately $ ...................... per month plus one-twelfth of annual taxes, fire insurance, and private mortgage insurance if required by lender. If this contract provides for the assumption of a loan, it is understood that the trust balances and down payment are approximate.

**SECOND TRUST**
To secure the balance of deferred purchase money, Purchaser is to: give seller [   ] place [   ] assume [   ] a second deed of trust on said property of approximately $ ...................... to be paid in monthly installments of $ ...................... including ......... percent interest per annum and may be prepaid at any time without penalty. This trust is due and payable in full .......... years from date of settlement. Said note may not be assumed without written consent of note holder.

**OWNER FINANCING**
Financing is contingent upon submission to Seller of employment verification and satisfactory credit report, paid for by Purchaser. Purchasers hereby release Agents from any liability and/or damage that may be caused by any statements in the credit report and authorize Agent to release credit information to Sellers. Said deed of trust and note shall require maker to provide the holder with written receipts or otherwise acceptable evidence of payment of real estate taxes and hazard insurance within ten business days of the due date thereof and the noteholder shall be provided with the original insurance policy and subsequent renewals thereof showing the noteholder as loss payee in the least amount of the then existing balance on said note. Failure to comply with the above shall consitute a default under said deed of trust note. Said deed of trust note shall be in default when any monthly payment is thirty days or more in arrears. A late charge of 5% of the monthly payment shall be due for any payment not received by the noteholder within fifteen days of the monthly due date. Should the premises securing the note be sold, transferred or conveyed in any manner, the entire balance shall be due and payable unless expressly approved in writing by the noteholder.

**LOAN CONTGY. & FEES [POINTS]**
Purchaser agrees, within seven (7) working days following ratification of contract to make loan application, or applications as may be necessary, and to file all necessary papers that are required for complete processing and to diligently pursue loan procurement, and Purchaser further agrees that failure to do so shall give the Seller the right of forfeiture of the deposit and to avail himself of other legal remedies. If new financing is to be arranged or if assumption of existing financing requires lender approval, then this contract is contingent upon said new financing or lenders approval upon the terms herein described, or approval cannot be obtained, this agreement shall become null and void, the deposit refunded in full to the Purchaser and all parties released from any further liability hereunder. Where financing is to be secured by a Purchaser, the Seller and Purchaser hereby agree to pay at time of settlement the prevailing loan discount required by the lending institution. It is understood and agreed the Purchase will pay no more than ............... % loan fee and the Seller shall pay up to but no more than ............... % loan fee.
Under FHA Loans there is a mortgage insurance premium (MIP). This fee [ ............... % of the loan amount] will be paid for by the Purchaser at settlement or the Purchaser may elect to add this MIP fee directly to the FHA First Deed of Trust, in which case, the loan fee to both the Purchaser(s) and Seller(s) as noted above may be based upon the "adjusted" loan amount. The V.A. requires the veteran Purchaser(s) to pay a funding fee in addition to the loan fee as noted above. The veteran purchaser(s) may elect to add this loan "funding fee" to the loan. In this event, the loan discount fee to the purchaser(s) and seller(s) may be based upon the gross "adjusted" loan amount.

**PURCHASER'S CONTGY.**
This contract is contingent until ........................... upon the sale of Purchaser's property located at ........................... ........................................................... or contract shall become null and void and deposit returned to Purchaser. However, the Purchaser has the right to proceed with this contract by removing the contingency by making alternative arrangements, which would allow the Purchaser to proceed to settlement. During contingency period, Seller's property shall remain on the market. Should Seller accept a back-up contract, the Purchaser shall have ............... after written notification to Purchaser or Purchaser's agency to remove this contingency, or Seller may void this contract and return deposit to the purchaser.

**OTHER TERMS**
................................................................................................

................................................................................................

................................................................................................

**SETTLEMENT DATE**
Purchaser and Seller are to make full settlement of this contract by ........................... or as soon thereafter as financing can be arranged or title defects, if any, can be corrected.

**ATTORNEY**
Purchaser makes it known he desires to employ as his settlement attorney or representative ...........................

**AGENTS**
Seller agrees to pay agent compensation on the sales price of the property as agreed upon between Seller and Listing Broker and to instruct the parties conducting settlement to deduct the same from the proceeds of the sale and to disburse ........................... to ........................... ........................... and the remaining amount of compensation to ........................... as Listing Broker

**V.A. OR F.H.A.**
When VA or FHA financing applies it is expressly agreed that notwithstanding any other provisions of this contract, the Purchaser shall not be obligated to complete the purchase of the property described herein or to incur any penalty by forfeiture of earnest money deposits or otherwise unless the Seller has delivered to the Purchaser a written statement issued by the FHA Commissioner or Veterans Administration, whichever is applicable, setting forth the appraised value of the property (excluding closing costs) of not less than $ ........................... which statement the Seller hereby agrees to deliver to the Purchaser promptly after such appraised value statement is made available to the Seller. The Purchaser shall, however, have the privilege and option of proceeding with the consumation of this contract without regard to the amount of appraised valuation made by the Veterans Administration or FHA Commissioner, whichever is applicable, providing that Purchaser agrees to do so within five (5) days of notification of said value. The appraised valuation is arrived at to determine the maximum mortgage the Department of Housing and Urban Development will insure. HUD does not warrant the value or condition of the property. The Purchaser should satisfy himself/herself that the price and the condition of the property are acceptable. (VA and FHA appraisals may require repairs to property, the completion of which is to be mutually agreed upon by Purchaser and Seller upon receipt of appraisal.)

## SBA FORMS

The Small Business Administration has ceased becoming a financial patsy for easy loans. It acts principally as a facilitator and guarantor for correspondent banks and loan-generating private lenders. The forms required by the SBA, before they underwrite a loan, are every bit as detailed, probing and meticulous as those from commercial banks. Here are a number of the commonly used forms for your study and guidance. In addition, forms for a business plan mandated by the SBA, but quite similar to one required by other lenders, is included. The execution of a business plan is a good idea in any event. The required, concentrated effort is needed by potential lenders and investors, but is also a sound guide for the applicant in the operation of his or her own business. The "Statements Required by Laws and Executive Orders" included with this form is given to every loan applicant. It offers a detailed explanation of the many types of loans available by the SBA and other federal agencies, as well as information that might be pertinent to a start-up or operational entrepreneur.

# SAMPLE SBA FORM 4, CERTIFICATION AND SCHEDULE OF COLLATERAL

OMB Approval No. 3245-0016
Expiration Date: 10-31-87

U.S. Small Business Administration

## Application for Business Loan

| Applicant | Full Address |
|---|---|

| Name of Business | Tax I.D. No. |
|---|---|

| Full Street Address | Tel. No. (Inc. A/C) |
|---|---|

| City | County | State | Zip | Number of Employees (Including subsidiaries and affiliates) |
|---|---|---|---|---|
| Type of Business | | | Date Business Established | At Time of Application _____ |
| Bank of Business Account and Address | | | | If Loan is Approved _____ |
| | | | | Subsidiaries or Affiliates _____ (Separate from above) |

| Use of Proceeds: (Enter Gross Dollar Amounts Rounded to Nearest Hundreds) | Loan Requested | SBA USE ONLY |
|---|---|---|
| Land Acquisition | | |
| New Construction/ Expansion/Repair | | |
| Acquisition and/or Repair of Machinery and Equipment | | |
| Inventory Purchase | | |
| Working Capital (Including Accounts Payable) | | |
| Acquisition of Existing Business | | |
| Payoff SBA Loan | | |
| Payoff Bank Loan (Non SBA Associated) | | |
| Other Debt Payment (Non SBA Associated) | | |
| All Other | | |
| Total Loan Requested | | |
| Term of Loan | | |

**Collateral**

If your collateral consists of (A) Land and Building, (D) Accounts Receivable and/or (E) Inventory, fill in the appropriate blanks. If you are pledging (B) Machinery and Equipment, (C) Furniture and Fixtures, and/or (F) Other, please provide an itemized list (labeled Exhibit A) that contains serial and identification numbers for all articles that had an original value greater than $500. Include a legal description of Real Estate offered as collateral.

| | Present Market Value | Present Loan Balance | SBA Use Only Collateral Valuation |
|---|---|---|---|
| A. Land and Building | $ | $ | $ |
| B. Machinery & Equipment | | | |
| C. Furniture & Fixtures | | | |
| D. Accounts Receivable | | | |
| E. Inventory | | | |
| F. Other | | | |
| Totals | $ | $ | $ |

**PREVIOUS SBA OR OTHER GOVERNMENT FINANCING:** If you or any principals or affiliates have ever requested Government Financing, complete the following:

| Name of Agency | Original Amount of Loan | Date of Request | Approved or Declined | Balance | Current or Past Due |
|---|---|---|---|---|---|
| | $ | | | $ | |
| | $ | | | $ | |

SBA Form 4 (2-85) Previous Editions Obsolete

**INDEBTEDNESS:** Furnish the following information on all installment debts, contracts, notes, and mortgages payable. Indicate by an asterisk (*) items to be paid by loan proceeds and reason for paying same (present balance should agree with latest balance sheet submitted).

| To Whom Payable | Original Amount | Original Date | Present Balance | Rate of Interest | Maturity Date | Monthly Payment | Security | Current or Past Due |
|---|---|---|---|---|---|---|---|---|
| | $ | | $ | | | $ | | |
| | $ | | $ | | | $ | | |
| | $ | | $ | | | $ | | |
| | $ | | $ | | | $ | | |

**MANAGEMENT** (Proprietor, partners, officers, directors and all holders of outstanding stock — <u>100% of ownership must be shown</u>). Use separate sheet if necessary.

| Name and Social Security Number | Complete Address | % Owned | *Military Service From | To | *Race | *Sex |
|---|---|---|---|---|---|---|
| | | | | | | |
| | | | | | | |
| | | | | | | |
| | | | | | | |

* This data is collected for statistical purposes only. It has no bearing on the credit decision to approve or decline this application.

**ASSISTANCE**     List the name(s) and occupation(s) of any who assisted in preparation of this form, other than applicant.

| Name and Occupation | Address | Total Fees Paid | Fees Due |
|---|---|---|---|
| Name and Occupation | Address | Total Fees Paid | Fees Due |

Signature of Preparers if Other Than Applicant

---

## THE FOLLOWING EXHIBITS MUST BE COMPLETED WHERE APPLICABLE. ALL QUESTIONS ANSWERED ARE MADE A PART OF THE APPLICATION.

For Guaranty Loans please provide an original and one copy (Photocopy is Acceptable) of the Application Form, and all Exhibits to the participating lender. For Direct Loans submit one original copy of application and Exhibits to SBA.

Submit SBA Form 1261 (Statements Required by Laws and Executive Orders). This form must be signed and dated by each Proprietor, Partner, Principal or Guarantor.

1. Submit SBA Form 912 (Personal History Statement) for each person e.g. owners, partners, officers, directors, major stockholders, etc.; the instructions are on SBA Form 912.

2. Furnish a signed current personal balance sheet (SBA Form 413 may be used for this purpose) for each stockholder (with 20% or greater ownership), partner, officer, and owner. Social Security number should be included on personal financial statement. Label this Exhibit B.

3. Include the statements listed below: 1, 2, 3 for the last three years; also 1, 2, 3, 4 dated within 90 days of filing the application; and statement 5, if applicable. This is Exhibit C (SBA has Management Aids that help in the preparation of financial statements.) All information must be signed and dated.

1. Balance Sheet          2. Profit and Loss Statement
3. Reconciliation of Net Worth
4. Aging of Accounts Receivable and Payable
5. Earnings projections for at least one year where financial statements for the last three years are unavailable or where requested by District Office.
    (If Profit and Loss Statement is not available, explain why and substitute Federal Income Tax Forms.)

4. Provide a brief history of your company and a paragraph describing the expected benefits it will receive from the loan. Label it Exhibit D.

## ALL EXHIBITS MUST BE SIGNED AND DATED BY PERSON SIGNING THIS FORM.

SBA Form 4 (2-85) Previous Editions Obsolete

SBA Form 4, Application for Loan, requires that all financial statements of the applicant small business concern and affiliates, if any, be signed and dated by the person signing the application form.

You may sign a Bank Form of Certification if required by a bank, or use the form shown below, or sign and date the face of each year and interim statement attached to your application.

## SAMPLE FORM

I, _____
(Pres., Vice Pres., Sec'y., Treas., Gen. Partner or Individual Owner) of


Do hereby certify that the foregoing Balance Sheet has been prepared from the company's book of account and that to the best of my knowledge and belief, it fairly presents the financial position of the company as of

| _____ | _____ | _____ |
| (Month) | (Day) | (Year) |

(Signature) _____

(Date Signed) _____

# SBA LOAN

## UNITED STATES SMALL BUSINESS ADMINISTRATION

## SCHEDULE OF COLLATERAL

## Exhibit A

| Applicant | | |
|---|---|---|
| Street Address | | |
| City | State | Zip Code |

## LIST ALL COLLATERAL TO BE USED AS SECURITY FOR THIS LOAN.

### Section I—REAL ESTATE

Attach a copy of the deed(s) containing a full legal description of the land and show the location (street address) and city where the deed(s) is recorded. Following the address below, give a brief description of the improvements, such as size, type of construction, use, number of stories, and present condition (use additional sheet if more space is required).

| LIST PARCELS OF REAL ESTATE | | | | | |
|---|---|---|---|---|---|
| Address | Year Acquired | Original Cost | Market Value | Amount of Lien | Name of Lienholder |
| | | | | | |

Description(s):

## SECTION II—PERSONAL PROPERTY

All items listed herein must show manufacturer or make, model, year, and serial number. Items with no serial number must be clearly identified (use additional sheet if more space is required).

| Description—Show Manufacturer, Model, Serial No. | Year Acquired | Original Cost | Market Value | Current Lien Balance | Name of Lienholder |
|---|---|---|---|---|---|
| | | | | | |
| | | | | | |
| | | | | | |
| | | | | | |
| | | | | | |
| | | | | | |
| | | | | | |
| | | | | | |
| | | | | | |
| | | | | | |
| | | | | | |
| | | | | | |
| | | | | | |
| | | | | | |
| | | | | | |
| | | | | | |
| | | | | | |
| | | | | | |
| | | | | | |
| | | | | | |
| | | | | | |
| | | | | | |

All information contained herein is TRUE and CORRECT to the best of my knowledge. I understand that FALSE statements may result in forfeiture of benefits and possible fine and prosecution by the U.S. Attorney General (Ref. 18 U.S.C. 100)

_____  Date_____

_____  Date_____

SBA Form 4 Schedule A (4/87) Previous Editions Obsolete

| | |
|---|---|
| **BUSINESS PLAN** | Applicant _____<br>City & State _____<br>_____ |

This "abbreviated" business plan is not all inclusive. More detailed publications are available from the U.S. Small Business Administration. The Management Assistance Personnel in the district office will provide more comprehensive business plans for your type of business or assist you in completing this form should you request it.

Use a separate sheet if necessary in answering questions to Part 1. Some answers, such as number 8, should identify what standards you have investigated and which ones you must conform to in your type of business. Part II must be completed by all applicants for direct EOL or 7(a) loans. Part III must be completed whenever such a direct loan application is to start a new business or in the other situations listed in that Part.

## PART I

## LOCATION

1. Why did you select your present or the proposed location?

2. Is the neighborhood: ☐ new ☐ established ☐ residential ☐ commercial

3. Who will be your customers and why will they come to you at this location?

4. What parking facilities are available to you? Will they be adequate?

5. What are the terms of your lease (enclose a copy of the lease), or the terms of your mortgage?

6. What is the physical condition of the building? ☐ good ☐ fair ☐ poor

7. What competition do you have in this location? How close?

8. Have you determined whether your building complies with local building codes and zoning ordinances? Occupational Health and Safety Regulations? Environmental Protection (air, water, and noise) Regulations? Others?

9. What licenses or permits are you required to have to start operations?

## PRICING AND ADVERTISING

10. Your merchandise will fall into what price range?
☐ high ☐ medium ☐ low

11. Will you sell for cash? ☐ yes ☐ no

12. If you offer credit, will your prices have to be higher?

13. How do your prices compare with your competitors? If yours are higher, why will people buy from you?

14. What type of advertising will you use ☐ radio ☐ TV ☐ handbill
☐ newspaper ☐ other (specify) _____
Why? How often? How much will it cost?

<table>
<tr><td colspan="2">PERSONAL FINANCIAL STATEMENT<br><br>As of _____, 19_____.</td><td>Return to:<br>Small Business<br>Administration</td><td>For SBA Use Only</td></tr>
<tr><td></td><td></td><td></td><td>SBA Loan No.</td></tr>
</table>

Complete this form if 1) a sole proprietorship by the proprietor; 2) a partnership by each partner; 3) a corporation by each officer and each stockholder with 20% or more ownership; 4) any other person or entity providing a guaranty on the loan.

| Name and Address, Including ZIP Code *(of person and spouse submitting Statement)*<br><br><br><br><br><br><br>SOCIAL SECURITY NO._____ | This statement is submitted in connection with S.B.A. loan requested or granted to the individual or firm, whose name appears below:<br><br>Name and Address of Applicant or Borrower, Including ZIP Code |
|---|---|
| Business *(of person submitting statement)* | |

**Please answer all questions using "No" or "None" where necessary**

| ASSETS | LIABILITIES |
|---|---|
| Cash on Hand & in Banks .. $ _____ | Accounts Payable ............. $ _____ |
| Savings Account in Banks .... _____ | Notes Payable to Banks ....... _____ |
| U.S. Government Bonds ....... _____ | (Describe below - Section 2) |
| Accounts & Notes | Notes Payable to Others....... _____ |
|   Receivable ........................ _____ | (Describe below - Section 2) |
| Life Insurance–Cash | Installment Account (Auto) ... _____ |
|   Surrender Value Only ........ _____ | .........Monthly Payments $ |
| Other Stocks and Bonds ...... _____ | Installment Accounts (Other) _____ |
|   (Describe - reverse side - Section 3) | .........Monthly Payments $ |
| Real Estate ......................... _____ | Loans on Life Insurance........ _____ |
|   (Describe - reverse side - Section 4) | Mortgages on Real Estate .... _____ |
| Automobile - Present Value ... _____ | (Describe - reverse side - Section 4) |
| Other Personal Property ....... _____ | Unpaid Taxes......................... _____ |
|   (Describe - reverse side - Section 5) | (Describe - reverse side - Section 7) |
| Other Assets......................... _____ | Other Liabilities .................... _____ |
|   (Describe - reverse side - Section 6) | (Describe - reverse side - Section 8) |
| | Total Liabilities...................... _____ |
| | Net Worth .............................. _____ |
| Total.................. $ _____ | Total.................. $ _____ |

| Section I. Source of Income *(Describe below all items listed in this Section)* | CONTINGENT LIABILITIES |
|---|---|
| Salary................................... $ _____<br>Net Investment Income.......... _____<br>Real Estate Income................ _____<br>Other Income *(Describe)*........ _____ | As Endorser or Co-Maker.. $ _____<br>Legal Claims and<br>   Judgments........................... _____<br>Provisions for Federal<br>   Income Tax ........................ _____<br>Other Special Debt............... _____ |

Description of Items listed in Section I _____

_____

_____

_____

_____

_____

\*Not necessary to disclose alimony or child support payments in "Other Income" unless it is desired to have such payments counted toward total income. Life Insurance Held *(Give face amount of policies — name of company and beneficiaries)* _____

_____

_____

_____

_____

_____

_____

## SUPPLEMENTARY SCHEDULES

Section 2. Notes Payable to Banks and Others

| Name and Address of Holder of Note | Amount of Loan | | Terms of Repayments | Maturity of Loan | How Endorsed, Guaranteed, or Secured |
|---|---|---|---|---|---|
| | Original Bal. | Present Bal. | | | |
| | $ | $ | $ | | |
| | | | | | |
| | | | | | |
| | | | | | |
| | | | | | |

## Section 3. Other Stocks and Bonds: Give listed and unlisted Stocks and Bonds *(Use separate sheet if necessary)*

| No. of Shares | Name of Securities | Cost | Market Value Statement Date | |
|---|---|---|---|---|
| | | | Quotation | Amount |
| | | | | |
| | | | | |
| | | | | |
| | | | | |
| | | | | |

## Section 4. Real Estate Owned. *(List each parcel separately. Use supplemental sheets if necessary. Each sheet must be identified as a supplement to this statement and signed). (Also advises whether property is covered by title insurance, abstract of title, or both).*

| Title is in name of | Type of Property |
|---|---|
| Address of property (City and State) | Original Cost to (me) (us)  $ _____<br>Date Purchased _____<br>Present Market Value  $ _____<br>Tax Assessment Value  $ _____ |
| Name and Address of Holder<br>of Mortgage (City and State) | Date of Mortgage _____<br>Original Amount  $ _____<br>Balance  $ _____<br>Maturity _____<br>Terms of Payment _____ |

Status of Mortgage, i.e., current or delinquent. If delinquent describe delinquencies

## Section 5. Other Personal Property. *(Describe and if any is mortgaged, state name and address of mortgage holder and amount of mortgage, terms of payment and if delinquent, describe delinquency.)*

## Section 6. Other assets. *(Describe)*

| Section 7. Unpaid Taxes. *(Describe in detail, as to type, to whom payable, when due, amount, and what, if any, property tax lien, if any, attaches)* |
| :--- |
|  |

| Section 8. Other Liabilities. *(Describe in detail)* |
| :--- |
|  |

(I) or (We) certify the above and the statements contained in the schedules herein is a true and accurate statement of (my) or (our) financial condition as of the date stated herein. This statement is given for the purpose of: *(Check one of the following)*

☐ Inducing S.B.A. to grant a loan as requested in application, of the individual or firm whose name appears herein, in connection with which this statement is submitted.

☐ Furnishing a statement of (my) or (our) financial condition, pursuant to the terms of the guaranty executed by (me) or (us) at the time S.B.A. granted a loan to the individual or firm, whose name appears herein.

| _____ | _____ | _____ |
| :---: | :---: | :---: |
| Signature | Signature | Date |

| PART II | PROJECTED CASH FLOW | | 1st Month | 2nd Month | 3rd Month | 4th Month | 5th Month |
|---|---|---|---|---|---|---|---|
| 1. Your Investment | $ | | | | | | |
| 2. Less Start-Up Costs | | | | | | | |
| 3. Remainder (*) | $ | | | | | | |
| 4. Beginning Cash | $ | | | | | | |
| Plus: Cash Sales | | | | | | | |
| Collections of A/R's | | | | | | | |
| Loans and other cash income | | | | | | | |
| 5. Total Available Cash | $ | | | | | | |
| Purchase of Inventory | | | | | | | |
| Employee Wages-Gross | | | | | | | |
| Payroll Taxes, etc. | | | | | | | |
| Outside Services | | | | | | | |
| Office Supplies | | | | | | | |
| Repairs and Maint. | | | | | | | |
| Advertising | | | | | | | |
| Car, Delivery, & Travel Exp. | | | | | | | |
| Acct'g, Legal, Etc. | | | | | | | |
| Rent | | | | | | | |
| Telephone | | | | | | | |
| Utilities | | | | | | | |
| Insurance | | | | | | | |
| Real Estate Taxes | | | | | | | |
| Interest on term loans | | | | | | | |
| Other Expenses | | | | | | | |
| 6. Total Expenses | $ | | | | | | |
| #5 less #6 | $ | | | | | | |
| Less Owner's Withdrawals | | | | | | | |
| 7. Balance | $ | | | | | | |
| Less payments due on fixed (term) payment loans | | | | | | | |
| Other loan payments | | | | | | | |
| 8. Ending Cash (**) | $ | | | | | | |

(*) This figure represents the beginning cash for the first month.
(**) The ending cash for one period is the beginning cash for the next month.
(***) This column must agree with projected income statement.

SBA FORM 1107 (7 85)

# PROJECTED CASH FLOW (con't)

| | 6th Month | 7th Month | 8th Month | 9th Month | 10h Month | 11th Month | 12th Month | Total (***) 1-12 Months |
|---|---|---|---|---|---|---|---|---|
| | | | | | | | | |

## PART III     START-UP COSTS

Whether you are starting a new business, moving to a new location, opening a new branch, or expanding your business, you will have some "start-up" or one-time expenses. In all applications for such purposes, complete the appropriate items below and transfer the total to Part II.

1. Real Estate, Furniture, fixtures, machinery, equipment:
   - a. Purchase Price (if paid in full with cash)          $ _____
   - b. Cash Down Payment (if purchased on contract)     $ _____
   - c. Transportation and Installation Costs            $ _____
2. Starting Inventory                                     $ _____

3. Decorating and Remodeling                              $ _____

4. Deposits
   - a. Utilities                                         $ _____
   - b. Rents                                             $ _____
   - c. Other (Identify)                                  $ _____
5. Fees
   - a. Legal, Accounting, Other                          $ _____
   - b. Licenses, Permits, etc.                           $ _____
   - c. Other (Identify)                                  $ _____
6. Initial Advertising Costs                              $ _____

7. Accounts Receivable (___ days sales)                   $ _____

8. Salaries and owner's draw until store opens for business  $ _____

9. Other                                                  $ _____

                                                          **TOTAL**     $ _____

# SAMPLE SBA FORM 1099

## PROJECTED PROFIT & LOSS

| | Start-up or Prior to Loan | 1st Month | 2nd Month | 3rd Month | 4th Month | 5th Month | 6th Month | 7th Month | 8th Month | 9th Month | 10th Month | 11th Month | 12th Month | Total for Year |
|---|---|---|---|---|---|---|---|---|---|---|---|---|---|---|
| 1. Total Sales (Net) | | | | | | | | | | | | | | 100% |
| 2. Cost of Sales | | | | | | | | | | | | | | |
| 3. Gross Profit (line 1 minus line 2) | | | | | | | | | | | | | | |
| 4. Expenses (operating) | | | | | | | | | | | | | | |
| 5. Salaries (other than owner) | | | | | | | | | | | | | | |
| 6. Payroll Taxes | | | | | | | | | | | | | | |
| 7. Rent | | | | | | | | | | | | | | |
| 8. Utilities (including phone) | | | | | | | | | | | | | | |
| 9. Insurance | | | | | | | | | | | | | | |
| 10. Professional Service (i.e., acct.) | | | | | | | | | | | | | | |
| 11. Taxes & Licenses | | | | | | | | | | | | | | |
| 12. Advertising | | | | | | | | | | | | | | |
| 13. Supplies (for business) | | | | | | | | | | | | | | |
| 14. Office Supplies (forms,postage,etc.) | | | | | | | | | | | | | | |
| 15. Interest (loans, contracts, etc.) | | | | | | | | | | | | | | |
| 16. Depreciation | | | | | | | | | | | | | | |
| 17. Travel (incl operating costs of veh) | | | | | | | | | | | | | | |
| 18. Entertainment | | | | | | | | | | | | | | |
| 19. Dues & Subscriptions | | | | | | | | | | | | | | |
| 20. Other | | | | | | | | | | | | | | |
| 21. | | | | | | | | | | | | | | |
| 22. Total Expenses (add lines 5 thru 21) | | | | | | | | | | | | | | |
| 23. Profit Before Taxes (line 3 minus 22) | | | | | | | | | | | | | | |

## FORECAST OF CASH FLOW

| | Start-up or Prior to Loan | 1st Month | 2nd Month | 3rd Month | 4th Month | 5th Month | 6th Month | 7th Month | 8th Month | 9th Month | 10th Month | 11th Month | 12th Month | Total for Year |
|---|---|---|---|---|---|---|---|---|---|---|---|---|---|---|
| 24. Income (cash received) | | | | | | | | | | | | | | |
| 25. Cash sales | | | | | | | | | | | | | | |
| 26. Collection of Accts. Receivable | | | | | | | | | | | | | | |
| 27. Other | | | | | | | | | | | | | | |
| 28. Total Income (add lines 25, 26, & 27) | | | | | | | | | | | | | | |
| 29. Disbursements (cash paid out) | | | | | | | | | | | | | | |
| 30. Owner's Draw | | | | | | | | | | | | | | |
| 31. Loan Repayments (principal only) | | | | | | | | | | | | | | |
| 32. Cost of Sales (line 2) | | | | | | | | | | | | | | |
| 33. Total Expenses (minus line 16) | | | | | | | | | | | | | | |
| 34. Capital Expenditures (equip, bldgs, veh., leasehold improvements) | | | | | | | | | | | | | | |
| 35. Reserve for Taxes | | | | | | | | | | | | | | |
| 36. Other | | | | | | | | | | | | | | |
| 37. Total Disbursements (add 30 thru 36) | | | | | | | | | | | | | | |
| 38. Cash Flow Monthly (line 28 minus 37) | | | | | | | | | | | | | | |
| 39. Cash Flow Cumulative (ln 38 + ln 39) | | | | | | | | | | | | | | |

Federal executive agencies, including the Small Business Administration, are required to withhold or limit financial assistance, to impose special conditions on approved loans, to provide special notices to applicants or borrowers and to require special reports and data from borrowers in order to comply with legislation passed by the Congress and Executive Orders issued by the President and by the provisions of various inter-agency agreements. SBA has issued regulations and procedures that implement these laws and executive orders and they are contained in Parts 112, 113 and 116, Title 13 Code of Federal Regulations Chapter 1, or SOPs.

This form contains a brief summary of the various laws and executive orders that affect SBA's business and disaster loan programs and gives applicants and borrowers the notices required by law or otherwise. The signatures required on the last page provide evidence that SBA has given the necessary notices.

## Freedom of Information Act

(5 U.S.C. 552)

This law provides that, with some exceptions, SBA must supply information reflected in agency files and records to a person requesting it. Information about approved loans that will be automatically released includes, among other things, statistics on our loan programs (individual borrowers are not identified in the statistics) and other information such as the names of the borrowers (and their officers, directors, stockholders or partners), the collateral pledged to secure the loan, the amount of the loan, its purpose in general terms and the maturity. Proprietary data on a borrower would not routinely be made available to third parties. All requests under this Act are to be addressed to the nearest SBA office and be identified as a Freedom of Information request.

## Privacy Act

(5 U.S.C. 552a)

Disaster home loan files are covered by this legislation because they are normally maintained in the names of individuals. Business loan files are maintained by business name or in the name of individuals in their entrepreneurial capacity. Thus they are not files on individuals and, therefore, are not subjuct to this Act. Any person can request to see or get copies of any personal information that SBA has in the requestor's file. Requests for information about another party may be denied unless SBA has the written permission of the individual to release the information to the requestor or unless the information is subject to disclosure under the Freedom of Information Act. (The "Acknowledgement" section of this form contains the written permission of SBA to release information when a disaster victim requests assistance under the family and individual grant program.)

NOTE: Any person concerned with the collection of information, its voluntariness, disclosure or routine use under the Privacy Act or requesting information under the Freedom of Information Act may contact the Director, Freedom of Information/Privacy Acts Division, Small Business Administration, 1441 L Street, N.W., Washington, D.C. 20416, for information about the Agency's procedures on these two subjects.

SBA FORM 1261 (4-89) REF:SOP 50 10 USE 12/86 Edition Until Exhausted

# Right to Financial Privacy Act of 1978

(12 U.S.C. 3401)

This is notice to you, as required by the Right to Financial Privacy Act of 1978, of SBA's access rights to financial records held by financial institutions that are or have been doing business with you or your business, including any financial institution participating in a loan or loan guarantee. The law provides that SBA shall have a right of access to your financial records in connection with its consideration or administration of assistance to you in the form of a Government loan or loan guaranty agreement. SBA is required to provide a certificate of its compliance with the Act to a financial institution in connection with its first request for access to your financial records, after which no further certification is required for subsequent accesses. The law also provides that SBA's access rights continue for the term of any approved loan or loan guaranty agreement. No further notice to you of SBA's access rights is required during the term of any such agreement.

The law also authorizes SBA to transfer to another Government authority any financial records included in an application for a loan, or concerning an approved loan or loan guarantee, as necessary to process, service or foreclose a loan or loan guarantee or to collect on a defaulted loan or loan guarantee. No other transfer of your financial records to another Government authority will be permitted by SBA except as required or permitted by law.

# Flood Disaster Protection Act

(42 U.S.C. 4011)

Regulations have been issued by the Federal Insurance Administration (FIA) and by SBA implementing this Act and its amendments. These regulations prohibit SBA from making certain loans in an FIA designated floodplain unless Federal flood insurance is purchased as a condition of the loan. Failure to maintain the required level of flood insurance makes the applicant ineligible for any future financial assistance from SBA under any program, including disaster assistance.

# Executive Orders -- Floodplain Management and Wetland Protection

(42 F.R. 26951 and 42 F.R. 2961)

The SBA discourages any settlement in or development of a floodplain or a wetland. This statement is to notify all SBA loan applicants that such actions are hazardous to both life and property and should be avoided. The additional cost of flood preventive construction must be considered in addition to the possible loss of all assets and investments in future floods.

# Lead-Based Paint Poisoning Prevention Act

(42 U.S.C. 4821 et seq.)

Borrowers using SBA funds for the construction or rehabilitation of a residential structure are prohibited from using lead-based paint (as defined in SBA regulations) on all interior surfaces, whether accessible or not, and exterior surfaces, such as stairs, decks, porches, railings, windows and doors, which are readily accessible to children under 7 years of age. A "residential structure" is any home, apartment, hotel, motel, orphanage, boarding school, dormitory, day care center, extended care facility, college or other school housing, hospital, group practice or community facility and all other residential or institutional structures where persons reside.

# Equal Credit Opportunity Act

(15 U.S.C. 1691)

The Federal Equal Credit Opportunity Act prohibits creditors from discriminating against credit applicants on the basis of race, color, religion, national origin, sex, marital status or age (provided that the applicant has the capacity to enter into a binding contract); because all or part of the applicant's income drives from any public assistance program, or because the applicant has in good faith exercised any right under the Consumer Credit Protection Act. The Federal agency that administers compliance with this law concerning this creditor is the Federal Trade Commission, Equal Credit Opportunity, Room 500, 633 Indiana Avenue, N.W., Washington, D.C. 20580.

# Civil Rights Legislation

All businesses receiving SBA financial assistance must agree not to discriminate in any business practice, including employment practices and services to the public, on the basis of categories cited in 13 C.F.R., Parts 112 and 113 of SBA Regulations. This includes making their goods and services available to handicapped clients or customers. All business borrowers will be required to display the "Equal Employment Opportunity Poster" prescribed by SBA.

# Executive Order 11738 -- Environmental Protection

**(38 F.R. 25161)**

The Executive Order charges SBA with administering its loan programs in a manner that will result in effective enforcement of the Clean Air Act, the Federal Water Pollution Act and other environmental protection legislation. SBA must, therefore, impose conditions on some loans. By acknowledging receipt of this form and presenting the application, the principals of all small businesses borrowing $100,000 or more in direct funds stipulate to the following:

1. That any facility used, or to be used, by the subject firm is not listed on the EPA list of Violating Facilities.

2. That subject firm will comply with all the requirements of Section 114 of the Clean Air Act (42 U.S.C. 7414) and Section 308 of the Water-Act (33 U.S.C. 1318) relating to inspection, monitoring, entry, reports and information, as well as all other requirements specified in Section 114 and Section 308 of the respective Acts, and all regulations and guidelines issued thereunder.

3. That subject firm will notify SBA of the receipt of any communication from the Director of the Environmental Protection Agency indicating that a facility utilized, or to be utilized, by subject firm is under consideration to be listed on EPA List of Violating Facilities.

# Occupational Safety and Health Act

**(15 U.S.C. 651 et seq.)**

This legislation authorizes the Occupational Safety and Health Administration in the Department of Labor to require businesses to modify facilities and procedures to protect employees or pay penalty fees. In some instances the business can be forced to cease operations or be prevented from starting operations in a new facility. Therefore, in some instances SBA may require additional information from an applicant to determine whether the business will be in compliance with OSHA regulations and allowed to operate its facility after the loan is approved and disbursed.

In all instances, signing this form as borrower is a certification that the OSHA requirements that apply to the borrower's business have been determined and the borrower is, to the best of its knowledge, in compliance.

# Debt Collection Act of 1982   Deficit Reduction Act of 1984

**(31 U.S.C. 3701 et seq. and other titles)**

These laws require SBA to aggressively collect any loan payments which become delinquent. SBA must obtain your taxpayer identification number when you apply for a loan. If you receive a loan, and do not make payments as they come due, SBA may take one or more of the following actions:

- Report the status of your loan(s) to credit bureaus
- Hire a collection agency to collect your loan
- Offset your income tax refund or other amounts due to you from the Federal Government
- Suspend or debar you or your company from doing business with the Federal Government
- Refer your loan to the Department of Justice or other attorneys for litigation
- Foreclose on collateral or take other action permitted in the loan instruments.

# Consumer Credit Protection Act

**(15 U.S.C. 1601 et seq.)**

This legislation gives an applicant who is refused credit because of adverse information about the applicant's credit, reputation, character or mode of living an opportunity to refute or challenge the accuracy of such reports. Therefore, whenever SBA declines a loan in whole or in part because of adverse information in a credit report, the applicant will be given the name and address of the reporting agency so the applicant can seek to have that agency correct its report, if inaccurate. If SBA declines a loan in whole or in part because of adverse information received from a source other than a credit reporting agency, the applicant will be given information about the nature of the adverse information but not the source of the report.

A recipient of an SBA disaster home loan may rescind such a loan within 3 days after the consummation of the transaction, in accordance with "Regulation Z" of the Federal Reserve Board (12 C.F.R. Part 226). This right of rescission is not applicable to other SBA loans which are extended primarily for business, commercial or agricultural purposes.

# Applicant's Acknowledgement

My (our) signature(s) acknowledge(s) receipt of this form, that I (we) have read it and that I (we) have a copy for my (our) files. My (our) signature(s) represents my (our) agreement to comply with the requirements the Small Business Administration makes in connection with the approval of my (our) loan request and to comply, whenever applicable, with the hazard insurance, lead-based paint, civil rights or other limitations contained in this notice.

My (our) signature(s) also represent written permission, as required by the Privacy Act, for the SBA to release any information in my (our) disaster loan application to the Governor of my (our) State or the Governor's designated representative in conjunction with the State's processing of my (our) application for assistance under the Individual and Family Grant Program that is available in certain major disaster areas declared by the President.

Business Name

_____ By _____
Date                              Name and Title

Proprietor, Partners, Principals and Guarantors

_____
Date                              Signature

_____
Date                              Signature

_____
Date                              Signature

_____
Date                              Signature

SBA FORM 1261 (4-89)    ＊U.S.GPO:1989-0-622-810

343

## SECURITY AGREEMENT

A Security Agreement is similar to a Promissory Note. It offers an item of worth, such as a building, vehicle, or major piece of machinery as collateral against a loan, usually in a commercial transaction. The debtor in such an agreement is enjoined from changing, misusing, or removing such collateral without the lender's approval, nor to use it as collateral in another transaction. Moreover, the lender can, should the agreement be violated, take the collateral as partial satisfaction against the incurred debt. The debtor in such an event is also responsible for the payment of any legal costs. In the case of the rental of a property, for example, an escrow deposit is usually given the owner of the property. The Security Agreement allows the landlord to take all or part of the deposit in satisfaction of the missed rent payment. A similar situation might exist when an automobile is leased or purchased and the vehicle itself is pledged as collateral, any down payment in such a case being forfeited.

# SECURITY AGREEMENT

STATE OF                    )

                               )    ss:

COUNTY OF               )

That, I, _____, of _____
                                         (Street Address)       (City)

_____, hereinafter called "Debtor," hereby grant
   (State)     (Zip)

to _____, of _____
                             (Street Address)     (City)     (State)

_____, hereinafter called the "Secured Party," a security interest in the
  (Zip)

following described property as collateral to secure payment of the obligations described herein.

## COLLATERAL

_____
_____
_____
_____

## OBLIGATION

_____
_____
_____
_____

      Default in the payment of all or any part of the obligation described is a default under this Agreement.

      Upon such default the Secured Party may declare all of the above-described obligation(s) immediately due and payable and shall have the remedies of a secured party under provisions of the Uniform Commercial Code. In the event legal action is required to enforce any provision of this Agreement, the prevailing party shall be entitled to recover reasonable attorney's fees and costs.

      The Debtor hereby agrees to exercise reasonable caution and care in use of the herein-described collateral; to adequately insure or keep insured the described collateral; not to attempt to sell, assign, or dispose of said collateral or his/her interest therein; not to encumber nor to permit any encumbrance against same; and not to remove said collateral from the county where the Debtor resides without written permission of the Secured Party.

      EXECUTED this _____ day of _____, 19_____.

                   (Signed)_____
                                               **Debtor**

                   (Signed)_____
                                     **Secured Party**

## SHAREHOLDER AGREEMENT CHECKLIST (FOR CLOSELY-HELD CORPORATIONS)

If you own a business in which others have invested money, you are in a fiduciary position of trust. Others have trusted you with their money and expect that you will protect this money to the best of your ability and to try and make it grow. The shareholder is then the owner of as little as one single share, or as many as several thousand shares of the stock of a corporation or mutual fund. A shareholder possesses usually a stock certificate indicating the number of shares owned in the company or fund. In a closely-held corporation a particularly personal relationship often exists that requires that all plans and projects be spelled out in fine detail. Such a shareholder agreement is one of the most important documents you can and must produce. It provides for the smooth functioning of your business, reduces the likelihood of confusion and contention, and helps to avoid lawsuits between the corporation and its shareholders or their heirs.

Since there is no such thing as a universal shareholder agreement, we have noted a series of nine points that you need to consider in writing a shareholder agreement specifically adapted to your company's needs. This checklist serves only to familiarize you with the multiple problems and to prepare you better to work out the final document with an attorney familar with such corporate agreements.

# SHAREHOLDER AGREEMENT CHECKLIST

## Corporate Governance

Who holds the power and controls the running of the company?
How are major capital investments for the company determined?
Payment of executive compensation. Is this determined by a management team or by majority vote of shareholders?

## Buy-and-Sell Arrangements

Assignment of shares upon death or total disability with a right-to-buy clause for surviving shareholder(s).
Share prices to be sold at a fair price formula.
Shares in a S corporation to be sold only if status of S corporation is protected.

## Funding of Buy-Out

At retirement or death of a shareholder, the buy-out needs to be provided for.
If current shareholders are to be given first option to purchase, the purchase price and funding method must be pre-determined.
If the corporation is to have first option to purchase, corporate funds must be available to exercise such an option through periodic fund set-asides.

## SUBCONTRACTING

A subcontractor performs only a part of the work for the General Contractor. He is responsible for only a portion of the work or service, spelled out by the General Contractor, in a written agreement. On the other hand, the subcontractor must also perform his end of the contract in a satisfactory and timely fashion. His relations with the customer or client are usually only through the General Contractor, unless otherwise instructed by the contract. Billing is also done by the subcontractor to the General Contractor. Subcontractors who are members of various trade subcontracting associations use their contracts and abide by the rules set up by those associations. Some of those contracts are shown here. This kind of symbiotic arrangement is beneficial to both parties. The General Contractor usually has the contacts and assumes overall responsibility; by employing one or more subcontractors, he reduces his need for people and products, especially when such work is often seasonal in nature.

As a subcontractor, read carefully through the "Addendum to Subcontract." These points have been carefully worked out with trade association attorneys and developed through long experience. Typical subcontract documents, developed by the Associated Specialty Contractors, Inc., an umbrella group for eight different subcontractors' groups, follow this introduction.

# Addendum to Subcontract

Contractor: _____ Project : _____

Subcontractor hereby accepts the terms of the attached subcontract subject to Contraactor's agreement with the terms set forth in this Addendum which shall supersede any conflicting term in any other contract document. Any of the Contractor's terms or conditions in addition or different from this standard addendum are objected to and shall have no effect. Contractor's agreement herewith shall be evidenced by Contractor's signature hereon or by permitting Subcontractor to commence work for the project.

1. Subcontractor shall be paid monthly progress payments on or before the 15th of each month for the value of work completed plus the amount of materials and equipment suitably stored on or off site. Final payment shall be due 30 days after the work described in the Proposal is substantially completed. No provision of this agreement shall serve to void the Subcontractor's entitlement to payment for properly performed work or suitably stored materials or to require the Subcontractor to continue performance if timely payments are not made to Subcontractor for suitably performed work or stored materials or to void Subcontractor's right to file a lien or claim on its behalf in the event that any payment to Subcontractor is not timely made.

2. The Contractor will withhold no more retention from the Subcontractor than is being withheld by the Owner from the Contractor with respect to the Subcontractor's work.

3. All sums not paid when due shall bear an interest rate of 1½% per month or the maximum legal rate permitted by law, whichever is less; and all costs of collection, including a reasonable attorney's fee, shall be paid by Contractor.

4. No backcharges or claim of the Contractor for services shall be valid except by an agreement in writing by the Subcontractor before the work is executed, except in the case of the Subcontractor's failure to meet any requirement of the subcontract agreement. In such event, the Contractor shall notify the Subcontractor of such default, in writing, and allow the Subcontractor reasonable time to correct any deficiency before incurring any cost chargeable to the Subcontractor.

5. Contractor is to prepare all work areas so as to be acceptable for Subcontractor work under the subcontract. Subcontrator will not be called upon to start work until sufficient areas are ready to insure continued work. The Contractor shall furnish all temporary site facilities including suitable storage space, hoisting, temporary electrical and water at no cost to Subcontractor.

6. Subcontractor shall be given a reasonable time in which to make delivery of materials and/or labor to commence and complete the performance of the contract. Subcontractor shall not be responsible for delays or defaults where occasioned by any causes of any kind and extent beyond its control, including but not limited to: delays caused by the owner, general contractor, architect and/or engineers, delays in transportation, shortage of raw materials, civil disorders, labor difficulties, vendor allocations, fires, floods, accidents and acts of God. Subcontractor shall be entitled to equitable adjustment in the subcontract amount for additional costs due to unanticipated project delays or accelerations caused by others whose acts are not the Subcontractor's responsibility and to time extensions for unavoidable delays. The Contractor shall make no demand for liquidated damages for delays in excess of the amount specified in the subcontract agreement and no liquidated damages may be assessed against Subcontractor for more than the amount paid by the Contractor for unexcused delays to the extent actually caused by Subcontractor.

7. The Subcontractor's equipment and work are guaranteed for a period of one year from the date of substantial completion or use by the Contractor or the Contractor's customer, whichever is earlier. THIS WARRANTY IS IN LIEU OF ALL OTHER WARRANTIES, EXPRESS OR IMPLIED, INCLUDING ANY WARRANTIES OF MERCHANTABILITY OR FITNESS FOR A PARTICULAR PURPOSE. The exclusive remedy shall be that Subcontractor will replace or repair any part of its work which is found to be defective. Subcontractor shall not be responsible for damage or defect caused by abuse, modifications not executed by the Subcontractor, improper or insufficient maintenance, improper operation or normal wear, tear and usage.

8. Work called for herein is to be performed during Subcontractor's regular working hours. All work performed outside of such hours shall be charged for at rates or amounts agreed upon by the parties at the time overtime is authorized.

9. Contractor shall, if the Owner does not, purchase and maintain all risk insurance upon full value of the entire work and/or materials delivered to the jobsite, which shall include the interest of Subcontractor.

10. The Subcontractor shall indemnify and hold harmless the Contractor, Owner, Architect or others from damages only to the extent such damages were caused by any negligent act or omission of the Subcontractor or anyone for whose acts the Subcontractor is liable.

Date: _____

Contractor: _____ Subcontractor: _____

_____     _____

By: _____     By: _____

Title: _____     Title: _____

## C  JOINT STANDARD FORMS

### Joint standard form 1:
### Standard subbid proposal

Subcontractor _____    Project _____

Address _____    Location _____

_____    _____

_____    _____

General Contractor _____    A&E _____

_____    _____

Address _____    Bid Time & Date _____

_____    Subbid Time & Date _____

Type of work (including specification sections) _____
_____
(List the category(ies) this proposal will cover, such as plumbing, heating, air conditioning and ventilation, electrical and elevators.)

This proposal includes furnishing all materials and performing all work in the category(ies) listed above, as required by the plans, specifications, general and special conditions and addenda _____
                          (Here list addenda by numbers)
Identify work to be **excluded** by specification paragraph otherwise the subcontractor will be responsible for all work in the above category(ies) required by the specifications and plans.

If this proposal, including prices, is accepted, the subcontractor agrees to enter into a subcontract and, if required, furnish performance and payment bonds from _____
                          (Name of surety company or agency)
guaranteeing full performance of the work and payment of all costs incident thereto, and the cost of the bond is **not** included in this proposal.

This proposal will remain in effect and will not be withdrawn by the subcontractor for a period of 30 days or for the same period of time required by the contract documents for the general contractor in regard to the prime bid, plus 15 days, whichever period is longer.


_____
Subcontractor

_____
By                          (Title)

# Joint standard form 2:
# Subcontractor's application for payment

TO:_____

FROM: _____
_____

PROJECT:

PAYMENT REQUEST NO. _____

PERIOD _____, 19____, to _____, 19____ .

STATEMENT OF CONTRACT ACCOUNT:

  1. Original Contract Amount                                  $_____

  2. Approved Changes (Net) (Add/Deduct) (As per attached breakdown)    $_____

  3. Adjusted Contract Amount                                   $_____

---

  4. Value of Work Completed to Date: (As per attached breakdown)    $_____

  5. Value of Approved Change Orders Completed to Date:           $_____

                      (As per attached breakdown)

  6. Materials Stored on Site: (As per attached breakdown)       $_____

  7. Total (4 + 5 + 6)                                           $_____

  8. Less Amount Retained (_____%)             ($ _____)

  9. Total Less Retainage                                   $_____

10. Total Previously Certified (Deduct)               ($ _____)

11. AMOUNT OF THIS REQUEST                     $_____

CERTIFICATE OF THE SUBCONTRACTOR:

    I hereby certify that the work performed and the materials supplied to date, as shown on the above represent the actual value of accomplishment under the terms of the Contract (and all authorized changes thereto) between the undersigned and _____relating to the above project.

    I also certify that payments, less applicable retention, have been made through the period covered by previous payments received from the contractor, to (1) all my subcontractors (sub-subcontractors) and (2) for all materials and labor used in or in connection with the performance of this Contract. I further certify I have complied with Federal, State and local tax laws, including Social Security laws and Unemployment Compensation laws and Workmen's Compensation laws insofar as applicable to the performance of this Contract.

    Furthermore, in consideration of the payments received, and upon receipt of the amount of this request, the undersigned does hereby waive, release and relinquish all claim or right of lien which the undersigned may now have upon the premises above described except for claims or right of lien for contract and/or change order work performed to extent that payment is being retained or will subsequently become due.

Date _____

Subscribed and sworn before me this_____day of
                      , 19____

Notary Public:_____
My Commission Expires:

                           SUBCONTRACTOR

BY: _____
                    (authorized signature)

TITLE: _____

# Joint standard form 3:
# Work authorization form

SHEET NO. ___ OF ___

DATE_____     CUSTOMER ORDER NO._____

PROJECT _____ JOB NO. _____

WORK PERFORMED BY _____ FOR _____

AUTHORIZED BY_____TITLE_____

DESCRIPTION OF WORK _____

_____

_____

**LABOR**                                    **MATERIAL**

| NAME | TRADE | Actual Hours Worked | | DESCRIPTION | QUANTITY |
| | | STRAIGHT TIME | PREMIUM TIME | | |
| --- | --- | --- | --- | --- | --- |
| | | | | | |
| | | | | | |
| | | | | | |
| | | | | | |
| | | | | | |
| | | | | | |
| | | | | | |
| | | | | | |
| | | | | | |
| | | | | | |
| | | | | | |

**EQUIPMENT & TOOLS**

| DESCRIPTION | TIME | DESCRIPTION | TIME |
| --- | --- | --- | --- |
| | | | |
| | | | |
| | | | |
| | | | |
| | | | |

**REMARKS:** _____

_____

CONTRACTOR _____   ARCHITECT OWNER _____   SUBCONTRACTOR _____

BY _____   BY _____   BY _____

BILLING ADDRESS_____   ADDRESS_____   BILLING ADDRESS_____

JOB COMPLETED  ☐ YES  ☐ NO

**WORK AUTHORIZATION NOT SIGNED BECAUSE:**

**NOTE:** COMPLETE A SEPARATE DAILY WORK ORDER   ☐ UNABLE TO CONTACT REPRESENTATIVE

FOR (1) EACH JOB (2) EACH DAY.   ☐ AUTHORIZED BY PHONE

(DO NOT ATTEMPT TO COMBINE JOBS OR DAYS)   ☐ FORM ISSUED FOR RECORD PURPOSE ONLY

AUTHORIZATION IN DISPUTE

# SUBCONTRACTOR PROPOSAL

## Conditions of Proposal

Project: _____

Acceptance of this proposal by Contractor shall be acceptance of all terms and conditions recited herein which shall supersede any conflicting term in any other contract document. Any of the Contractor's terms and conditions in addition or different from this proposal are objected to and shall have no effect. Contractor's agreement herewith shall be evidenced by Contractor's signature hereon or by permitting Subcontractor to commence work for project.

1. Subcontractor shall be paid monthly progress payments on or before the 15th of each month for the value of work completed plus the amount of materials and equipment suitably stored on or off site. Final payment shall be due 30 days after the work described in the Proposal is substantially completed. No provision of this agreement shall serve to void the Subcontractor's entitlement to payment for properly performed work or suitably stored materials or to require the Subcontractor to continue performance if timely payments are not made to Subcontractor for suitably performed work or stored materials or to void Subcontractor's right to file a lien or claim on its behalf in the event that any payment to Subcontractor is not timely made.

2. The Contractor will withhold no more retention from the Subcontractor than is being withheld by the Owner from the Contractor with respect to the Subcontractor's work.

3. All sums not paid when due shall bear an interest rate of 1½% per month or the maximum legal rate permitted by law, whichever is less; and all costs of collection, including a reasonable attorney's fee, shall be paid by Contractor.

4. No backcharges or claim of the Contractor for services shall be valid except by an agreement in writing by the Subcontractor before the work is executed, except in the case of the Subcontractor's failure to meet any requirement of the subcontract agreement. In such event, the Contractor shall notify the Subcontractor of such default, in writing, and allow the Subcontractor reasonable time to correct any deficiency before incurring any cost chargeable to the Subcontractor.

5. Contractor is to prepare all work areas so as to be acceptable for Subcontractor work under the subcontract. Subcontrator will not be called upon to start work until sufficient areas are ready to insure continued work. The Contractor shall furnish all temporary site facilities including suitable storage space, hoisting, temporary electrical and water at no cost to Subcontractor.

6. Subcontractor shall be given a reasonable time in which to make delivery of materials and/or labor to commence and complete the performance of the contract. Subcontractor shall not be responsible for delays or defaults where occasioned by any causes of any kind and extent beyond its control, including but not limited to: delays caused by the owner, general contractor, architect and/or engineers, delays in transportation, shortage of raw materials, civil disorders, labor difficulties, vendor allocations, fires, floods, accidents and acts of God. Subcontractor shall be entitled to equitable adjustment in the subcontract amount for additional costs due to unanticipated project delays or accelerations caused by others whose acts are not the Subcontractor's responsibility and to time extensions for unavoidable delays. The Contractor shall make no demand for liquidated damages for delays in excess of the amount specified in the subcontract agreement and no liquidated damages may be assessed against Subcontractor for more than the amount paid by the Contractor for unexcused delays to the extent actually caused by Subcontractor.

7. The Subcontractor's equipment and work are guaranteed for a period of one year from the date of substantial completion or use by the Contractor or the Contractor's customer, whichever is earlier. THIS WARRANTY IS IN LIEU OF ALL OTHER WARRANTIES, EXPRESS OR IMPLIED, INCLUDING ANY WARRANTIES OF MERCHANTABILITY OR FITNESS FOR A PARTICULAR PURPOSE. The exclusive remedy shall be that Subcontractor will replace or repair any part of its work which is found to be defective. Subcontractor shall not be responsible for damage or defect caused by abuse, modifications not executed by the Subcontractor, improper or insufficient maintenance, improper operation or normal wear, tear and usage.

8. Work called for herein is to be performed during Subcontractor's regular working hours. All work performed outside of such hours shall be charged for at rates or amounts agreed upon by the parties at the time overtime is authorized.

9. Contractor shall, if the Owner does not, purchase and maintain all risk insurance upon full value of the entire work and/or materials delivered to the jobsite, which shall include the interest of Subcontractor.

10. The Subcontrator shall indemnify and hold harmless the Contractor, Owner, Architect or others from damages only to the extent such damages were caused by any negligent act or omission of the Subcontractor or anyone for whose acts the Subcontractor is liable.

11. The subcontract form used between the Subcontractor and the Contractor will be AIA Standard Form Subcontract Document A401. Where there is a conflict between provisions of either the AIA Standard Form, or the contract documents between the Owner and Contractor and this Proposal, then this Proposal shall govern.

Date: _____

Contractor: _____         Subcontractor: _____

_____         _____

By: _____            By: _____

Title: _____           Title: _____

## LIMITED WARRANTY

(Or Limited Guaranty) A warranty is a promise or guarantee given to a purchaser that the goods or services obtained will perform as promised. If there is a failure of such a product or service, an exchange is promised, a refund given, or repair made at no charge or at a proportionate reduction in price. Warranties usually become effective when the manufacturer or supplier receives an application from the buyer, not on the date of purchase or performance. Such warranties are usually limited by a specified period of time or by a statement that limits responsibility on the manufacturer's or provider's part to defect caused only by the latter, and not by the purchaser or ultimate user.

# LIMITED WARRANTY

These goods are warranted free from defects in workmanship and materials on purchase. If the goods are defective, they will be repaired or replaced, at the vendor's option, without charge on return to the vendor within _____ days from date of purchase with satisfactory proof of purchase from the vendor and date of purchase.

This warranty is given only to the original purchaser of the goods and is void if the goods have been

___ damaged by negligence or accident after purchase;

___ used other than for the purpose for which they are intended to be used or not used in accordance with any operating instructions supplied with the goods;

___ adapted or repaired other than by the vendor or an approved service center; or

___ added on to or used with other goods which may affect the integrity, performance, safety, or reliability of these goods.

This warranty is given in place of all other warranties and assurances, whether express or implied, including but not limited to matters of quality, fitness for purpose, or merchantability and the vendor accepts no liability, under any circumstances whatsoever, for any consequential damage or loss suffered by anyone as a result of using or being unable to use the goods.

Certain jurisdictions have consumer protection laws which give you additional rights.

(Company Signature or Logo)

## WILLS

Last Wills and Testaments are necessary so that the executor of such an instrument can dispose of his property in the manner he or she wishes it to be disposed of. Without such a will a deceased's property will be divided according to a court's decision, is often subject to much acrimonious litigation by the survivors, and usually does not conform with the deceased's wishes. Wills are usually filed with the Register of Wills in the county of the executor's residence. If an attorney is employed or an executor appointed, a copy of the will is retained by this legal agent. Lawyers, trust officers of banks, or a close and favored relative or friend are usually named by the executor of the will as their post-mortem administrator.

The form presented here is a short form of a Last Will and Testament, perfectly legal when the executor's property is simple. Attorneys draw up wills when much property or complicated circumstances exist. Such instruments can be many pages in length and cost several hundred dollars. All wills should be signed by a witness or two to make them effective and legal in most jurisdictions.

# 𝕷𝖆𝖘𝖙 𝖂𝖎𝖑𝖑 𝕬𝖓𝖉 𝕿𝖊𝖘𝖙𝖆𝖒𝖊𝖓𝖙
# 𝕺𝖋

_____

I,_____ of _____, _____County,
_____, being of full age and of sound and disposing mind and memory, do make,
publish and declare this to be my Last Will and Testament, hereby revoking all wills and codicils
by me heretofore made.

**ITEM I:**    I direct that all of my just and enforceable debts and funeral expenses
be paid out of my estate as soon as practicable after the time of my decease.

All estate, inheritance, succession and other death taxes which shall become
payable by reason of my death, shall be paid out of my estate as an administration expense.

**ITEM II:**    I give, devise and bequeath my entire estate, whether real property or
personal property, of every kind, name and description, whatsoever and where-
soever situated, which I now own or hereafter acquire, to _____ ,
as Trustee(s) of the _____ Trust, to be held, managed and disposed of
in accordance with the provisions of said Trust which was established by a
Declaration of Trust dated _____, 19 ____, between_____ ,
as the Settlor (s), and _____, as the Trustee(s), and which is now in
existence.

**ITEM III:**    I nominate and appoint my spouse,_____ , to be the
Execut___ of this, my Last Will and Testament, hereby authorizing and empow-
ering my said Execut___ to compound, compromise, and settle and adjust  all
claims and demands which may be presented against my estate or which may
be due to my estate; and to sell at private or public sale, lease or exchange, at
such prices and upon such terms of credit or otherwise as she may deem best,
the whole or any part of my real or personal property; and to execute, acknowledge and deliver deeds or other proper instruments of conveyance thereof to the
purchaser or purchasers, all without license or leave of court. In connection with
the sale of any real estate, I authorize my Execut___to employ real estate brokers
and to pay them standard commissions for their services. I request that no bond
be required of my said Execut___.

In the event my spouse, _____ , does not survive me, shall be
incapable of serving as Execut___, shall elect not so to serve, or for any reason
is unable to complete the administration of my estate, then I appoint, _____
_____ as Alternate Execu_____, to serve with the same powers
aforesaid and also to serve without bond.

IN WITNESS WHEREOF, I have hereunto set my hand to this, my Last Will and Testament, at _____, _____ this, _____ day of _____ 19 _____.

_____

Signed by the said _____ and by h___ acknowledged to be h___ Last Will and Testament, before us and in our presence and by us subscribed as attesting witnesses, in her presence and at her request, and in the presence of each other, the day and year last aforesaid.

_____ residing at _____

_____ residing at _____

_____ residing at _____

# BIBLIOGRAPHY

BASIC BOOK OF BUSINESS AGREEMENTS, Hartnett Enterprise, 1990, $74.45 ppd.

THE CONTRACT AND FEE SETTING GUIDE FOR CONSULTANTS AND PROFESSIONALS, Howard L. Shenson; John Wiley & Sons, 1990, $14.95.

WRITE YOUR OWN BUSINESS CONTRACTS: What Your Attorney Won't Tell You, E. Thorpe Barrett; PSI Research/Oasis Press, 1990, $39.95.

CONTRACT DOCUMENTS, Associated Specialty Contractors, Bethesda, MD, 1987, $20.

STANDARD LEGAL FORMS & AGREEMENTS FOR SMALL BUSINESS, Steve Sanderson; Self-Counsel Press, 1990, $14.95.

HOW TO PROTECT YOUR BUSINESS, Better Business Bureaus; Benjamin/Prentice-Hall, 1985, $8.95.

THE COMPLETE LEGAL KIT, Consumer Law Foundation; Running Press, 1988, $19.95.

DO YOUR OWN LEGAL WORK, Charles F. Abbott; Advocate Publishers, 1977, $14.95.

WRITE YOUR OWN CONTRACTS, R.O.Cottrell; Ogden Shepard, 1986, $16.95.

BUSINESS FORMS & CONTRACTS (IN PLAIN ENGLISH), Leonard D. DuBoff; Madrona, 1986, $19.95.

THE BUSINESS PLANNING GUIDE, Bangs and Osgood; Upstart, 1976, rev. 1988, $19.95.

THE SMALL BUSINESS HANDBOOK, Irving Bursteiner; Prentice-Hall, 1989, $16.95.

MONTHLY BOOKKEEPING SYSTEM, Keith Clark; 1988, $8.95.

SMALL TIME OPERATOR, Bernard Kamoroff; and Books, 1989, $14.95.

MASTER FORMS FOR YOUR COPIER, Deflecto/ Bantam Books, 1982, $29.95.

SALES MANAGER'S COMPLETE MANUAL OF FORMS, AGREEMENTS, POLICIES & PROCEDURES, Carlsen and Boxley; Prentice-Hall, 1990, $69.95.

THE ENTREPRENEUR'S GUIDE TO DOING BUSINESS WITH THE FEDERAL GOVERNMENT, Bevers-Christie-Price; Prentice-Hall, 1989, $14.95.

J.K.LASSER LEGAL FORMS FOR SMALL BUSINESS, Simon and Schuster, 1988, $19.95.

FINANCIAL RECORD KEEPING FOR SMALL STORES, SBA Management Series #32, 1976, $1.55 (#045-000-00142-3).

TEN-SECOND BUSINESS FORMS, Bob Adams Inc., 1989, $12.95.

BUSINESS FORMS ON FILE, Facts on File, 1988, looseleaf, $95; update, $35.

THE COMPLETE BOOK OF CORPORATE FORMS, Ted Nicholas; Enterprise Publishing, looseleaf, $74.95.

THE SMALL BUSINESS LEGAL ADVISOR, William A. Hancock; McGraw Hill, 1992 (2nd ed.), $16.95.

# Index of Terms and Agreements